2024

Training

mit Original-Prüfungen

Realschule Niedersachsen

Englisch 10. Klasse

STARK

Bildnachweis

Deckblätter
S. 1 Deckblatt „Übungsaufgaben zu den Kompetenzbereichen" © Willselarep|Dreamstime.com
S. 127 Deckblatt „Abschlussprüfung" © wavebreakmedia. Shutterstock

Listening
S. 6ff. Illustrationen © Paul Jenkinson
S. 7 Business Class © Richair|Dreamstime.com; Economy Class (1B/C) © Aleksandr Kurganov|Dreamstime.com; Taxi © Roland Nagy|Dreamstime.com; Bus © Tupungato|Dreamstime.com; Zug © Johnscoolphotos/shutterstock
S. 8 London © QQ7. Shutterstock; Strand © MartiniDry. Shutterstock; Park © Peter Radacsi/shutterstock; Flughafen © Rob Wilson. Shutterstock; Café © Kevin George|Dreamstime.com; Wohnzimmer © Ambient Ideas. Shutterstock; Taxis © Innershadows|Dreamstime.com; Frühstücksbüffet © Supparsorn Wantarnagon|Dreamstime.com; Bänke © Tupungato|Dreamstime.com
S. 12 Nugget © Steffen Foerster. Shutterstock
S. 13 Kind © Nikol Senkyrikova|Dreamstime.com

Reading
S. 22 Mountainbike © 123rf.com; Feuerstelle © Valery Ivashchenko|Dreamstime.com; Flugzeug © WojciechBeczynski. Shutterstock; Handtasche © Zaclurs|Dreamstime.com
S. 23 Architekt © Can Stock Photo Inc./michaeljung; Pärchen © Can Stock Photo Inc./mimagephotography; Familie © Can Stock Photo Inc./Goodluz
S. 24 Mann © Can Stock Photo Inc./photography33; Frau © Leonardo2012|Dreamstime.com
S. 27 Harry © Mikie Flippo. Shutterstock; Brooke © kurhan. 123rf.com; Amy © stockyimages. Shutterstock; Rory © Lasse Kristensen. Shutterstock; Harper © Kinga. Shutterstock
S. 28 Blut © Can Stock Photo/Lonely11
S. 29 George Washington © Scott Catron, lizensiert unter CC-BY-2.5
S. 32 Fußballspielerinnen mit Ball © Wavebreak Media Ltd. 123rf.com
S. 34 Sydney © Taras Vyshnya. Shutterstock; indisches Essen © Alex Hubenov. Shutterstock; Wal © Sasin Tipchai. Shutterstock; Kreuzfahrtschiff © Finadiz|Dreamstime.com
S. 37 Junge © Gualtiero Boffi|Dreamstime.com

Mediating
S. 44f. Schilder @ Paul Jenkinson
S. 47 Ernte © 123rf.com; Schafe © Tania Zbrodko. Shutterstock
S. 48 Schilder (Aufgabe 5) © Paul Jenkinson
S. 51 afrikanisches Dorf © Paul Jenkinson
S. 52 Würstchenbude © Paul Jenkinson
S. 57 Straßencafé © Giancarlo Liguori. Shutterstock
S. 58 Begrüßung © franz12/shutterstock
S. 60 Sonne © LEWEB. Shutterstock
S. 62 Fenster © Jürgen Fälche – Fotolia.de; München © Stefan Kühn, lizensiert unter CC BY-SA 3.0; Mädchen beim Schaukeln © Pavel Lysenko – Fotolia.de; Restaurant © Sebastian Czapnik|Dreamstime.com
S. 63 Quadfahren im Schlamm © Can Stock Photo/BrandonSeidel; Quadfahren am Strand © Can Stock Photo/james74

Writing
S. 75 Junge nach Mobbingvorfall © mandy godbehear|123RF
S. 78 Piloten © Tea|Dreamstime.com
S. 82 London © boybehindacamera/shutterstock
S. 85 Briefumschläge mit E-Mail-Symbol © Can Stock Photo Inc./vasabii
S. 86 Schnipsel © 123rf.com
S. 86/91 Hintergrund Brief © 123rf.com
S. 89 Frau © PathDoc. Shutterstock; Baustelle © Devin_Pavel. Shutterstock; Hotelzimmer © Dreamshot|Dreamstime.com; Kakerlake © 607708. Shutterstock
S. 92 Golden Gate Bridge © Jay Beiler|Dreamstime.com; Cable Car © Minyun Zhou|Dreamstime.com
S. 95 Tagebuch © Dana Rothstein|Dreamstime.com;
S. 96 Schreiben © Ditty_about_summer. Shutterstock
S. 98 Mädchen mit Smartphone © Syda Production|Dreamstime.com
S. 99 Mädchen mit Gedankenblasen © Martinmark|Dreamstime.com
S. 100 Smartphone © bloomua. Shutterstock

Speaking
S. 108 zwei Frauen © Jan Martin Will|Dreamstime.com
S. 110 Mädchen vor Computer © Monkey Business Images Ltd.|Dreamstime.com; Kinder im Klassenzimmer © Dawn Shearer Simonetti. Shutterstock;
S. 112 Notizzettel © amasterphotographer. Shutterstock; Mädchen im Klassenzimmer © Emil Kudahl Christensen|Dreamstime.com; World AIDS Day © Allies Interactive Services Private Limited|Dreamstime.com; Holzzug © Ntcandrej|Dreamstime.com; Hund © Susan Schmitz. Shutterstock; Umweltschützer*innen © Wavebreakmedia Ltd|Dreamstime.com

Weitere Fotos und Grafiken © Stark Verlag

18. ergänzte Auflage
www.stark-verlag.de

Inhalt

Inhalt

Realschulabschlussprüfung 2023 ...... www.stark-verlag.de/mystark

Sobald die Original-Prüfungsaufgaben 2023 freigegeben sind, können sie als PDF auf der Plattform MyStark heruntergeladen werden (Zugangscode vgl. Umschlaginnenseite).

MP3-Dateien

Listening Test 1: Short dialogues
Listening Test 2: Short texts
Listening Test 3: The German exchange
Listening Test 4: Off the sofa and do it!
Listening Test 5: My Norfolk
Listening Test 6: Things you didn't know about London
Listening Test 7: The California Gold Rush
Listening Test 8: The Stolen Generations
Listening Test 9: What can be done?
Listening Test 10: Environment views
Listening Test 11: Five-star hotel or wilderness?
Listening Test 12: What's on your plate?
Abschlussprüfung 2020
Abschlussprüfung 2021
Abschlussprüfung 2022
Abschlussprüfung 2023

Hinweis: Die MP3-Dateien sind ebenfalls auf der Plattform MyStark verfügbar.

Listening tests 1–12 gesprochen von: Eva Adelseck, Esther Gilvray, Rees Jeannotte, Daria Kozlova, Jennifer Mikulla, Julian Powell, Ben Tendler, Roger Voight

Die **Hintergrundgeräusche** in den Tracks (Listening Tests 1–12) stammen von Freesound, Pacdv und Soundsnap.

Autorinnen und Autoren

Listening: Paul Jenkinson, Redaktion
Reading: Paul Jenkinson, Redaktion
Mediating: Paul Jenkinson, Redaktion
Writing: Heinz Gövert, Paul Jenkinson, Caroline Neu-Costello, Redaktion
Speaking: Birte Bendrich, Paul Jenkinson, Redaktion

digitale Aufgaben: Patrick Charles, Walter Düringer, Heinz Gövert, Paul Jenkinson, Elke Lüdeke, Caroline Neu-Costello, Redaktion
digitale Kurzgrammatik: Redaktion

Vorwort

Liebe Schülerin, lieber Schüler,

dieses Buch hilft dir bei der selbstständigen Vorbereitung auf **Klassenarbeiten und die Prüfung zum Erwerb des Realschulabschlusses** im Fach Englisch.

- Die **Übungsaufgaben** widmen sich den Kompetenzbereichen *Listening, Reading, Mediating, Writing* und *Speaking*. In den ersten Abschnitten erfährst du jeweils, welche Anforderungen auf dich zukommen können und wie du dich am besten darauf vorbereitest. Anhand der Übungen kannst du trainieren, wie man mit möglichen Aufgabenstellungen umgeht und sie erfolgreich löst.
- Im Anschluss findest du eine Sammlung von **Original-Prüfungsaufgaben** der letzten Jahre. Damit kannst du deine Kenntnisse „unter Prüfungsbedingungen" testen.
- Eine Auswahl **hilfreicher Wendungen**, die dir in den unterschiedlichsten Bereichen nützlich sein werden, erleichtert dir das selbstständige Verfassen von Texten sowie die Vorbereitung auf die mündliche Prüfung. Diese wichtigen Wortschatzelemente kannst du auch digital üben. Die sogenannten „MindCards", interaktive Vokabelkärtchen, sind für die Arbeit am Smartphone oder Tablet bestens geeignet. Du kannst sie über die QR-Codes oder über die beiden Links einfach und schnell abrufen:
  https://www.stark-verlag.de/mindcards/writing-1
  https://www.stark-verlag.de/mindcards/speaking-1

  Writing

  Speaking
- Auf der Plattform **MyStark** (Zugangscode vgl. Umschlaginnenseite) kannst du auf viele **digitale Aufgaben zum Grundwissen** in den Bereichen **Grammatik** und **Wortschatz** zugreifen.
- Auf **MyStark** findest du außerdem folgende digitale Inhalte:
  - die **Original-Prüfungsaufgaben 2023** als PDF,
  - **MP3-Dateien** zu den Hörverstehenstexten der Übungsaufgaben und der Original-Prüfungsaufgaben,
  - viele **interaktive Aufgaben** zu den Bereichen *Listening, Reading, Mediating und Writing*. Neben allen Aufgaben, die du am Computer oder Tablet bearbeiten kannst, findest du im Buch dieses Symbol:
  - eine **digitale Kurzgrammatik**, in der du nachschlagen kannst, wenn du in der Grammatik einmal unsicher bist sowie
  - **Lernvideos** zu wichtigen grammatischen Strukturen und zu Strategien, wie du am besten Vokabeln lernst (auch über QR-Code abrufbar).

  Lernvideos

Ein separater Band (Best.-Nr. D03150L) enthält zu allen Aufgaben dieses Buches **ausführliche Lösungsvorschläge** mit **hilfreichen Tipps**.

Viel Spaß beim Üben und viel Erfolg in der Prüfung!

Auf alle **digitalen Inhalte** kannst du online über die Plattform **MyStark** zugreifen. Deinen persönlichen **Zugangscode** findest du auf der Umschlaginnenseite.

Hinweise zur Abschlussprüfung

Die folgenden Hinweise zum schriftlichen Teil der Abschlussprüfung im Fach Englisch zum Erwerb des **Sekundarabschlusses I** – Realschulabschluss – gelten für alle Schulformen, die nach den Kerncurricula der Realschule unterrichten. Die Prüfungsaufgaben werden auf der Grundlage der Kerncurricula und der Bildungsstandards erstellt. Die sprachlichen Anforderungen im Fach Englisch orientieren sich am mittleren Niveau des Gemeinsamen Europäischen Referenzrahmens (B1).

Bearbeitungsdauer

Die Bearbeitungszeiten für die schriftlichen Prüfungen wurden vom Kultusministerium festgelegt. Im Fach Englisch beträgt die zur Verfügung stehende Zeit 120 Minuten.

Ablauf der schriftlichen Prüfung

- Die schriftliche Prüfung besteht aus mehreren Teilen. In der Abschlussprüfung 2020 wurde neben den Bereichen *Listening, Reading* und *Writing* auch der Bereich *Mediating* geprüft. In den Folgejahren ist die Sprachmittlung jedoch entfallen. **Erkundige dich unbedingt vorab bei deiner Lehrkraft, welche Bereiche Teil der Abschlussprüfung 2024 sein werden.**
- Zunächst hast du 15 Minuten Zeit, beide Aufgabensets zum Kompetenzbereich *Writing* zu sichten und dich für ein Aufgabenset zu entscheiden. Das nicht gewählte Set wird wieder abgegeben. Erst jetzt beginnt der eigentliche Prüfungszeitraum von 120 Minuten.
- Für den Prüfungsteil *Listening* stehen dir ca. 30 Minuten zur Verfügung. Die Länge dieses Prüfungsteils hängt von der Spiellänge der verwendeten Audioquelle ab.
- Für die restlichen Aufgaben des Pflichtteils und die Bearbeitung des Wahlteils stehen dann insgesamt noch ca. 90 Minuten zur Verfügung.
- In allen Teilen der Prüfung darf ein zweisprachiges Wörterbuch oder ein elektronisches Wörterbuch verwendet werden. Von der Benutzung von Wörterbüchern im Prüfungsteil *Listening* wird jedoch aufgrund der zur Verfügung stehenden Zeit abgeraten.

Sollten nach Erscheinen dieses Bandes wichtige Änderungen in der Abschlussprüfung vom Kultusministerium bekannt gegeben werden, findest du aktuelle Informationen dazu auf der Plattform MyStark.

Übungsaufgaben zu den Kompetenzbereichen

1 Listening

Hörverstehenstexte und die dazugehörigen Aufgabenstellungen können sehr unterschiedlich sein. Die Texte, die du im Rahmen von Klassenarbeiten und in der Abschlussprüfung zu hören bekommst, spiegeln meist **reale Sprechsituationen** wider, d. h., man kann solche oder ähnliche Texte im „wirklichen Leben“ hören. Die Inhalte der Texte können von der Begrüßungsansprache eines Piloten über die Lautsprecheransagen an einem Bahnhof bis hin zu Nachrichtenmeldungen, Radiointerviews oder Alltagsgesprächen reichen. Es kann sich auch einfach um kurze Berichte oder Podcasts zu den unterschiedlichsten Themen handeln. Genauso vielfältig wie die verschiedenen Arten von Hörtexten können auch die Aufgabenstellungen ausfallen. In diesem Kapitel werden dir die häufigsten Textarten und Aufgabenstellungen zum Kompetenzbereich „Listening“ vorgestellt.

1.1 Strategien zum Bereich „Listening“

Vorgehen in der Prüfung

In einer Klassenarbeit oder Prüfung hörst du den **Hörverstehenstext meist zweimal**.

Arbeitsschritt **1**

Vor dem ersten Vorspielen des Textes hast du in der Regel genügend Zeit, dir die **Aufgabenstellungen** auf dem Arbeitsblatt **anzusehen**. Lies sie dir sorgfältig durch und überlege genau, um welche Art von Aufgabe es sich handelt und was von dir verlangt wird. Überlege schon vor dem ersten Hören, auf welche Kerninformationen es in den Aufgaben ankommt. Darauf musst du dich dann während des Hörens ganz besonders konzentrieren.

Arbeitsschritt **2**

Nun hörst du den Text zum ersten Mal. Zu den Aufgaben, die du während oder nach dem ersten Hören bereits beantworten kannst, kannst du gleich die **richtige Antwort aufschreiben oder abhaken**. Versuche, möglichst viele Aufgaben **während des Hörens** zu lösen, da die Pause nach dem ersten Hördurchgang oft recht kurz ist. Wenn du bei einer Aufgabe unsicher bist, grüble nicht darüber nach, wie die richtige Antwort lauten könnte, um nicht Gefahr zu laufen, die Lösungen zu den darauffolgenden Aufgaben zu verpassen. Lass einfach eine Lücke und versuche, die restlichen Aufgaben zu lösen. Du brauchst nicht nervös zu werden, wenn du nach dem ersten Hören noch nicht alle Lösungen notiert hast. Lass dich auch nicht verunsichern, wenn du nicht alles auf Anhieb verstehst. Die Texte enthalten absichtlich unbekannte Wörter, da du im Alltag auch in solche Situationen kommen wirst.

Arbeitsschritt 3

Beim zweiten Hördurchgang kannst du zum einen deine **Antworten** noch einmal **überprüfen und** zum anderen die **noch verbleibenden Aufgaben beantworten**. Die Aufgabenstellungen folgen beim Hörverstehen der Textchronologie, d. h., wenn du z. B. die letzte Aufgabe zu einem Text nicht beantworten konntest, solltest du besonders am Ende des Textes aufpassen.

Tipp

- Vor dem ersten Hören: Worum geht es? Lies die Aufgabenstellungen genau durch.
- Während des ersten Hörens (und ggf. in der kurzen Pause danach): Trage die Lösungen zu den Aufgaben ein, die du schon beantworten kannst. Welche Informationen fehlen dir noch?
- Während des zweiten Hörens (und ggf. in der kurzen Pause danach): Löse die restlichen Aufgaben. Überprüfe noch einmal die Aufgaben, die du bereits beim ersten Hördurchgang gelöst hast.

Vorgehen beim Üben

Zu Übungszwecken kannst du dir die Hörverstehenstexte ruhig so oft anhören, wie du möchtest. Lies sie aber nicht durch! Versuche, die Arbeitsaufträge nur durch Zuhören zu beantworten. Nur wenn du überhaupt nicht auf die richtige Lösung kommst, solltest du die Hörverstehenstexte im Anhang dieses Buches lesen. Bei der Bearbeitung der Hörverstehensaufgaben in diesem Buch solltest du wie folgt vorgehen:

- Lies die Aufgabenstellungen genau durch. Hast du sie alle verstanden? Kläre unbekannte Wörter mithilfe eines Wörterbuches.
- Höre dir den entsprechenden Text einmal an, sodass du weißt, worum es darin geht.
- Höre dir den Text noch einmal an, wenn du den Text noch nicht so gut verstanden hast. Diesen Schritt kannst du so oft wiederholen, wie es für dich hilfreich ist.
- Versuche, während des Hörens die Aufgaben zu lösen.
- Wenn du alle Aufgaben bearbeitet hast, solltest du die Richtigkeit deiner Lösungen überprüfen, indem du dir den Text ein weiteres Mal anhörst.
- Anschließend überprüfst du deine Antworten am besten anhand des zugehörigen Lösungsbuchs. Wenn du viele Fehler gemacht hast, dann überlege genau, wie sie zustande gekommen sind. Hast du den Hörtext nicht genau verstanden? Hast du die Fragestellung falsch verstanden? Lies gegebenenfalls den Hörverstehenstext durch und wiederhole die gesamte Aufgabe ein paar Wochen später.
- Versuche, mit der Bearbeitung jeder weiteren Hörverstehensaufgabe in diesem Buch die Zahl der Hördurchgänge zu reduzieren, bis du bei der in der Prüfung üblichen Anzahl angelangt bist. In der Prüfung werden die Texte in der Regel nur zweimal vorgespielt.

1.2 Häufige Aufgabenstellungen zum Bereich „Listening“

Multiple choice

Dieser Aufgabentyp ist dir bestimmt schon vertraut: Dir wird eine Frage mit mehreren möglichen Antworten vorgegeben und du musst entscheiden, welche Antwort am besten zum Inhalt des Textes passt. Meist weicht dabei die Formulierung der Aufgabenstellung etwas von der im Text ab. In manchen Aufgaben hast du mehrere Bilder zur Auswahl. Hier musst du entscheiden, welches Bild am besten zum Hörtext passt.

Beispiel

Text:	"I'm sorry I'm late. The bus didn't come so I had to walk home and get my bike."
Task and answer:	Tick (✓) the correct answer: Why was the man late? ☐ Because the bus was late and he cycled. ☐ Because he walked. ☑ Because there was no bus.

Filling in the missing information

Hier musst du fehlende Informationen meist in einer Tabelle ergänzen. Es ist aber auch möglich, dass du Sätze vervollständigen oder Formulare ausfüllen sollst. Da bei diesem Aufgabentyp detailgenaues Verstehen gefordert ist, ist es besonders wichtig, dass du die Aufgabenstellung bereits vor dem Hören des Textes aufmerksam durchliest, damit du weißt, worauf du beim Hören achten musst. Arbeite ganz konzentriert, damit du die geforderten Wörter beim Hören nicht verpasst. Wenn du ein Wort nicht sofort verstehst, grüble nicht darüber nach, sondern versuche, die restlichen Lücken auszufüllen. Dieses eine Wort kannst du beim zweiten Hördurchgang nachtragen.

Beispiel

Text:	The man's smartphone rang in the bus queue. He turned away to talk. When he turned around, the bus had gone without him.
Task and answer:	Fill in the missing information. The man missed the bus because he had _turned away_ from it.

True or false

Auch diesen Aufgabentyp kennst du sicher schon lange aus dem Unterricht. Du sollst jeweils entscheiden, ob eine Aussage zum Hörtext richtig oder falsch ist. Auch hier wird die Formulierung in der Aufgabenstellung variiert.

Beispiel

Text:	"It was twenty minutes to the bus station."
Task:	Decide whether the statement is *true* or *false*.
Answer:	It was a long way to the bus station. true ☑ false ☐.

Matching

Eine weitere Aufgabenstellung, die häufig in Klassenarbeiten vorkommt, aber auch Teil der Abschlussprüfung sein kann, ist „matching“. Bei dieser Aufgabenstellung hörst du häufig kurze Äußerungen verschiedener Personen zu einem Thema, denen du dann die entsprechenden Aussagen *(statements)*, die dir schriftlich vorliegen, zuordnen musst.

Beispiel

Text:	**Jane:** “I hate flying but sometimes I have to do it because of my job …” **Mike:** “You’re lucky – I always have to work in the office.”
Task:	*Decide who could have said the following sentence:* “Travelling is part of my work.”
Answer:	☑ Jane ☐ Mike

1.3 Übungsaufgaben zum Bereich „Listening“

Listening Test 1: Short dialogues

You will hear six short conversations. There is one question for each of the conversations.
Tick (✓) the correct answer to each question.

1. What must Rob buy?

A ☐

B ☐

C ☐

2. What time does Tom arrive in school?

A ☐

B ☐

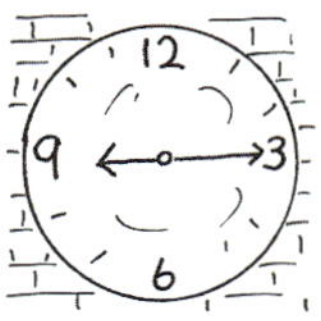

C ☐

3. Which poster do Vicky and Pete put on the school wall?

A ☐

B ☐

C ☐

4. Where does Mary post the letter?

A ☐

B ☐

C ☐

5. Which present doesn't June buy for her nephew?

A ☐

B ☐

C ☐

6. Where will John and Lynn go on holiday this year?

A ☐

B ☐

C ☐

Listening Test 2: Short texts

You will hear six recordings. There is one question for each recording.
Tick (✓) the correct answer to each question.

1. Which group of people get onto the plane second?

A ☐

B ☐

C ☐

2. How will Daniel get home if his mum can't meet him?

A ☐

B ☐

C ☐

3. Which is the correct way to the hotel?

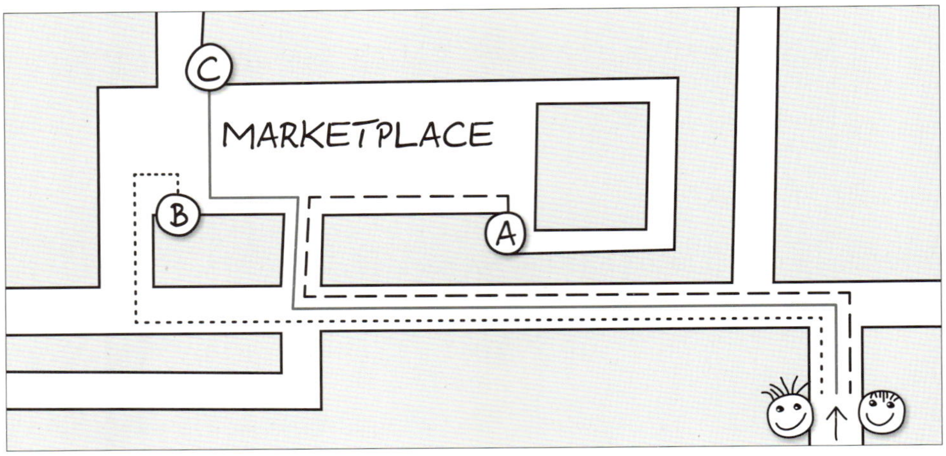

A ☐ B ☐ C ☐

4. What is Tom going to do now on Saturday?

A ☐

B ☐

C ☐

5. Where will each group of friends wait?

A ☐

B ☐

C ☐

6. Where was Lilly when she found out that she'd lost her camera?

A ☐

B ☐

C ☐

Listening Test 3: The German exchange

You will hear Aiden talking to his teacher, Mrs Jackson, about the German exchange.
Tick (✓) the correct answer to each question.

1. Why didn't Aiden receive the information?
   a) ☐ He was playing sport in a competition.
   b) ☐ He wasn't very interested at first.
   c) ☐ He wasn't feeling very well.

2. Does Mrs Jackson know when the exchange will be?
   a) ☐ She hasn't decided yet.
   b) ☐ Not exactly, but she knows which months.
   c) ☐ She is waiting to hear from Germany about the dates.

3. If Aiden goes, will he have a girl as a partner?
   a) ☐ No, he won't.
   b) ☐ Yes, he will.
   c) ☐ It is a possibility.

4. What happens on Friday?
   a) ☐ The English pupils and their partners go sightseeing all day.
   b) ☐ Everyone goes ice-skating.
   c) ☐ The English pupils meet their partners in the afternoon.

5. How do the group get to the school?
   a) ☐ They are met and taken to school.
   b) ☐ They go by train.
   c) ☐ Their partners' parents collect them from the airport.

6. What do the English group eat on the last evening?
   a) ☐ a Chinese meal
   b) ☐ something typically German
   c) ☐ pizza and pasta

Listening Test 4: Off the sofa and do it!

Listen to Sam and Beth talking about a windsurfing course.
Tick (✓) the correct sentence endings.

1. Sam was in town …
   a) ☐ because he was meeting his friends.
   b) ☐ to buy a birthday present.
   c) ☐ to get some details about something.

2. To do the course you must …
   a) ☐ be able to swim.
   b) ☐ be able to swim well in the sea.
   c) ☐ have tried windsurfing before.

3. Beth knows where the beach is because …
   a) ☐ she takes her children there.
   b) ☐ she went there when she was young.
   c) ☐ she likes walking there.

4. To get to the sailing club you have to …
   a) ☐ turn left after the car park.
   b) ☐ drive through the car park.
   c) ☐ turn left before the car park.

5. The first lesson is …
   a) ☐ on land.
   b) ☐ on the lake.
   c) ☐ on the sea.

6. On the windsurfer, you must stand …
   a) ☐ between the arrows.
   b) ☐ on the lines.
   c) ☐ where the footprints are.

7. What is difficult is …
   a) ☐ getting the sail out of the water.
   b) ☐ climbing back onto the windsurfer after falling off it.
   c) ☐ turning the windsurfer around.

Listening Test 5: My Norfolk

You will hear John Watson talking about three big country houses in Norfolk. Answer the questions.

When did King Edward buy Sandringham House?	1. ______
When can't you visit Sandringham House?	2. ______
What is around Holkham Hall?	3. ______
Name the ways Holkham Hall earns money.	4. ______ 5. ______ open air concerts
Who was the first owner of Houghton Hall?	6. the first ______
What is Houghton Hall now being used for?	7. as an ______

Listening Test 6: Things you didn't know about London

You will hear someone talking about London and some unusual facts about it. Complete the sentences.

London sees about …	1. ______ visitors a year.
Oslo's present for London is for …	2. ______
The money from *Peter Pan* goes to a …	3. ______
The Tube was the world's …	4. ______
While a station was being made the builders found …	5. ______
The Shard, a famous building in London, is …	6. ______ high.
Many tall buildings have …	7. ______

Listening Test 7: The California Gold Rush

Listen to a television presenter and an expert talking about the California Gold Rush. Tick (✓) the correct ending to each sentence.

a gold nugget

1. The first person to find gold was …
   a) ☐ a Native American.
   b) ☐ a settler.
   c) ☐ an Englishman.

2. The gold nugget was discovered in …
   a) ☐ a sawmill.
   b) ☐ the hills of California.
   c) ☐ a river.

3. On the nugget there are …
   a) ☐ teeth marks.
   b) ☐ many chips missing.
   c) ☐ three tests done.

4. The news about the nugget …
   a) ☐ went quickly across America.
   b) ☐ was stopped at first by the government.
   c) ☐ travelled slowly.

5. People in New York first learnt about gold in California …
   a) ☐ through a newspaper article.
   b) ☐ from stories about it.
   c) ☐ from a member of Congress.

6. People travelling west to seek gold …
   a) ☐ usually did not have a family.
   b) ☐ often had wrong expectations.
   c) ☐ knew they would have to work hard.

7. Van Valen's wife …
   a) ☐ moved to California to help her husband.
   b) ☐ only earned $ 500 in two years.
   c) ☐ had a very difficult life.

8. Most of the gold seekers …
   a) ☐ were successful enough to have comfortable lives.
   b) ☐ did not make a lot of money.
   c) ☐ returned home after a few years.

9. One result of the gold rush was that California …
   a) ☐ now appeared on maps.
   b) ☐ became very rich.
   c) ☐ joined the USA.

Listening Test 8: The Stolen Generations

You will hear a radio interview between the presenter, Greg Masters, and his guest, Jenny Green, talking about Australia's "Stolen Generations".

Decide whether each sentence is true or false.
Put a tick (✓) in the correct box *true* or *false*.

	true	false
1. The Aboriginal children were taken away from their families up until about 1970.	☐	☐
2. The governments wanted to help Aboriginal people integrate.	☐	☐
3. Most Aboriginal people thought their culture was better than the whites'.	☐	☐
4. Most children were put into homes close to their families.	☐	☐
5. The children had to take new names and speak English.	☐	☐
6. In the homes, Aboriginal children received a good education.	☐	☐
7. The government has never said sorry to the Aboriginal community.	☐	☐
8. The problem has still not been completely solved.	☐	☐

Listening Test 9: What can be done?

Read the following sentences carefully and then listen to the radio interview about the problems that some young people have today. Are the sentences *true* or *false?* Tick (✓) the correct box.

	true	false
1. Two of the main problems have got better.	☐	☐
2. There is still some cigarette advertising.	☐	☐
3. Smoking is expensive in Britain.	☐	☐
4. Small children regularly drink alcohol as well.	☐	☐
5. Real situations are used for alcohol awareness.	☐	☐
6. British people don't have ID cards.	☐	☐
7. Computers are a problem for young people.	☐	☐

Listening Test 10: Environment views

You will hear a radio interview where two young people are talking to the presenter about the environment. Decide whether each sentence is *true* or *false.* Put a tick (✓) in the correct box *true* or *false.*

	true	false
1. New energy sources are always welcomed.	☐	☐
2. It's quicker for Lewis's mum to take the car than to walk.	☐	☐
3. Public transport used to be better.	☐	☐
4. People could be encouraged to leave their cars at home.	☐	☐
5. Tourism can only make places better.	☐	☐
6. There's a danger that the same mistakes will happen again.	☐	☐
7. Cooperation is on the wish list.	☐	☐

Listening Test 11: Five-star hotel or wilderness?

Listen to the survey. Some people are talking about how they usually spend their holidays. Who thinks what? Write the correct letters in the chart.
Be careful: There is one more statement than you need.

A We can't afford to stay at a hotel.

B I usually go on city trips.

C I don't want to be a tourist in the traditional sense. I want to meet local people and see their home town through their eyes.

D I always visit my best friend, who lives far away.

E Couchsurfing is too risky.

F I like camping, but I don't want to sleep on the forest floor.

G I love being outdoors.

H I want nature, silence and luxury.

John	Olivia	Hailey	Carter	Josh	Sara	Lara

Listening Test 12: What's on your plate?

Listen to the survey. Some people are talking about their eating habits.
Who thinks what? Write the correct letters in the chart.
Be careful: There is one more statement than you need.

A I don't eat any animal products at all.

B I want to eat fewer sweets.

C Cooking for me means heating up what's in the freezer.

D Cooking is too much work for one person.

E I grow my own fruit and vegetables.

F I'm a meat-eater and I love barbecues.

G I always eat out at expensive restaurants.

H I'm not a strict vegetarian.

Henry	Liam	Clare	Finn	Colin	Hanna	Tessa

2 Kompetenzbereich: Reading

Es gibt viele verschiedene Arten von Texten, wie z. B. Werbetexte, Kochrezepte, Bedienungsanleitungen, Bewerbungsschreiben und Lebensläufe, E-Mails und Briefe, Tagebuch- oder Blogeinträge, Zeitungs- und Zeitschriftenartikel, Interviews, Kritiken und literarische Texte. Ebenso vielfältig wie die Textsorten können auch die Aufgabenstellungen dazu sein. Die Textsorten und Aufgabentypen, die am häufigsten in Klassenarbeiten und in der Abschlussprüfung vorkommen, werden dir hier vorgestellt.

2.1 Strategien zum Bereich „Reading"

Je nachdem, welche Art von Lesetext oder welche Art von Aufgabenstellung du bearbeiten musst, unterscheidet sich die Vorgehensweise. Manchmal musst du die Gesamtaussage des Textes erfassen *(reading for the gist)* und manchmal sollst du Details aus dem Text herausfinden. Du musst dann den Text nach den geforderten Informationen durchforsten (*skimming* oder *scanning*).

Arbeitsschritt 1

Zunächst einmal ist es sinnvoll, den Text an sich ganz genau zu betrachten. Manchmal kannst du bereits am **Layout**, d. h. an der Gestaltung des Textes, erkennen, um welche **Textsorte** es geht. Wenn du weißt, ob der dir vorliegende Text eine Werbeanzeige, ein Zeitungsartikel oder ein Interview ist, dann bist du schon einen Schritt weiter. Da der Bereich „Reading" in der Abschlussprüfung aus mehreren Teilen besteht, kommen darin auch verschiedene Textsorten, wie z. B. Werbeanzeigen und Sachtexte, vor.

Arbeitsschritt 2

Als Nächstes solltest du den **Text** einmal **genau lesen**. Die meisten unbekannten Wörter kannst du ganz leicht aus dem **Sinnzusammenhang erschließen**. Lass dich also nicht aus der Ruhe bringen, wenn dir das eine oder andere Wort unbekannt ist. Schlage nur die Wörter im Wörterbuch nach, die du nicht erschließen kannst, die aber für das Verständnis des Textes wichtig sind. Ganz entscheidend ist, dass du dir bei diesem Arbeitsschritt einen guten **Überblick über den Inhalt** des Textes verschaffst.

Arbeitsschritt 3

Nun solltest du die **Aufgabenstellungen genau lesen**, damit du weißt, unter welchen Aspekten du den Text bearbeiten sollst. Wenn du jetzt den Lesetext im Hinblick auf die jeweiligen Aufgabenstellungen liest, kannst du dabei ganz gezielt wichtige **Schlüsselwörter** bzw. **Textpassagen markieren**, damit du sie bei der Bearbeitung der Aufgaben schnell wiederfindest.

Nun bist du für die Beantwortung der Aufgaben gut gerüstet!

Tipp

- Schaue dir den Lesetext genau an. Kannst du vom „Layout" auf die Textsorte schließen?
- Lies den Text genau durch und verschaffe dir so einen guten Überblick über den Inhalt.
- Lies die Aufgabenstellungen sorgfältig. Markiere beim nochmaligen Lesen des Textes wichtige Textaussagen im Hinblick auf die Aufgabenstellungen.

2.2 Häufige Aufgabenstellungen zum Bereich „Reading"

True or false

Hier musst du entscheiden, ob **Aussagen** zum Text **richtig** oder **falsch** sind. Es ist wichtig, dass du sowohl den Text als auch die „statements" genau liest, denn ein einziges Wort kann ausschlaggebend sein, ob ein Satz korrekt ist oder nicht. Manchmal wird darüber hinaus von dir verlangt, dass du deine Entscheidung belegst. Du musst dann in der Regel die betreffenden Zeilen angeben; gelegentlich sollst du die genaue Textstelle zitieren.
Der Aufgabentyp „true or false" kommt in der Abschlussprüfung oft in Verbindung mit mehreren Werbeanzeigen, aber auch mit Sachtexten, vor.

Beispiel

Text:	The first U.S. American boot camp for teenagers was created in the 1980s to reduce the number of young criminals.
Task:	Decide whether the following statement is *true* or *false*.
Statement:	Boot camps have existed in the USA for about 15 years. true ☐ false ☑
Hinweis:	*Da seit den 1980er-Jahren schon weit mehr als 15 Jahre vergangen sind, ist diese Aussage falsch. Als Beleg könntest du „first U.S. American boot camp … created in the 1980s" angeben.*

Dieses Buch soll dir beim Üben helfen, also rate nicht einfach. Wenn du die Antwort nicht weißt, dann lass eine Lücke. Markiere die Fragen, bei denen du dir nicht sicher bist. Schaue im Lösungsteil erst dann nach, wenn du die ganze Übung bearbeitet hast, und versuche zu verstehen, warum die Antwort so und nicht anders lauten muss. Am besten wiederholst du diese Aufgabe zu einem späteren Zeitpunkt.

Matching

Es gibt verschiedene Arten von Zuordnungsaufgaben. Häufig sollst du einzelnen Textabschnitten eine passende Überschrift zuordnen oder umgekehrt: Dir werden Überschriften vorgegeben, zu denen du passende Abschnitte im Text finden musst. Manchmal musst du auch verschiedenen Personen, Ländern, Organisationen etc. Informationen oder Aussagen zuordnen.
In der Abschlussprüfung liegen dir meist einige Personenbeschreibungen vor. Du sollst diesen Personen dann einzelne kurze Texte oder Textabschnitte zuordnen, in denen es z. B. um Hobbys, Nebenjobs oder Reiseziele geht. Fast immer ist es so, dass mehr Auswahlmöglichkeiten als Personen vorgegeben sind – du musst also ganz genau hinsehen und darfst dich nicht in die Irre führen lassen.

Text:	① Harry studies English literature at university. He likes the theatre but he doesn't like musicals or comedy very much. One of his favourite plays is coming to London soon so he and a few friends are going to watch it. ② Sam … ③ Kim … **A** Macbeth **B** The Lion King **C** The Phantom of the Opera
Task:	Match each person (e. g. ① – ③) to the show they are going to watch (e. g. A – C)
Answer:	

Harry	Sam	Kim
A	…	…

Multiple choice

Bei diesem Aufgabentyp werden dir der Anfang eines Satzes und **verschiedene Satzenden** oder Fragen mit mehreren Antwortmöglichkeiten vorgegeben. Aus diesen Möglichkeiten musst du diejenige auswählen, die am besten zum Inhalt des Textes passt, und **das richtige Kästchen abhaken**. Oft wird in der Aufgabe nicht genau dieselbe Formulierung verwendet wie im Text; du musst also nach Schlüsselwörtern mit einer ähnlichen Bedeutung suchen und den Text und die Wahlmöglichkeiten genau vergleichen.

Beispiel

Text: In South Africa, young people born after 1994 – the year when Nelson Mandela was elected the first black president – are often referred to as "born frees". They are the first generation to grow up in a free and democratic society, the first who no longer experienced the system of racial segregation that had characterised South Africa for almost half a century.

Task and answer: Tick (✓) the correct box.
"Born frees" …
☐ are young people who were born in 1993 or earlier.
☐ never knew Nelson Mandela in their lifetime.
☑ were born when racial segregation had already been abolished.

Short answers / Filling in gaps

Manchmal sollst du auch Fragen zum Text beantworten oder Beispiele für bestimmte Sachverhalte aus dem Text heraussuchen. Lies den Text bezüglich der Aufgabenstellung aufmerksam durch und markiere die entsprechenden Textstellen. Meist reicht es, wenn du in Stichpunkten antwortest, gelegentlich musst du aber auch einen ganzen Satz formulieren. Es kann auch vorkommen, dass bereits ein Satz vorgegeben ist und du nur eine Lücke vervollständigen musst. Lies also die Aufgabenstellung ganz genau und halte dich an die Vorgaben.

Beispiel

Text:	Many projects for volunteers in Australia focus on the protection of wildlife, such as looking after endangered animals like the tree kangaroo or the southern hairy-nosed wombat. By collecting rubbish or planting trees, volunteers can help to restore the typical living space of these species.
Task and answer:	What can volunteers do to protect the living space of endangered species? Give two examples from the text: ▶ collect rubbish ▶ plant trees

2.3 Übungsaufgaben zum Bereich „Reading“

Reading Test 1: What can we do today?

On holiday, the Meyers saw some interesting adverts for different activities and places to visit. Read the adverts on the next page carefully, then decide whether the statements below are *true* or *false*. Tick (✓) the correct boxes.

	true	false
1. If it's raining, you can't go sky walking.	☐	☐
2. The Westwoods know some ghost stories.	☐	☐
3. Children can feed some of the animals.	☐	☐
4. You can't choose what you eat on your picnic.	☐	☐
5. Lord and Lady Westwood love people visiting their new house and gardens.	☐	☐
6. Sky Walking is open to everyone.	☐	☐
7. You can visit Westwood House at any time during the day.	☐	☐
8. A day's driving may cost you more than £ 150.	☐	☐
9. You can't go to the zoo on a Saturday.	☐	☐
10. Famous people stayed at Westwood House.	☐	☐

1

Then walk through the treetops! Try our course through the trees at heights of 15 metres above the ground – jump, climb, swing and much more.

Open dry days only:
Daily 9.00 a.m. – 6.00 p.m.
Price: **£ 8.50** – **no under 16-year-olds**

No booking, just arrive – safety lessons given, and then off you go.

2

Westwood House and Gardens

Lovely 15th-century house with beautiful gardens.

Book a visit now and have a tour around the house by the owners, Lord and Lady Westwood.

Listen to the stories and see the rooms where people came and made history – ghosts and more.

Open for private tours only. Tel: 0781/5678
Prices: £ 9.45 adults / £ 7.50 children under 16

3

TIGBY ZOO

Enjoy a great day out at Tigby Zoo.

Tigers, lions, bears and lots more - look down on the apes and the monkeys from the treetop walk.
Visit our restaurant; feed the animals in the Children's Corner.

Prices:
£ 12.50 adults
£ 6.50 children under 16

Open: Mon - Sat
9.00 a.m. - 8.00 p.m.

4

Picnic in style

We provide the elegant picnic with homemade food, you choose one of our 20 old cars.

from £ 150 a day (10 hours)

We'll even suggest where to go and what to see.

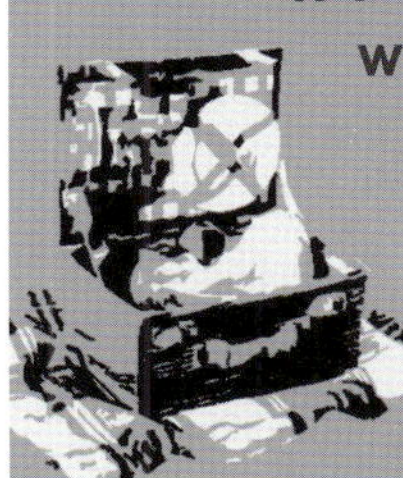

CARS and more
0716/44552

Reading Test 2: A birthday present

Holly and Luke are looking for a birthday present for their mum, who is adventurous, but not very good at sports. They have found some very interesting adverts. Read the adverts carefully, then decide if each statement is *true* or *false*. Tick (✓) the correct box.

1

THE Mountain Bike Experience

Four different levels of tracks to follow:
blue for **beginners** to **black** for **experienced mountain bikers**.

- Bikes can be hired by the hour or by the day.
- We even have a limited number of e-mountain bikes (booking in advance).

To book in advance, send an **e-mail** to: info@forestbikes_centre.uk
Phone: 09765/45670

Price: £ 3.50 (hour) / £ 20 (day)
Open: April 1st until November 15th–10 a.m. to 6 p.m.

2

Back to the Wild

With our experienced leaders, you'll learn how to camp without a tent and what to cook without going to the supermarket!

Interested? Phone **0379/232323** today for a brochure with all the details, dates and prices, or look on our website: www.bewild_hillside.co.uk

3

Every weekend in July and August
we offer 30-minute
flying experiences
in the afternoons
from 1 p.m. – 6 p.m.

It's a great present for someone – or something just for yourself.
Whatever the reason, book now! It'll be the best 30 minutes of your week!

Each plane can take 1–3 people. Price per take-off: £ 40
Phone the airport and ask for Sabrina.

4

CHOCOLATE DAY

Chocolate is beautiful! Listen to the history of how chocolate came to Britain and watch how we do wonderful things with it. Then try making any chocolate fantasy you have yourself – from a **chocolate handbag** to **chocolate-covered strawberries**!

Phone: Jenny and Jason on 0921/39678 to book a place on the "Chocolate dream course" or fill in the form on our website: **www.chocfan.smallbusiness.com**

	true	false
1. All you need to bring is a tent.	☐	☐
2. It is cheaper if there are three people.	☐	☐
3. E-bikes are available all year.	☐	☐
4. You can only go flying during the week.	☐	☐
5. If you have a dream, you might be able to make it.	☐	☐
6. There is a route for everyone.	☐	☐
7. You will need to bring your own food.	☐	☐
8. You can only phone to book this special present.	☐	☐
9. They show participants what they can do first.	☐	☐
10. Holly and Luke's mum would go on the black track if her birthday present was "The Mountain Bike Experience".	☐	☐

Reading Test 3: Charities

1. Who supports which charity? There are seven charities. Each of the five people or groups of people (①–⑤) have a favourite charity. Decide who supports which charity. Write the name of the charity next to the numbers.

Mr Davies is an architect. He works in London but loves going into the countryside looking at castles and other interesting buildings. He always takes photographs of them and sometimes he imagines how he could make them into something else. Last year he bought an old windmill and then spent twelve months making it into his own home. He's really proud of it and says he'll never sell it.

Jenny and her husband met when they were in Kenya. He was working as a doctor in a small village hospital and she was teaching the children there. She laughs about the school now because it only had one classroom and fifty children of all different ages. She now works in a school with over 1,000 pupils and lots of everything, but she misses her work in Africa and the feeling of really making a difference.

The Smith family have got two children. They live in a small village in the north of England where they recently moved to from London because they want to live in an unpolluted environment. They have two dogs and two cats and the whole family loves riding horses. The children always play outside somewhere or in their big garden.

4 

Mike loves the weekends. Last year he went on a sailing course on a lake near where he lives. Now he and a friend go sailing every weekend. The lake was boring once he had learnt to sail so now they go to Brancaster, which is on the coast. The coast there is beautiful and he loves the peace and quiet. It is fun sailing on the sea but it can be dangerous.

5 

At 13, Charlie was spending most of her time drinking vodka with her mates in an old disused factory. At 15, she was pregnant, and at 17, she was in a young people's prison. When she got out, she met Ralph, who helped her get a job and to stay away from her old life. She's now 34 and her life is getting better every year.

Action Now

Action Now helps very poor families and their children in different parts of the world to have a better future. For many children in developing countries, life is a daily fight to survive. With little food, polluted drinking water, disease and no schools, the future is not good for these people.

Action Now helps these poor families and their children.

- It starts village schools so children can learn to read, write and do maths.
- It helps with other projects, too, like providing the materials needed to bring fresh water to a village.

We help these poor families and their villages to help themselves so that they can have a better future.

The RNLI

The Royal National Lifeboat Institution is an emergency service for the sea.
We get no money from the government and we have few employees.

- *Most people are volunteers.*
- *Our members risk their lives every day saving other people.*

Sometimes a boat's engine has broken down or sometimes someone is very ill on a yacht and needs to go to hospital quickly, sometimes we rescue people who have fallen down a cliff, and sometimes we even have to rescue someone's pet that is stuck on the rocks.

► *The service is free but to keep it we need your money.*

WILD TRUST

Wild Trust was started about fifteen years ago. It helps to protect the countryside in many different ways.

- It looks after the birds and the animals found on its land.
- It tries to bring people closer to nature and shows them how important it is for everyone.
- We make special projects, too, for example building paths for countryside walks.
- We even have our own hospital for injured animals and birds that are found not just by us but by people in the area.

Our future plans are to buy a forest and keep it as a place of special interest for people to enjoy. We also want to try and protect an area of the coast so that people can see how it should be and not full of litter and tourists.

Don't Fall Down

Have you ever seen wonderful old buildings not looked after? They look dirty, high grass takes over the gardens and ivy grows quickly up the walls and over the roofs. The roofs then often collapse, windows become broken and walls get damaged. Suddenly, a beautiful old building becomes a ruin.

We want to look after these historic buildings.
We like to rebuild them and make them beautiful again.

Sometimes they become museums or activity centres but whatever they become they are given a life once again. Instead of being a horrible broken-down eyesore, they are returned to how they once were. If you support Don't Fall Down, then you're supporting your heritage for future generations to enjoy.

Care

Lots of old people have problems, especially in villages with only one shop, few buses and no doctor. Often they need small repairs done to their houses, too, but most businesses aren't interested in doing five-minute jobs.

What do we do? We have:

- a free car service for old people.
- lots of young people who mow lawns and do gardening.
- many specialists, from electricians to builders, who have recently stopped working or give up a few hours a week to help.

But these services need money – for petrol, for tools and for many other things. Please help us continue our good work.

Off the Streets

Off the Streets began about 3 years ago when its founders, Harry and Kate, saw that young people in a poor area of Manchester had little to do and nowhere to go. These young people were bored: they vandalised things, joined gangs and started drinking and using drugs.

Harry and Kate knew they could help.

- They rented an old school building with a field.
- They got a group of the kids to say what they needed: a skateboard area, a football pitch, table tennis tables, and a lot more.

Off the Streets was a huge success. Harry and Kate now want to start another centre in Leeds. Can you help to finance this?

Lakeland Mountain Rescue Centre

What could be better than walking up high mountains for a fantastic view over the lakes of Northern England or testing your skills by climbing some of the rock faces in the area? But accidents happen. Last year alone:

- we saved the lives of 72 people: some got lost in thick fog; some had fallen and broken a leg or an arm.
- it cost £ 200,000 to save lives and to keep our vehicles and equipment up to date.
- each of our volunteers worked for an average of 120 hours – for free.

If you love walking or climbing and the mountains, then help us keep this service.

	name of the charity
①	
②	
③	
④	
⑤	

2. Fill in the chart with the information from the adverts.

① problems in developing countries (4 aspects)	• • • •
② what a ruin often looks like (3 aspects)	• • •
③ problems which old people in small villages often have to deal with (2 aspects)	• •
④ charities that save injured people (2 charities)	• •
⑤ a charity which owns land	
⑥ serious problems among bored young people in a troublespot in Manchester (3 aspects)	• • •
⑦ what Care uses the donated money for (2 examples)	• •
⑧ what rebuilt or renovated buildings are sometimes used as (2 examples)	• •
⑨ what a charity offers young people in order to prevent them from getting into trouble (2 aspects)	• •
⑩ a charity which wants to raise awareness for the environment	

Reading Test 4: The Royal Theatre

1. The following five people (①–⑤) all want to go to the theatre. Everyone goes to see a different performance (A–G). Decide who goes where. Write the correct letter of the theatre production under the person's name.

① 

Harry is studying English at university. At the moment he's reading some well-known plays. He loves one play especially. It's a power struggle with lots of evil things happening and strong characters in it. Harry thinks this theatre performance, therefore, would be good to watch.

② 

Brooke, who is not easily scared, loves true stories and especially older ones that are a bit strange. She doesn't like musicals that much but if a friend wants to go to one she will. Today she's by herself so she can decide on something she really wants to watch.

③ 

Amy wants to give her grandchildren a surprise. The children and their parents are going on holiday to France soon. Amy isn't going with them because the children asked her to look after their animals. They're all animal mad. She's looking forward to seeing them again after Easter and then she can give them her surprise.

④ 

Rory has just started his own band and is a great America fan. He'd love to go to the States but he hasn't got much money. He always criticises a lot of pop stars for singing songs without any meaningful lyrics. Tonight he's going to the theatre with some of his friends.

⑤ 

Harper works in a busy office and has two younger brothers and a sister – she loves the idea of going somewhere with them all and having lots of fun and adventures. She's bought everyone a ticket to see this show because it might give them an idea for next year.

ROBINSON CRUSOE (A)

Wonderful family entertainment to begin the summer holidays. Everyone knows the story of Robinson Crusoe and how he has to live alone on a small island. But this story starts before Daniel Defoe's famous book. First the hero is attacked by pirates, then he goes to America. After that, when sailing to South America, he finally ends up on the island by himself until he saves Man Friday from the cannibals who arrive for their barbecue! There's lots of fun for all the family. It's a story for anyone over 7 years old.

B

Summer Holiday

A real summer holiday musical for the family. It makes you laugh, it makes you happy and it makes you sing the songs for weeks after you've left the theatre. It's just fun, fun and more fun, with lots of '50s and '60s music, too.

A group of young people decide to go "where the sun shines brightly" in a red, London double-decker bus which they have converted into a very big camper. They travel across Europe having fun and enjoying themselves but they're always being chased by the mother of Bobby, one of the young people. Bobby isn't just any normal girl, she's a famous singer in disguise. Her agent also wants her back in England, so he, too, wants to catch up with the group of young people.

C

Macbeth

Witches, blood, murder. What more could anyone want for a good night at the theatre? Shakespeare's Macbeth has something for everyone. The play starts with Macbeth on his way home after a battle meeting three horrible old witches in the middle of a storm.

They tell him he will become King of Scotland, which Macbeth wants very much. Macbeth and his wife murder the King and then Macbeth takes over. But the ending is not a happy one for Lady Macbeth or the new King of Scotland. Fast, brutal and the best play this year.

D

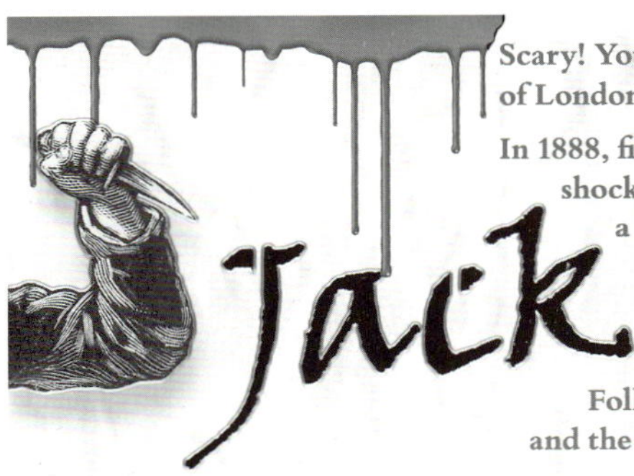

Scary! You won't want to walk down the East End streets of London at night after this performance.

In 1888, five women were violently murdered. The crime shocked everyone because they had been killed in such a terrible way. Who did it?

This play will have you looking at the evidence that the police had and you can come to your own conclusion.

Follow this true story and be shaken by the brutality and the struggle to find a killer.

E

Pickles

Pickles is a loveable dog that lives on the streets. Her story begins as a Christmas present to the Borrowdales' children. After a few months, having a puppy around isn't fun anymore. So, when her owners no longer want her, they take her into the middle of London, open the car door and throw her out. She has to find somewhere to sleep and somewhere to get food and water. A sad tale with a great happy ending and lots of adventures in between. A real family story with bad people you'll hate and good people you'll love.

The Door

F

A strange title that gets the hairs on the back of your neck standing up even before you've decided to go. The Door is a mysterious entrance to one family's future. Every time a member of the family goes through the door, they see a different version of the future. But whose future is the real one for the family? A good old-fashioned drama with lots of twists and turns in the plot. Don't tell your friends how it ends, though – you'll spoil the play for them.

G

This fantastic new musical from America follows the life of George Washington from his early days as the poor second son whose future takes a new direction after a family death. Playing an ever-increasing role in the struggle for independence, he fights against the French and then the British. Eventually he becomes the first President of America.

This is a modern musical with good solid rap songs to tell the tale and fantastic dance routines. A fast-moving performance with songs you'll remember for months afterwards.

Washington

① Harry	② Brooke	③ Amy	④ Rory	⑤ Harper

2. Answer the following questions about the theatre performances. Write short answers.
   a) Who wrote *Robinson Crusoe*? ______
   b) Where exactly were the women murdered? ______
   c) What type of theatre performance is *The Door*? ______
   d) When did the dog join the family? ______
   e) Who is Bobby? ______
   f) Who do the witches talk to? ______
   g) Who was Washington's first enemy? ______

Reading Test 5: "We may be 'born free', but ..."

In South Africa, young people born after 1994 – the year when Nelson Mandela was elected the first black president – are often referred to as "born frees". They are the first generation to grow up in a free and democratic society, the first who no longer experienced the system of racial segregation that had characterised South Africa for almost half a century.

During the so-called apartheid era, the population was divided into the following four racial groups: White, Bantu (black Africans), Coloured (of mixed ethnic origin) and Asian. While people with British or Dutch roots enjoyed lots of privileges, the non-white groups (especially black people) were systematically oppressed. For example, they were not allowed to vote and were forced to live in particular areas called "homelands". Public facilities were usually segregated into white and non-white zones so that white people didn't have to share the same space with members of the other groups.

Sign from the apartheid era in South Africa

For "born frees" like Mbali Legodi, a black young woman from Cape Town, this period seems far away. "Of course, my parents and grandparents have often told me about it, but I can't really imagine what it must have been like. I think for most of our generation it's normal to move around freely or be allowed to vote." Young South Africans nowadays take many of the hard-won privileges for granted, which has led some of the older generation to think of the "born frees" as spoiled or naive. Yet today's youngsters have to cope with problems of their own.

"Many of my friends are unemployed, there simply aren't enough jobs," Mbali says. According to recent statistics, about 60 per cent of South Africans between the ages of 15 and 24 are out of work. Black Africans seem to be particularly at risk of facing long-term joblessness. In addition, those who do find work also earn considerably less than the average white person. "I guess if you look at it from that perspective, not so much has changed. Even so many years after the end of apartheid, the old inequalities are still in place."

Has she ever considered leaving South Africa and moving to another country? "I knew you would ask that. But no, never. I mean, just look around you: I live in the most beautiful country in the world. There are so many creative people, people who want to change things. We may be 'born free', but there's still a lot for us to do in this society."

(419 words)

Read the article published in a youth magazine and then tick (✓) the correct sentence endings. There is only one correct solution for each statement.

1. The term "born frees" refers to ...
   a) ☐ black people who were released from prison.
   b) ☐ the children of President Nelson Mandela.
   c) ☐ South Africans born after the end of apartheid.

2. Through the apartheid system, non-whites ...
   a) ☐ lost their political voice.
   b) ☐ had to live in poor areas.
   c) ☐ oppressed other minority groups.

3. A lot of young South Africans ...
   a) ☐ have no respect for the older generation.
   b) ☐ have never even heard of apartheid.
   c) ☐ consider it normal to be living in a democratic society.

4. Over half of young South Africans ...
   a) ☐ earn average wages today.
   b) ☐ now have a positive future.
   c) ☐ face difficult employment prospects.

5. Today, the inequalities of apartheid ...
   a) ☐ have completely disappeared.
   b) ☐ can still be felt.
   c) ☐ have been made illegal.

6. Mbali Legodi wants to ...
   a) ☐ stay in her country.
   b) ☐ start a new life abroad.
   c) ☐ study in Europe.

7. Many born frees want to ...
   a) ☐ build a new South Africa.
   b) ☐ leave their country.
   c) ☐ create a new lifestyle.

Reading Test 6: Young Refugees Learn about U.S. on the Soccer Field

Young refugees in the United States are learning about each other and their new country on the soccer field. One player is 13-year-old Win La Bar. His family is from Myanmar, also known as Burma. Win was born in Thailand after his family fled their Burmese homeland. Now he is one of about 200 refugee children who play at the North Phoenix Christian Soccer Club, in the western state of Arizona. The players in the club's twelve teams are between six and eighteen years old.

Win and his nine family members share two apartments. Win has his own bedroom, but his sister sleeps in a room with her three young children. Win's parents and three other children live in another apartment. He loves his new home: "I've got a better chance to get a better education, and I get to play more soccer without worrying about gunshots."

The soccer club has helped him make friends and learn about his new home. His coaches have taught his family about life in the United States. Win says it was "very different, very hard to adapt into this world", because he had never seen cars or planes.

Alondra Ruiz works for the soccer club. She brings the players to games and drives them home. Sometimes she drives for hours a day, and hundreds of kilometers a week. During the rides the students ask her many questions about the United States. Ruiz tells them "you're not different. You're here. And you can become anything you want."

"Being part of this club, and keeping kids busy is very rewarding to me because it's good for them, and it's good for the future," she says. "What I hear often is that they're being treated different at school, that they're not being accepted. I relate to that 100 percent. I wasn't accepted coming from Mexico."

Ruiz was an immigrant child who grew up in the United States. Whereas her husband has permission to work in the U.S., she is not here legally.

Zara Doukoum knows what the other refugee students have dealt with, including when people did not understand what they were saying when they were just learning to speak English. "Every refugee in America went through that," she says. This year she will graduate from Central High School, the public school attended by most of her teammates. It will be four years since she arrived in Phoenix with her mother and three sisters. She wants to attend college, where she may play soccer or tennis. *(430 words)*

Adapted from: Christopher Jones-Cruise, Anna Matteo, Voice of America Learning English, January 25, 2016.

Read the web article. Then tick (✓) the correct sentence endings.

1. Win's place of birth was …

   a) ☐ the USA.

   b) ☐ Myanmar.

   c) ☐ Thailand.

   d) ☐ Burma.

2. Win …
   a) ☐ and his parents live together.
   b) ☐ lives together with three of his younger siblings.
   c) ☐ and his parents have separate flats.
   d) ☐ and his family have a lot of living space.

3. Win no longer has to worry about …
   a) ☐ his education.
   b) ☐ being in danger.
   c) ☐ making friends.
   d) ☐ playing soccer.

4. At the soccer club, the refugee children …
   a) ☐ get additional lessons in English.
   b) ☐ can learn more than just soccer rules.
   c) ☐ also learn how to choose the right college.
   d) ☐ can learn how to drive a car.

5. Alondra tries to …
   a) ☐ help the refugees financially.
   b) ☐ motivate the refugees.
   c) ☐ arrange the refugees' matches for them.
   d) ☐ avoid the refugees' questions.

6. Alondra also understands when the refugee children talk about the problem of …
   a) ☐ being an illegal.
   b) ☐ not speaking the language.
   c) ☐ their parents getting a work permit.
   d) ☐ integration.

7. Every refugee struggles …
   a) ☐ because of the discrimination shown.
   b) ☐ but they can succeed.
   c) ☐ but is supported by teammates.
   d) ☐ because they are different.

Reading Test 7: Cruise ships can seriously damage your health

http://laylastravelblog.co.uk

Most popular post

Cruise ships can seriously damage your health

I love holidays but I hate cruise ships. I'll admit it. Last year, I decided to visit a city called Cádiz in the southwest of Spain. Cádiz has about 120,000 inhabitants and began life more than 3,000 years ago. It sounded an interesting place to visit but when I got there three huge cruise ships were in the harbour: three cruise ships with thousands of passengers on them who invaded the city centre like an attacking army – and ruined it. That's my experience.

The ships were also running their engines: black smoke was bellowing out of their funnels, polluting the air, covering the city with dirt particles and producing constant noise. Venice is also suffering an invasion of cruise ships in the same way that Cádiz is, and the city wants to ban them. Dubrovnik has major problems, too: last year – I checked – 800,000 cruise ship visitors descended on the medieval city, which only has a population of just over 42,000. It, too, is looking at ways to stop the invasion.

I saw an advert last week when I was online about a cruise in the Arctic where the ship stopped at isolated communities on the coast. It showed pictures of polar bears in their natural environment, local people hunting and fishing and their traditions. Some of these communities had fewer than 500 inhabitants. The ship, though, could carry more than 1,400 passengers. Imagine how the way of life there will change – hunting and fishing to selling coffee, cakes and postcards?

I wanted to discover more about this popular way of having a holiday nowadays and found many things that shocked me. The daily emissions from a cruise ship are the same as those from one million cars and on one ship the air pollution on its upper deck is as bad as any major city's. With an estimated 24 million passengers a year, the cruise ship industry is huge and continually increasing in spite of cruises being expensive.

It's not just the pollution from emissions that is the problem: cruise ships need vast quantities of water, their guests produce a huge amount of waste and they have a long-lasting and devastating impact on beautiful places around the world and the people who live there. And is the situation getting worse? The largest cruise ship has nearly 9,000 people on it – 6,800 guests, and the rest are crew. Would you like three or four of those ships to stop in your beautiful city?

Read the blog entry and then tick (✓) the correct sentence endings.

1. Cádiz has …
   a) ☐ only recently become an important city.
   b) ☐ a long history attached to it.
   c) ☐ a very good name as a tourist destination.

2. The author of the blog does not like …
   a) ☐ the army.
   b) ☐ the ships arriving.
   c) ☐ the mass of visitors from the ships.

3. Some Mediterranean cities are …
   a) ☐ enjoying the economic benefits.
   b) ☐ finding that the air is becoming increasingly polluted.
   c) ☐ considering taking action to halt the trend.

4. The author found out about the Arctic cruise …
   a) ☐ from a newspaper advert.
   b) ☐ from a website.
   c) ☐ from friends who had been on the trip.

5. Visitors to isolated communities will …
   a) ☐ change them completely.
   b) ☐ make them wealthy.
   c) ☐ help them move into the modern world.

6. People booking holidays on cruise ships …
   a) ☐ have decreased in number recently.
   b) ☐ are finding them more expensive than before.
   c) ☐ do not seem to worry about the cost of their trips.

7. The biggest cruise ship at the moment has …
   a) ☐ a large number of employees.
   b) ☐ about 9,000 holidaymakers on it.
   c) ☐ received a lot of criticism.

Reading Test 8: Volunteering in Australia

Australia has long been one of the top gap-year destinations for young people from around the globe who have just finished school and want to travel for a year before starting a job or continuing their education. Many of them feel they want to do "something useful" during this time and decide to do voluntary work for a few weeks.

There are all sorts of projects in Australia in need of volunteers who are willing to get their hands dirty for a while. Most of those projects focus on the protection of wildlife, such as looking after endangered animals like the tree kangaroo, the flatback sea turtle or the southern hairy-nosed wombat. By collecting rubbish, planting trees or removing plants that do not naturally belong to the Australian landscapes volunteers can help to restore the typical living space of these species[1]. Constructing and maintaining walking trails or building fences in national parks are also very common activities. Sometimes volunteers also get the chance to assist in research programmes, setting up cameras to monitor endangered species, for example.

Some of these volunteers are international travellers, but Australia is also known as a nation of volunteers with 38 % of women and 34 % of Australian men volunteering regularly. Apart from spending an adventurous time and making new friends, many volunteers also cherish the feeling of learning something about the environment and contributing to its protection. Amber, from Arizona, says, "This program has taught me a great deal about conservation and what it takes to keep parts of a country safe for animals and plants. Life is too precious not to help the world and give something back." It is especially young people who set out on a gap year who feel that volunteering also makes a difference to themselves. "I've grown as a person and conquered so many fears," says Maggie from Canada.

(312 words)

1 species – type of plants or animals

Read the text about young people doing voluntary work in Australia. Decide if each statement is *true* or *false*. Tick (✓) the correct box "true" or "false" and give the lines in which you can find the relevant information.

	true	false	line(s)
1. Australia attracts the most people taking gap years in the world.	☐	☐	____
2. There are many one-year projects available.	☐	☐	____
3. Many projects are concerned with nature.	☐	☐	____
4. Some areas need to be made suitable for rare species.	☐	☐	____
5. Volunteers are used to create national parks.	☐	☐	____
6. Volunteers have to take photographs of animals as part of their job.	☐	☐	____
7. Not all volunteers are from abroad.	☐	☐	____
8. Meeting other young people and having fun is an extra benefit of the projects.	☐	☐	____
9. Gaining self-confidence is another result of volunteering during a gap year.	☐	☐	____

Reading Test 9: The Double Life of Cassiel Roadnight

I was in a hostel[1], a stop-off for impossible kids in east London somewhere. I'd been there a couple of days, walked in off the streets half-starved, because I had to. [...]

They gave me old clothes, washed thin and mended and almost the right size. They asked me lots of questions in return for two meals and a dry place to sleep. [...]

"I'm Gordon," [the man] said. "And the lady's name is Ginny."

"Well done," I said. "Good for you."

"And you are?" he said.

I looked at my shoes, somebody else's shoes, black and lumpy and scuffed. [...]

"I'm nobody," I said. [...]

The Ginny woman came with something in her hand, a piece of paper. "Can I have a word?" she said.

Gordon got up and they left me in the room on my own again. I could hear them on the other side of the door. They were whispering, but I could still hear.

She said, "I only saw it this morning. Pure coincidence."

"Bloody hell."

"He's been gone nearly two years."

"Well. I. Never."

"Do you think it's him?"

"Look at it. It's got to be."

The door handle moved. [...] When they came back in they were altered, careful, like I was a bomb that might go off, a sleeping tiger, a priceless vase about to fall. [...]

"Cassiel?" [Ginny] said.

I looked straight at her. I didn't know what was going on. "What?"

"Cassiel Roadnight?" she asked.

My name is not Cassiel Roadnight. It never has been. [...]

"Who, *me?*" I said. Gordon gave me the piece of paper. It was a printout, a picture of a boy with the word MISSING across his forehead. [...]

"Oh my God," I said, and took in a breath and I held it. [...]

My face exactly – my nose, my mouth, my chin. [...] I kept my eyes on the picture. There was something wrong with it.

Here are some things I know for sure about my face. I see them every time I look in the mirror.

One. I have two scars. [...]

Two. I have three piercings in my left ear and two in my right. [...]

Three. My teeth are bad. [...]

In the picture there were no scars on my face, no piercings. I had perfect teeth. I was happy and well fed and wholesome.

In other words, it wasn't me.

I tried to tell them. I looked up from the picture and I said, "No."

"Cassiel," Gordon said. He crossed his legs. His trousers and his mouth made a shushing noise.

I shook my head. "Not me." [...]

"What are the odds," Gordon said to Ginny, like I wasn't there, "of there being two *identical* missing boys?"

"*Billions* to one," Ginny said, like that settled it.

"I don't care what the odds are," I said. "It's not me." [...]

They didn't believe me. They wanted it to be right, I could tell that. They were going to insist on it. It doesn't matter what you say to people like that. When they have made up their minds they stop listening.

I breathed in hard and I tried not to think. I looked at the boy in the picture. I thought how incredible it was to have a double like that, somewhere out there in the world, to look exactly like a total stranger. I looked at Cassiel Roadnight's happy, flawless, fearless face. And the thought occurred to me then, that I could be him, if I wanted. [...]

There were people looking for Cassiel Roadnight, but they were people who cared. He had a family and friends. He had loved ones. He had a life I could step right into. And what did I have?

Nobody. Nothing [...].

I always wanted to be someone else. Doesn't everyone?

"OK," I said to the thought, so quietly I almost didn't say it at all.

"What?" Gordon said.

They looked at each other and then back at me. It was like they'd been holding everything in. Suddenly there was this noise in the room of them breathing.

"OK," I said.

"Good," said Ginny, and Gordon said, "Your name is Cassiel Roadnight?"

"Yes," I told him. "My name is Cassiel Roadnight," and I watched the smile spread and stick to his face.

1 hostel – here: shelter for homeless people

Adapted from: Valentine, Jenny. 2010. The Double Life of Cassiel Roadnight. *London: HarperCollins, pp. 7–17*

1. Read the extract of the novel and tick (✓) the correct sentence endings.

   a) The narrator comes to the hostel ...
   - [ ] while he is on holiday in London.
   - [ ] because he desperately needs something to eat.
   - [ ] to buy some second-hand clothes.

   b) The narrator's real name is ...
   - [ ] Gordon.
   - [ ] not mentioned.
   - [ ] Cassiel Roadnight.

   c) The man and woman suddenly treat the narrator differently because they ...
   - [ ] think he might be dangerous.
   - [ ] think he might be a missing person.
   - [ ] want him to identify another boy.

d) The narrator is sure that the picture shows …
- ☐ him.
- ☐ a person he does not know.
- ☐ someone he knows.

e) Eventually, the narrator decides to …
- ☐ take on a new identity.
- ☐ return to his family.
- ☐ stay at the hostel for longer.

2. Fill in the chart with the information from the text.

what the narrator gets at the hostel (2 aspects)	• •
what the narrator looks like (2 aspects)	• •

3. Decide if each statement is *true* or *false*. Tick (✓) the correct box and give the lines in which you can find the relevant information.

	true	false	line(s)
a) The narrator does not say where exactly the hostel is located.	☐	☐	____
b) The story begins right after the narrator arrives at the shelter.	☐	☐	____
c) Cassiel Roadnight has been missing for almost two years.	☐	☐	____
d) The narrator does not immediately decide to take on the missing boy's identity.	☐	☐	____
e) The narrator is quite satisfied with his life as it is.	☐	☐	____

3 Mediating

Was versteht man unter „Mediating"? Eine „Mediating"-Aufgabe ist eine Sprachmittlung, d. h., du erhältst einen (oder mehrere kurze) Texte auf Englisch oder Deutsch. Deine Aufgabe ist es, den Textinhalt zu verstehen und wichtige Informationen in die jeweils andere Sprache zu übertragen: Du musst also Informationen eines englischen Textes auf Deutsch bzw. bestimmte Details eines deutschen Textes auf Englisch wiedergeben. Häufig sollst du Fragen zu den Texten beantworten oder anderen Personen in einem Gespräch über den Textinhalt berichten. Manchmal musst du auch zwischen zwei Personen, die sich nicht verständigen können, dolmetschen. Aber Achtung: „Mediating" ist keine wörtliche Übersetzung!

3.1 Strategien zum Bereich „Mediating"

- Lies die Arbeitsanweisungen und die Texte aufmerksam durch. Halte dich bei der Bearbeitung der Aufgaben genau an die Vorgaben.
- Denke daran, dass es nicht deine Aufgabe ist, wortwörtlich zu übersetzen! Stattdessen sollst du die relevanten Informationen **sinngemäß** in eine andere Sprache übertragen. Gerate deshalb nicht in Panik, wenn du einmal die genaue Bedeutung eines englischen Wortes nicht kennst. Versuche einfach, aus dem Zusammenhang herauszufinden, was gemeint ist.
- Wenn du auf Englisch schreibst, formuliere keine zu komplizierten Sätze; so kannst du unnötige Fehler vermeiden. Denke aber daran, vollständige Sätze zu schreiben, es sei denn, die Arbeitsanweisungen verlangen etwas anderes.
- Liegt dir ein deutscher Text vor, der schwierige Wörter enthält, die du auf Englisch nicht weißt, umschreibe die Bedeutung oder formuliere deinen Satz so, dass du die unbekannte Vokabel gar nicht brauchst. Lasse jedoch keinesfalls eine Lücke.
- Denke daran, dass die Satzstellung im Englischen von der im Deutschen abweichen kann.
  Die englische Wortstellung in einem Aussagesatz ist *subject – verb – object*.
- Antworten auf Deutsch geben zu müssen klingt leicht, aber viele Schüler machen auch im Deutschen Fehler. Beantworte die Fragen in gutem Deutsch und lies anschließend das, was du geschrieben hast, noch einmal aufmerksam durch.
- Dolmetschst du in einem Gespräch, achte auf die richtige Perspektive. Wenn z. B. eine Person von sich selbst spricht, verwendet sie die 1. Person. Wenn du nun einem weiteren Gesprächsteilnehmer über diese Person berichtest, musst du die 3. Person verwenden. Es ändert sich also u. a. das Personalpronomen.

- Achte darauf, dass in einem Gespräch deine Äußerungen zu den vorhergehenden und nachfolgenden Gesprächsbeiträgen passen müssen. Lies also am Ende den gesamten Dialog noch einmal durch und überprüfe, ob deine Lösungen im Zusammenhang einen Sinn ergeben.
- Deine Äußerungen sollen **adressatengerecht** sein – überlege also genau, mit wem du sprichst bzw. für welche Person du einen Text zusammenfasst. Du wirst z. B. deiner kleinen Schwester oder deinem kleinen Bruder Dinge auf andere Art und Weise erklären müssen als beispielsweise deinen Großeltern.
- Wenn dir eine Übung große Schwierigkeiten bereitet, schaue dir in den Lösungen die Beispielantworten an. Wiederhole diese Übung zu einem späteren Zeitpunkt.

Tipp

- Lies die Arbeitsanweisungen und den Text genau. Markiere ggf. wichtige Textabschnitte in Farbe.
- Beim „Mediating" sollst du nicht wortwörtlich übersetzen, sondern bestimmte Informationen sinngemäß und adressatengerecht in die jeweils andere Sprache übertragen.
- Achte auf einen guten sprachlichen Ausdruck sowie Fehlerfreiheit.
- Lies dir deinen Text oder den vervollständigten Dialog am Ende noch einmal durch und kontrolliere, ob alle gefragten Informationen enthalten sind.

3.2 Häufige Aufgabenstellungen zum Bereich „Mediating"

Die Übungen in diesem Kapitel sollen dir helfen, mit den deutschen und englischen Texten und den jeweiligen Aufgabenformaten umzugehen. Die erste Aufgabe dient einer ersten Annäherung an die Sprachmittlung. Alle weiteren Aufgaben zeigen dir die große Bandbreite an Aufgabenstellungen auf. Bearbeite am besten zuerst die leichteren Aufgaben zu Beginn des Kapitels, bevor du dich dann an die längeren und schwierigeren Aufgabenstellungen machst.
Grundsätzlich unterscheidet man zwischen Sach- und Gebrauchstexten. Im Bereich „Mediating" können dir beide Arten von Texten begegnen. Häufig wirst du dich jedoch mit **Gebrauchstexten**, also z. B. mit Schildern, Formularen, Werbetexten/Anzeigen, Informationsbroschüren oder Mitteilungen, auseinandersetzen müssen. Auch Alltagsgespräche, Interviews oder Chats sind typische Texte für Sprachmittlungen.
Im Folgenden stellen wir dir die häufigsten Aufgabenformate vor.

Informationen aus einem Text in einer anderen Sprache zusammenfassen

Deine Aufgabe kann es sein, relevante Informationen aus einem Text in der jeweils anderen Sprache zusammenzufassen. Lies die Aufgabenstellung genau, denn sie kann wichtige Informationen enthalten, für wen du einen Text zusammenfassen musst. Es ist ein Unterschied, ob du einem kleinen Kind oder einem Erwachsenen etwas erklärst.

Beispiel

Text:

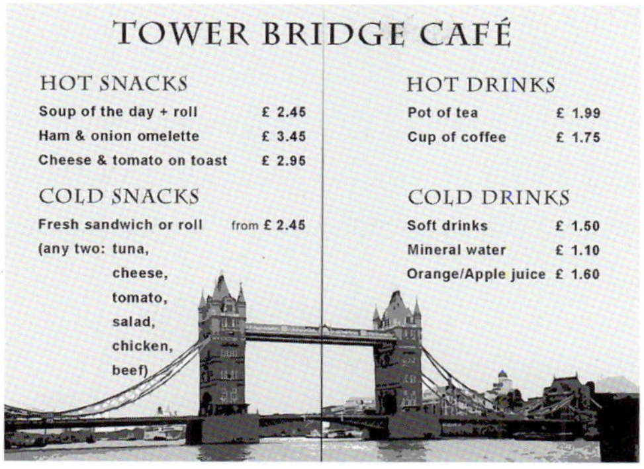

Task: Du gehst mit deiner kleinen Schwester in ein Café, während deine Eltern noch ein Museum in London besuchen. Erkläre deiner Schwester, was auf der Speisekarte steht und sage auch, was du gerne essen möchtest.

Answer: *Es gibt heiße und kalte Imbisse, aber keine große Auswahl. Es gibt . . .*

Auf Grundlage eines Textes ein Gespräch vervollständigen

Oftmals sollst du konkrete Fragen zu einem Text beantworten. Achte dabei darauf, dass du auf alle gefragten Aspekte eingehst und dass deine Äußerungen in den Sinnzusammenhang des Gesprächs passen. Meist liegt dir ein deutschsprachiger Text vor, zu dem du ein Gespräch auf Englisch vervollständigen sollst. Es kommt aber auch vor, dass du zu einem englischen Text einen Dialog auf Deutsch ergänzen sollst.

Beispiel

Text:

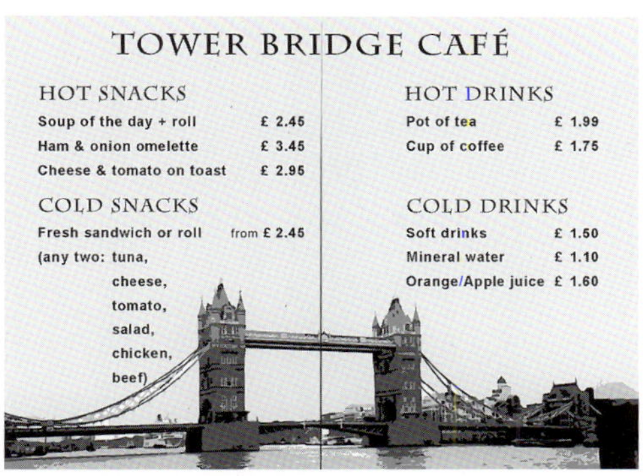

Task: Du gehst mit deiner kleinen Schwester in ein Café, während deine Eltern noch ein Museum in London besuchen. Beantworte die Fragen deiner Schwester mithilfe der Speisekarte.

Answer: **Schwester:** Ich habe großen Hunger. Was gibt es denn hier alles zu essen?

Du: *Es gibt nur Kleinigkeiten, aber wir finden bestimmt etwas für dich. Sie haben kleine warme und kalte Gerichte.*

Schwester: Mich friert es total. Ich hätte lieber etwas Warmes. Und du weißt ja, dass ich keinen Käse mag.

Du: *Es gibt eine Tagessuppe . . .*

In einem Gespräch dolmetschen

Hier wird von dir verlangt, dass du zwischen zwei Personen, die sich nicht miteinander verständigen können, dolmetschst, d. h., du musst Informationen oder Fragen sowohl vom Englischen ins Deutsche als auch vom Deutschen ins Englische übertragen. Denke hier an die richtige Perspektive und passe z. B. die Pronomen an.

Beispiel

Task: Du bist in einem Café in London. Am Nebentisch sitzt ein deutsches Ehepaar, das Schwierigkeiten bei der Bestellung hat. Du bietest deine Hilfe an. Vervollständige das Gespräch.

Answer: **Du:** Entschuldigen Sie, kann ich Ihnen helfen?

Frau: Das ist sehr nett von dir. Ich habe unsere Kellnerin leider nicht verstanden. Könntest du bitte nachfragen, was sie gesagt hat?

Du (zur Kellnerin): Could you say that again, please?

Kellnerin: Of course. I just said that today's special is a really delicious pumpkin soup.

Du: Es gibt heute Kürbissuppe. Die Kellnerin sagt, sie sei sehr lecker . . .

3.3 Übungsaufgaben zum Bereich „Mediating"

1. Talking about signs
   a) Schaue die drei Schilder an. Erkläre deinem kleinen Bruder auf Deutsch, was sie bedeuten.

1

2

3

Schild 1

____

____

____

Schild 2

____

____

____

Schild 3

____

____

____

b) Look at the German signs. Explain what they mean to your English friend who does not understand German.

Sign 1

____

____

Sign 2

____

____

Sign 3

____

____

2. Du bist mit deiner Familie im Urlaub in Großbritannien. Gerade seid ihr am Flughafen in Stansted, da ihr heute schon wieder nach Hause fliegen müsst. Deine kleine Schwester sieht dieses Schild und möchte wissen, was dort erklärt wird. Fasse die Information für deine Schwester zusammen.

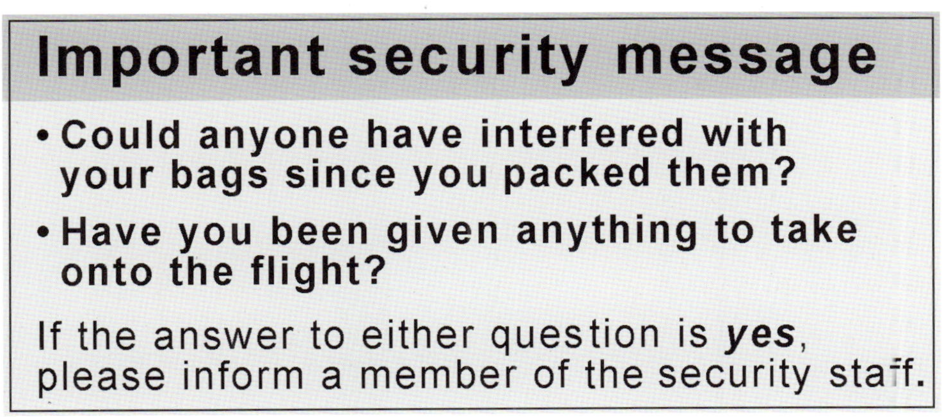

____

____

____

____

3. Im Unterricht besprecht ihr, wie weltweit versucht wird, die Kriminalität in Städten zu bekämpfen. Du hast im Internet recherchiert und einen älteren Artikel auf einer englischen Website gefunden, der über einen interessanten Versuch der englischen Polizei berichtet, gegen Verbrechen vorzugehen. Fasse die wichtigsten Punkte für deine Klassenkamerad*innen zusammen.

NEWS · NEWS · NEWS · NEWS · NEWS · NEWS · NEWS · NEWS · NEWS

Can you believe your eyes?

Have you seen a police officer? Are you really sure it was a police officer?

In England the police are trying a new idea to save money and to have more police around towns and cities. The idea is simple: if people see a police officer, they don't do anything wrong. That means that the police officer doesn't have to do anything, he or she just has to be there.

Petrol stations at night, for example, often have problems. Sometimes people fill up their cars with petrol and then drive away without paying, but if there is a policeman or woman in the garage shop, they don't. This idea works in supermarkets, too. If people see a police officer, they do not steal things.

The English police, therefore, have photographed themselves and have made cardboard police officers to stand in petrol stations and supermarkets. They have been quite successful but some have already been stolen!

Except for looking for stolen policemen or women, the police now have more time to do other things.

4. Du bist Mitglied der Umwelt-AG deiner Schule. Während deines Urlaubs in England siehst du unten stehendes Poster. Du findest den ökologischen Ansatz, den die Besitzer der Farm verfolgen, sehr interessant, und bittest deine Eltern, mit dir zu dem Bauernhof zu fahren.

a) Du telefonierst gerade mit einem Freund aus der Umwelt-AG und beschreibst ihm, wie *Highfields Farm* bewirtschaftet wird. Gehe auf **einen** der drei Ansätze ein.

___

___

___

___

___

b) Du bist gerade mit deiner Familie auf dem Bauernhof. Deine kleine Schwester Louisa ist total begeistert und will einer jungen Katze hinterherlaufen, die in einer Blumenwiese verschwindet. Erkläre ihr, wie sie sich generell auf dem Hof zu verhalten hat.

☞ Farm awareness

- Farms are work places; do not touch machinery or climb on it.
- Please keep to our paths and do not walk on the crops or pick the wild flowers.
- Always wash your hands after touching animals or plants.

____

____

____

____

5. Du bist mit deinem jüngeren Cousin für ein paar Tage nach London gefahren. Es ist Freitag und halb zwölf, und ihr habt Hunger. Ihr seid gerade in einer Straße, in der es viele Restaurants gibt. Da du besser Englisch sprichst als dein Cousin, erklärst du ihm, welche Möglichkeiten ihr habt.

Jakob: Ich bin echt hungrig. Was gibt es in dieser Straße alles zu essen?

You: ____

____

Jakob: Wir haben im Urlaub noch gar keine Fish & Chips gegessen. Was genau steht auf dem Schild?

You: ____

____

Jakob: Hm. Auf Pizza hätte ich allerdings auch Lust. Warum stehen denn auf dem Schild zwei unterschiedliche Preise?

You: ____

____

Jakob: Das ist nicht so teuer, oder? Wann macht die Imbissbude auf?

You: ____

Jakob: Ich habe aber so großen Hunger. Wenn die Imbissbude vielleicht erst in einer Stunde aufmacht, dann halte ich das nicht aus! Und mir tun auch echt die Füße weh vom vielen Herumlaufen. Können wir uns denn irgendwo reinsetzen?

You: ____

____

Jakob: Super. Wann macht das indische Restaurant auf?

You: ____

Jakob: Lass uns dorthin gehen. Auf ein Currygericht hätte ich auch echt Lust. Ist das Essen dort sehr teuer? Was meinst du?

You: ____

____

6. Du möchtest mit deinem Freund Ben während der Sommerferien verreisen. In einer Zeitschrift hast du eine Anzeige für einen Abenteuerkurs in England gefunden. Du bist total begeistert und rufst Ben an. Beantworte seine Fragen.

You: Hi Ben, ich habe eine richtig coole Idee für unsere Sommerferien. Ich habe nämlich eine Anzeige für ein Abenteuercamp in England gesehen. Man kann dort unter anderem verschiedene Sportarten ausprobieren oder lernen, aber auch andere spannende Dinge unternehmen.

Ben: Was genau könnten wir dort alles machen?

You: ______________________________

____

____

____

Ben: Wie lang dauert das Camp und wo findet es statt?

You: ______________________________

____

Ben: Das klingt interessant. Wer kann denn daran teilnehmen?

You: ______________________________

____

Ben: Das hört sich echt gut an. Ich spreche mal mit meinen Eltern. Steht in der Anzeige auch, was das Camp kostet und was bei dem Preis alles mit dabei ist?

You: ______________________________

____

Ben: Das ist nicht billig, aber OK, oder? Falls meine Eltern noch mehr über das Camp erfahren möchten, wo können sie nachfragen oder nachsehen?

You: ______________________________

____

7. Kim ist Schülerin der River High School. Im Sommer wird sie Besuch von ihrer Freundin Jana aus Deutschland bekommen. Kim möchte in dieser Zeit gerne an einem Wohltätigkeitslauf an ihrer Schule teilnehmen und versucht, Jana dazu zu überreden, auch mitzumachen. Die beiden telefonieren gerade und Kim beantwortet Janas Fragen auf Deutsch.

Kim: Hi Jana. Ich muss dir etwas erzählen. Ich habe gerade ein Plakat über einen Wohltätigkeitslauf gesehen. Hast du Lust, dass wir beide da mitmachen, wenn du mich besuchst?

Jana: Ein Wohltätigkeitslauf? Das muss ich mir noch überlegen … Wann und wo findet der Lauf denn statt?

Kim: ______________________________

____

Jana: OK, an dem Tag wäre ich ja auf jeden Fall schon da. Wofür soll denn Geld gesammelt werden?

Kim: ______________________________

____

Jana: Das Dorf hat keinen Brunnen? Wo kommt denn das Wasser bisher her?

Kim: ______________________________

____

Jana: Oje, wenn ich mir vorstelle, ich müsste vor der ersten Stunde so weit gehen, da wäre ich zu nichts zu gebrauchen … Ähm, wie weit müssten wir denn bei dem „Charity Run“ laufen?

Kim: ______________________________

____

Jana: Ein paar Runden würde ich schon schaffen … OK, ich mache auch mit. Muss ich mich irgendwo anmelden?

Kim: ______________________________

____

Running Water

Charity run: 20th August · River High School

We want to raise **$ 10,000** to bring water to the **African village** where our **partner school** is.

Why? Every morning the children have to collect the **day's water** for the family – the well is **5 kms away**. As a result they miss lessons or are very tired at school. If there is water in the village, the children will get a better education because they will have more time to learn.

- **800 m course: people can sponsor each lap up to a maximum of 10 laps**
- **Prize for the most money raised**
- **Food and craft stalls and plenty of extra activities**

If you want to run, please register via email: **runningwater@RHS.org**
For details of how to sponsor someone, visit our website: **www.RHS.org**

8. Your English friends are visiting you. Explain what the sign means so that they can decide what they want to eat.

9. Today is Tuesday. Your parents' American friends want to drive into the town centre themselves to go shopping. They do not know how long they want to stay. Explain the parking fees to them.

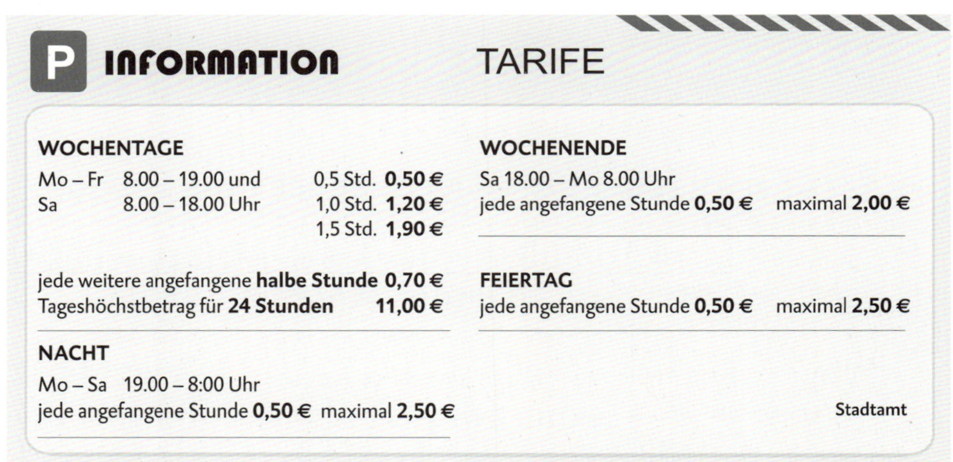

10. You see an advert for a great pop festival in your newspaper while your English friend Megan is staying with you. Answer your friend's questions in English.

You: There's a weekend rock festival at Schloss Battenburg. That's near here. Would you like to go?

Megan: That sounds good. Who's playing?

You: ______________________________

____

____

Megan: Cool. How much are the tickets?

You: ______________________________

____

Megan: That's not too bad. If we go for the weekend, where can we stay?

You: ______________________________

____

Megan: How much is the campsite?

You: ______________________________

____

Megan: Great. And when does the festival start and finish?

You: ____

____

Megan: Would we have to take our own food and drink?

You: ____

____

Megan: Ok, let's go for the weekend!

11. Your English friend, Beth, has just passed her driving test and she is going to drive to Germany for the first time. You have found a website giving foreign visitors some useful information about driving in Germany. You want to tell Beth the main points. Complete the dialogue by answering Beth's questions.

http://www.sicherautofahrenindeutschland.de

Allgemeines

In Deutschland gilt **Rechtsverkehr**. Autofahrer aus Ländern, in denen Linksverkehr herrscht und die auf deutschen Straßen mit dem eigenen Fahrzeug unterwegs sind, beachten bitte Folgendes: Da das Lenkrad in diesen Fahrzeugen auf der rechten Seite angebracht ist, befindet sich der Fahrer nicht in der Straßenmitte, sondern neben dem Gehsteig.
Für eine Liste der Länder mit Rechtsverkehr klicken Sie bitte hier.

Geschwindigkeits-begrenzungen

Dass man auf deutschen **Autobahnen** so schnell fahren darf, wie man möchte, ist weltweit bekannt. Doch diese Aussage ist nicht allgemeingültig: Auf viel befahrenen oder gefährlichen Strecken, in Baustellenbereichen, Tunneln oder bei Staugefahr gelten bestimmte Geschwindigkeitsbegrenzungen. Man beachte hier also die Verkehrsschilder und Anzeigen an den Autobahnen. Geschwindigkeiten werden in „Kilometern pro Stunde" angegeben. Zur Umrechnungstabelle von Meilen pro Stunde in Kilometer pro Stunde gelangen Sie hier.
Alle Autofahrer sollten generell umsichtig fahren – auch in Bereichen, in denen die Geschwindigkeit nicht eingeschränkt ist, muss das Fahrverhalten an die Verkehrssituation angepasst werden.
Auf **Landstraßen** beträgt die Geschwindigkeitsbegrenzung i.d.R. 100 km/h, in **Städten** normalerweise 50 km/h. Die gelben Ortsschilder zeigen, wo ein Ort beginnt und wo er endet. In verkehrsberuhigten Gebieten darf man allerdings nur 30 km/h oder Schrittgeschwindigkeit fahren. Hier gilt rechts vor links. Weitere Informationen erhalten Sie hier.

Vorfahrts-regelungen

Die Vorfahrt wird in Deutschland meist durch Ampeln oder Verkehrsschilder geregelt. Ist dies nicht der Fall (z.B. in verkehrsberuhigten Bereichen), so gilt „rechts vor links".
Vorsicht an Kreuzungen mit Ampeln! Wenn man als Autofahrer grün hat und abbiegen will, muss man dennoch anhalten, wenn Fußgänger oder Radfahrer die Straße überqueren möchten. Sie haben Vorrang.

Tanken

An einer Tankstelle muss man zwei Wörter kennen: „Benzin" bedeutet „petrol", „Diesel" bedeutet natürlich „diesel".

Wir wünschen eine gute und sichere Fahrt auf unseren Straßen!

You: Hi Beth. I found a German website that has lots of information and some tips about driving in Germany. Are you interested?

Beth: Yes, of course, I know you drive on the right but is there an easy way to remember that?

You: ______________________________

Beth: That's easy. What are the speed limits?

You: ______________________________

Beth: How do I know where a town starts and ends?

You: ______________________________

Beth: It's all very easy! Is there anything else I should know about?

You: ______________________________

Beth: Those two things are good to know. My car uses petrol – what's that in German?

You: ______________________________

Beth: Thanks a lot. See you next week.

You: Have a safe journey! See you then.

12. Your English friend, Jake, loves music and saw an article about a Samba festival in Germany, but he only understood the heading! Complete the dialogue.

Samba ... in Oberfranken!!

Kaum zu glauben, aber wahr! Die kleine Stadt Coburg in Oberfranken ist Veranstaltungsort des größten Sambafestivals außerhalb Brasiliens – und das schon seit 1992. Das Festival findet seitdem jedes Jahr am zweiten Wochenende im Juli statt* und zieht inzwischen mehr als 200,000 Besucher an, obwohl die Stadt selbst nur rund 45,000 Einwohner hat.

Im ersten Jahr war das Festival mit nur 20 teilnehmenden Gruppen recht klein, doch mittlerweile machen über 100 Sambagruppen aus aller Welt mit. Das Festival geht von Freitag bis Sonntag. Es gibt zahlreiche Open-Air-Bühnen, auf denen sowohl lokale als auch internationale Gruppen auftreten, und viele Workshops und Aktivitäten für Kinder. Natürlich gibt es auch Verkaufsstände, an denen z. B. bunte Kleidung oder Sambamusik erworben werden können. Auch Essens- und Getränkestände dürfen nicht fehlen. Höhepunkt der Veranstaltung ist der farbenfrohe und mitreißende Umzug durch die Stadt.

Das Festivalgelände ist weitläufig abgesperrt und darf nur mit Armband, das die Festivalbesucher an den Kassen erhalten, betreten werden.

Coburg ist an diesem Wochenende im Ausnahmezustand, doch nicht alle Bewohner*innen der Stadt sind darüber begeistert, denn es geht hoch her beim Samba-Festival. Lärmempfindliche Coburger*innen suchen für diese Zeit lieber das Weite!

* Während der Corona-Pandemie wurde das Festival in digitaler Form abgehalten.

Jake: When and where does this Samba festival take place?

You: ______________________________

____

Jake: How many groups are there and is it very popular?

You: ______________________________

____

Jake: Really? That's much bigger than I expected.

You: ______________________________

____

Jake: The biggest? Wow, that's impressive! What's on the programme?

You: ______________________________

____

____

____

Jake: It sounds great. Everyone in Coburg must be really happy to have such an amazing festival.

You: ______________________________

____

Jake: I can understand them but it's only for one weekend.

13. You are sitting outside a café when you see the woman at the next table open her bag and take out her own sandwiches and a drink. An angry-looking waitress comes out of the café and starts to talk to the woman. There is a language problem, but you think you can help. Complete the dialogue.

Kellnerin: *Sie können Ihre belegten Brote nicht hier essen!*

Frau: I'm sorry, I don't understand. I don't speak German.

Kellnerin: *Typisch! Essen Sie Ihre Brote nicht hier!*

Du: *Ich glaube, dass sie nur Englisch spricht. Vielleicht kann ich Ihnen helfen.*

Kellnerin: *Sagen Sie ihr, dass sie ihre belegten Brote hier nicht essen kann.*

Du: ______________________________

____

Frau: Oh dear. I thought these were just normal seats. I didn't realise they belonged to the café.

Du: Sie entschuldigt sich. ______________________________

____

____

Kellnerin: *Sie kann dort sitzen bleiben, wenn sie etwas bestellt. Wenn nicht, kann sie in den Park dort drüben gehen.*

Du: ______________________________

____

Frau: I think I've annoyed her. Can you ask her for a cup of coffee and one of those nice strawberry cakes, please?

Du: Yes, of course. That's no problem. *(zur Kellnerin)* ______________

____

____

Kellnerin: *O.K. Sagen Sie ihr, das kostet 4,50 € – und kein Sandwich hier!*

Du: ______________________________

____

Frau: She said something about sandwiches, too, didn't she?

Du: Yes, she did.

____

____

Frau: Thank you for helping me – she's not very friendly, though, is she?

14. Your exchange partner from England has just arrived. Your parents would like to talk to her, too, but her German and their English are not very good. You must act as the mediator and explain things in English to your exchange partner and in German to your parents. Complete the conversation.

Vater: *Hallo, Chloe. Hattest du eine gute Reise?*

Du: ______________________________

____

Chloe: Yes, it was fine, thanks, but very long. I'm quite tired now.

Du: ______________________________

____

Mutter: *Vielleicht will sie duschen. Ich habe schon Handtücher in ihr Zimmer gebracht. Kannst du ihr das sagen?*

Du: ______________________________

____

Chloe: That would be nice, thank you. We travelled overnight and we couldn't shower this morning.

Du: ______________________________

____

____

Vater: *Ich erinnere mich auch an solche Reisen. Sag Chloe, dass du ihr nach dem Duschen zeigen wirst, wo alles ist. Wenn sie fertig ist, können wir zu Mittag essen.*

Chloe: What did your father say?

Du: ______________________________

____

____

Mutter: *Isst Chloe alles? Gibt es irgendetwas, das sie nicht mag?*

Du: ______________________________

____

Chloe: The only thing I really hate is spinach.

Du: ______________________________

Vater: *Ich esse auch keinen Spinat. Spinat ist wirklich fürchterlich.*

Du:

15. Du nimmst an einem Austauschprogramm teil, bei dem du und dein Partner jeweils drei Monate an der Schule des anderen verbringt. Dein amerikanischer Austauschpartner Sammy hat heute seinen ersten Schultag in Deutschland. Ihr seid im Büro des Schulleiters, der Sammy begrüßen möchte. Da Sammys Deutsch noch nicht so gut ist, dolmetschst du zwischen den beiden.

Schulleiter: *Guten Morgen, ich bin Herr Schwarz, der Schulleiter. Hattest du einen guten Flug?*

You:

Sammy: Yes, I did, thanks, but it was very long and I'm still a bit tired.

You:

Schulleiter: Bitte sag ihm, dass ich ihn herzlich an unserer Schule begrüßen möchte und dass ich ihm drei unvergessliche Monate bei uns wünsche. Falls es Probleme geben sollte, kann er sich jederzeit an mich wenden – am besten mit dir als Dolmetscher!

You:

Sammy: Oh, that's nice! I hope my German will get better so that I can talk to him without you soon.

You:

Nach dem Treffen mit dem Schulleiter gehst du mit Sammy zum Unterricht. Dein Klassenlehrer gibt euch ein Infoblatt zu den Hitzefrei-Regelungen für diese Woche. Lies den Flyer durch und teile Sammy mit, welche Voraussetzung erfüllt sein muss, damit es Hitzefrei gibt und wann die Unterrichtsstunden verkürzt werden.

Liebe Schülerinnen und Schüler,

die erste Hitzewelle des Jahres steht an, daher hier zur Erinnerung die Hitzefrei-Regelungen an unserer Schule:

- Nur wenn die Temperaturen in den Klassenräumen bereits um 10 Uhr morgens die 25 °C-Marke überschreiten, können Unterrichtsstunden ausfallen. Die Temperaturmessung erfolgt an verschiedenen Standorten im Schulgebäude durch den Hausmeister.
- Über den Ausfall von Stunden bestimmen die Schulleiter*innen aller Schulen der Region gemeinsam. Die Abfahrtszeiten der Schulbusse werden koordiniert und entsprechend vorverlegt.
- Liegen die Temperaturen mehrere Tage lang bereits am Vormittag über 25 °C, so werden alle Stunden des Schultages auf 35 Minuten verkürzt. Eine solche Regelung wird ggf. bis spätestens 12 Uhr des Vortages bekannt gegeben.
- Bei extremen Temperaturen und erhöhten Ozonwerten findet kein Sportunterricht im Freien statt. Die Neigungsgruppen Fußball und Leichtathletik müssen dann entfallen, der reguläre Sportunterricht wird in die Sporthalle verlegt.
- Während der Hitzewelle ist das Trinken von Wasser im Unterricht selbstverständlich erlaubt.

gez. Die Schulleitung

You:
- ______________________________
- ______________________________

Sammy: That's cool. At home we have to work in the heat! What about sport?

You: ______________________________

Sammy: Are we allowed to drink in lessons when it is so hot? And how do we get back to your house when the school closes early?

You:
- ______________________________
- ______________________________

16. You and your family are behind an American at an information desk at Munich airport . The American is having language problems since the employee's English is very poor. You decide to help.

You: Can I help? I can speak English and German.

American: Thank you. I'm looking for a typical Bavarian hotel but not in the city.

You: I'll ask. ______________________________

____

Employee: Das „Hotel Bavaria München" ist sehr gut. Es ist ein wunderschönes Landhotel in der Nähe von München. Hier ist ein Hotelprospekt.
(Der Angestellte gibt dir den Prospekt auf der nächsten Seite).

You: ______________________________

____

American: That sounds great – and the photos look good, too. Can you ask him if he has the brochure for me in English?

You: ______________________________

____

Employee: Nein, leider nicht. Die englischsprachigen Prospekte sind aus.

The American explains that he's got a rental car but doesn't want to drive into Munich and asks whether it is possible to visit the city using public transport. He'd also like to try some local food but his wife doesn't and they don't want a noisy hotel. Give him the information about these three points from the brochure.

- ______________________________
  ____
- ______________________________
  ____
- ______________________________
  ____

Add two more pieces of information which you think are relevant.

- ______________________________
  ____
- ______________________________
  ____

Hotel Bavaria München ☆☆☆

Ankommen und rundum wohlfühlen

Verbringen Sie entspannte Urlaubstage in unserem idyllischen Landhotel, welches dank seiner naturnahen Lage am Stadtrand Münchens viel Ruhe und Erholung bietet.

Dennoch können Sie aufgrund der ausgezeichneten Verkehrsanbindung alle Sehenswürdigkeiten Münchens mit dem Bus oder der S-Bahn bequem und schnell erreichen. Ihr Auto können Sie währenddessen sicher in unserer hoteleigenen Garage lassen.

Kinder dürfen sich auf dem neu errichteten Spielplatz an der frischen Luft austoben und der bestens ausgestattete Fitnessraum kann von unseren erwachsenen Gästen rund um die Uhr genutzt werden.

Unser hauseigenes Restaurant serviert neben internationaler und bayerischer Küche auch vegetarische Gerichte sowie Diätkost. Teilen Sie uns am besten vorab telefonisch Ihre Wünsche mit.

Weitere Informationen und Buchung:

www.hotel-bavaria-munich.de

Tel.: 089/723489

Bezahlen können Sie selbstverständlich bar oder mit Kreditkarte.

17. Your older cousin from Australia, who loves excitement, is visiting you. She was looking at a holiday brochure for things to do near the Baltic coast, because you are going there together for a week. Some photographs of people on quad bikes caught her eye. She wants you to help her understand the German.

Liebst du **DIE GESCHWINDIGKEIT** und das **ABENTEUER** ...

... und möchtest unsere **OSTSEE-INSEL RÜGEN** auf unkonventionelle Art und Weise kennenlernen? Dann bist du bei uns genau richtig!

Komm zu **QUADABENTEUER** und entdecke auf unserer spannenden Offroad-Tour viele wunderschöne und unberührte Orte der größten deutschen Insel – abseits vom Trubel. Mit unseren erfahrenen Guides befährst du eine abwechslungsreiche Strecke, die über Felder, entlang eines Flussbetts, durch Wasser und Schlamm, über steiniges Terrain und Sandstrände führt.

Wenn du Lust hast, dir den Fahrtwind um die Nase wehen zu lassen und Rügen mit dem Quad zu erkunden, schreibe einfach eine kurze E-Mail an:

info@QuadAbenteuer.com

Unsere Mitarbeiterin Marie beantwortet alle deine persönlichen Fragen, z. B. was die Sicherheit, Einweisung, passende Kleidung und Kosten betrifft, zeitnah.

Wir bieten rund ums Jahr Touren für 2 bis 10 Personen an – schlechtes Wetter und Schnee sind kein Hindernis!

Ava: I found some photos of quad biking with something in German about it. It looks great fun. Where do they do this?

You: ______________________________

____

Ava: It looks like they go off-road. Can you tell me more?

You: ______________________________

____

____

____

Ava: That sounds exciting, doesn't it? What happens if it rains?

You: ____

____

Ava: I wouldn't want to go when it's snowing, but we shouldn't have that problem in August! Is Rügen far away from where we're staying at the Baltic Sea? I'd really love to go quad biking.

You: No, it isn't. Actually, it's only about an hour's drive away, so we can definitely take you there.

Ava: Great! I still have some questions, though. How can I find out more about the quad bike tour?

You: ____

But would you like me to write the email for you? It's got to be in German, of course.

Ava: Thanks, that'd be great. I'd like to know if they provide everything – clothes and a helmet – or do I need to bring them or anything else? Could you please also ask what time the trips take place and if they take place every day? Oh, I nearly forgot – how much does everything cost and would it be a problem that I don't speak German?

You: No problem – I'll do it now.

Du schreibst für Ava eine E-Mail an Marie. Achte darauf, dass du auf alle Fragen von Ava eingehst.

TO: Info@QuadAbenteuer.com

SUBJECT: Fragen zur Quad-Tour

Hallo Marie,

meine Cousine Ava würde gerne im August eine Tour bei *QuadAbenteuer* buchen, aber sie hat vorab noch ein paar Fragen. Es wäre super, wenn Sie die folgenden Fragen beantworten könnten.

____

____

____

____

____

____

____

Herzlichen Dank für die Beantwortung der Fragen.
Viele Grüße und bis bald,
(dein Name)

4 Writing

Viele Schüler*innen sind der Meinung, dass sie sich auf den Bereich „Schreiben“ nicht vorbereiten können, da die Aufgabenformen sehr stark variieren und die Note ohnehin stark von der individuellen Einschätzung der Lehrer*innen abhänge. Erschwerend kommt im Fach Englisch noch die Fremdsprache und die damit verbundene Fehleranfälligkeit hinzu. Aus diesen Gründen beschäftigen sich manche Schüler*innen erst gar nicht mit dem Kompetenzbereich „Writing“, was umso schlimmer ist, wenn man bedenkt, dass dieser Bereich bereits ein Drittel bis ein Viertel der Note in den meisten Klassenarbeiten und in deiner Abschlussprüfung ausmacht.
Mache nicht den gleichen Fehler! Lies die folgenden Seiten gut durch. Du wirst sehen: Eine sinnvolle und erfolgreiche Vorbereitung auf das Schreiben englischer Texte ist möglich. Aus diesem Grund enthält dieser Übungsteil auch vorbereitende Aufgaben, die dir helfen, Texte abwechslungsreicher zu formulieren und beim Schreiben zusammenhängender Texte sicherer zu werden.

4.1 Strategien zum Bereich „Writing“

Langfristige Vorbereitung

Auf das Schreiben von Texten in Klassenarbeiten und in der Abschlussprüfung kannst du dich nur langfristig gut vorbereiten. Wenn du dir erst zwei Tage vor der Prüfung überlegst, dass du in diesem Bereich noch Schwächen hast, dann ist es für eine sinnvolle Beschäftigung mit diesem Thema definitiv zu spät.

Solltest du beim Schreiben von Texten feststellen, dass du in der Grammatik manchmal unsicher bist, bietet es sich an, die **digitalen Zusätze** auf **MyStark** (Zugangscode vgl. Umschlaginnenseite) zu nutzen. Hier kannst du durch die Bearbeitung vieler **interaktiver Aufgaben zum Grundwissen** ganz gezielt Lücken in der **Grammatik** schließen, **Lernvideos** zu Grammatikthemen ansehen, mit denen erfahrungsgemäß viele Lernende Schwierigkeiten haben, oder Regeln mithilfe der **Kurzgrammatik** wiederholen. Auch zur Wiederholung, Erweiterung und Festigung des **Wortschatzes** sind die Aufgaben zum Grundwissen ideal. Methode 1

Schaue bzw. höre dir englischsprachige Interviews mit deinen Lieblingsstars im Internet (z. B. bei YouTube) oder im Fernsehen an. Sieh dir Filme im Original an, entweder im Kino – falls sie in deiner Stadt im Original vorgeführt werden – oder auf DVD bzw. über einen Streaming-Dienst im Internet (z. B. Netflix). Als Hilfe kannst du dir – falls möglich – auch die englischen Untertitel einblenden lassen und die Dialoge mitlesen. Methode 2

Methode 3

Versuche, möglichst viel in englischer Sprache zu lesen; auch hier wirst du im Internet fündig. Du kannst dich z. B. über Themen, die dich interessieren, im Online-Lexikon Wikipedia informieren. Hier gibt es übrigens auch den Bereich „Simple English", falls dir die Texte zu schwierig sind. Oder probiere, Romane und Geschichten auf Englisch zu lesen. Du wirst sehen: Mit der Zeit verstehst du mehr und mehr, und viele Ausdrücke und Redewendungen kommen dir immer vertrauter vor, sodass du sie für deine eigenen Texte verwenden kannst.

Methode 4

Eine gute Übung ist es auch, sich viel in der Fremdsprache zu unterhalten. Sprich hin und wieder mit deinen Freund*innen oder deinen Geschwistern englisch. So wird dir das eigenständige Formulieren von Mal zu Mal leichter fallen.

Wichtig ist also, dass du dich mit der englischen Sprache auch in deiner Freizeit beschäftigst. Dabei geht es nicht nur darum, das Verfassen englischer Texte zu üben, sondern ganz generell sollst du möglichst viel mit dem Englischen in Kontakt kommen. So kannst du deinen Wortschatz erweitern und Sicherheit im Gebrauch der Fremdsprache erwerben, die du beim Schreiben brauchst.

Das Schreiben eines Textes

Es gibt viele verschiedene Arten von Texten, wie z. B. Briefe oder E-Mails, Artikel und Blogs. Ganz gleich, welche Art von Texten du schreiben musst, die Vorgehensweise ist dabei immer ähnlich.

Arbeitsschritt 1 – Aufgabe(n) lesen

Lies die Aufgabenstellung(en) gut durch und überlege genau, was darin von dir verlangt wird. In der Abschlussprüfung sind oft bestimmte Aspekte vorgegeben, die unbedingt in deinen Texten vorkommen müssen. In Klassenarbeiten können die Themen aber auch freier formuliert sein.

Arbeitsschritt 2 – Aufgaben(set) auswählen

Manchmal kannst du in Klassenarbeiten zwischen mehreren Aufgabenstellungen wählen. In deiner Abschlussprüfung musst du mehrere Schreibaufgaben unterschiedlicher Länge verfassen. Du kannst zwischen zwei Aufgabensets, die meist aus jeweils zwei oder drei Aufgaben bestehen, auswählen. **Suche dir die Aufgaben aus, mit denen du dich am besten auskennst.** Vermeide nach Möglichkeit Themen, zu denen du nichts zu sagen hast. Es macht keinen Sinn, einem Freund oder einer Freundin in einem Brief von den Abenteuern beim Skifahren zu erzählen, wenn du noch nie etwas mit Wintersport zu tun hattest.
Hast du dich für ein Set entschieden, beginne mit der Aufgabe, bei der du dich am sichersten fühlst. Die Aufgaben steigen im Schwierigkeitsgrad und in der Textlänge bzw. bauen sogar manchmal aufeinander auf, sodass es in der Regel sinnvoll ist, mit der ersten Aufgabe anzufangen.

Arbeitsschritt 3 – Notizen machen

Lies dir die (erste) Aufgabenstellung aufmerksam durch und überlege, was du dazu schreiben könntest. Beachte dabei genau die Vorgaben aus der Aufgabenstellung – die darin genannten Aspekte kannst du meist schon als grobe Gliederung für deinen Text verwenden. Überlege als Nächstes, was du noch hinzufügen musst – fallen dir z. B. schon Beispiele zu den einzelnen Aspekten oder nützliche Formulierungen ein? Dann solltest du sie gleich **auf einem Blatt**

notieren. Gleiche deine Notizen anschließend noch einmal mit der Aufgabenstellung ab, um sicherzugehen, dass du wirklich alle geforderten Aspekte berücksichtigt hast.

Arbeitsschritt 4 – Text schreiben

Nun musst du den **Text formulieren**. Gehe dabei Schritt für Schritt die Aufgabenstellung durch und formuliere die einzelnen Sätze aus. Gute inhaltliche Ideen sind dabei genauso wichtig wie ein **klarer Aufbau** deines Textes. Versuche, Abhängigkeiten, Folgen etc. durch entsprechende Konjunktionen, also durch Bindewörter, wie z. B. „because" oder „although", deutlich zu machen. Schreibe kurze, überschaubare Sätze; so kannst du Grammatikfehler leichter vermeiden. Achte dennoch darauf, dass du nicht jeden Satz gleich aufbaust, sondern unterschiedliche Strukturen verwendest. Auch beim Wortschatz solltest du abwechseln, d. h. nicht immer die gleichen Wörter wiederholen. Greife auf Redewendungen zurück, die du gelernt hast. Wenn du etwas nicht ausdrücken kannst oder dir der Wortschatz fehlt, dann versuche, die Begriffe zu umschreiben oder notfalls einen anderen Aspekt zu finden, zu dem dir die Vokabeln leichter einfallen. In Kapitel 4.2 findest du eine Zusammenstellung vieler nützlicher Formulierungen, die dir beim Aufsatzschreiben helfen werden. Lerne sie auswendig. Du wirst sie immer wieder einsetzen können.
Achte auch darauf, in etwa die geforderte **Wortzahl** einzuhalten, da dir ansonsten Punkte abgezogen werden können.

Arbeitsschritt 5 – Text korrigieren

Nimm dir auf jeden Fall die Zeit, **deinen Text** abschließend noch einmal in Ruhe **durchzulesen**. Ist alles logisch aufgebaut? Sind die einzelnen Sätze sinnvoll miteinander verknüpft oder gibt es irgendwo Gedankensprünge? Bist du auf alle in der Aufgabenstellung genannten Aspekte *(prompts)* eingegangen? Wichtig ist auch, dass du noch einmal gezielt nach Rechtschreib- und Grammatikfehlern suchst und diese entsprechend verbesserst.

Vielleicht kommen dir die beschriebenen Arbeitsschritte eher zeitaufwendig und umständlich vor. Versuche aber dennoch, nach diesem Schema vorzugehen: Du wirst merken, dass dir das bei den Hausaufgaben, in Klassenarbeiten und natürlich erst recht in der Prüfung wertvolle Zeit spart. So wird es kaum passieren, dass du eine falsche Aufgabe oder ein Aufgabenset auswählst, das dir nicht liegt, und das erst merkst, wenn du schon mitten im Schreiben bist. Klar sollte dir allerdings auch sein, dass du dieses Verfahren üben musst.

Tipp

- Lies die Aufgabenstellung(en) genau und analysiere sie.
- Wähle die für dich geeignete(n) Aufgabe(n) aus.
- Notiere dir zu der Aufgabe, die du zuerst bearbeiten möchtest, einige Stichpunkte.
- Überprüfe, ob du alle Aspekte der Aufgabenstellung berücksichtigt hast.
- Formuliere den Text anhand der Aufgabenstellung und der vorgegebenen *prompts* Schritt für Schritt aus.
- Lies deinen Text abschließend noch einmal genau durch und überprüfe dabei, ob alles logisch aufgebaut und verständlich geschrieben ist. Verbessere Rechtschreib- und Grammatikfehler.
- Gehe bei allen weiteren Schreibaufgaben genauso vor.

Writing

4.2 Hilfreiche Wendungen

Die folgenden Wörter und Ausdrücke helfen dir beim Schreiben von Texten. Du solltest sie auswendig lernen. Die Wendungen sind übrigens auch als digitale „MindCards" verfügbar, mit denen du am Smartphone oder Tablet üben kannst.

Formulierungshilfen für E-Mails und Briefe

Anrede und Schlussformeln in formellen E-Mails und Briefen (z. B. Geschäftsbrief / Anfrage)

wenn du den Namen des Ansprechpartners nicht kennst:

Sehr geehrte Damen und Herren,	*Dear Sir / Madam,* *Dear Sir or Madam,* *To whom it may concern:*
Mit freundlichen Grüßen	*Yours faithfully,*

wenn du den Namen des Ansprechpartners kennst:

Sehr geehrte Frau Roberts,	*Dear Mrs Roberts,*
Sehr geehrter Herr James,	*Dear Mr James,*
wenn du nicht weißt, ob die Frau verheiratet ist oder nicht	*Dear Ms Bell,*
Mit freundlichen Grüßen	*Yours sincerely,*

Layout eines Geschäftsbriefes

24 Castle Street Blackburn Lancashire LK6 5TQ	Absender (ohne Namen)[1]
6th March 20…	Datum[2]
Mrs J. Fox Dane Cleaners 3 Arthur Road Doddington NE3 6LD	Name + Adresse des Empfängers (bei Geschäftsbriefen)
Dear Mrs Fox,	Anrede
Thank you for your letter …	
Yours sincerely,	Schlussformel
Adam Smith	Unterschrift
Adam Smith	Name

1 Die Adresse des Absenders kann auch auf der linken Seite stehen.
2 Das Datum kann auch links stehen. Die Schreibweisen 6 March 20… / March 6, 20… / March 6th, 20… sind alternativ möglich.

Tipp

In formellen E-Mails und Briefen musst du die Langformen der Verben verwenden (z. B. „I am" anstelle von „I'm").

Anrede und Schlussformeln in persönlichen E-Mails und Briefen

Liebe Jane,	*Dear Jane,*
Viele Grüße / Liebe Grüße	*Best wishes,* *Love,* (nur bei sehr guten Freunden; von Frauen viel häufiger verwendet als von Männern)

Mögliche Einleitungs- und Schlusssätze

Danke für …	*Thank you for …*
Ich habe … erhalten.	*I received …*
Ich hoffe, dass …	*I hope (that) …*
Wie geht es dir?	*How are you?*
Im letzten Brief hast du mir von … erzählt.	*In your last letter you told me about . .*
Im letzten Brief hast du mir erzählt, dass …	*In your last letter you told me (that) …*
Entschuldige, dass ich … vergessen habe, aber …	*Sorry that I forgot to …, but …*
Sage bitte … / Richte … bitte aus …	*Please tell …*
Es wäre schön, wenn wir uns treffen könnten.	*It would be nice if we could meet.*
Bitte richte … (schöne) Grüße aus.	*Best wishes to … /* *Please give my (best) regards to … /* *Please say hi / hello to … from me.*
Bitte schreibe mir bald zurück.	*Please write soon.*
Ich freue mich darauf, bald von dir zu hören.	*I'm looking forward to hearing from you soon. / I hope to hear from you soon.*
Ich freue mich auf deinen Brief.	*I'm looking forward to your letter.*
Ich werde dich anrufen.	*I'll call / ring you.*

Weitere häufig vorkommende Redewendungen / Ausdrücke

sich entschuldigen	*I'm sorry …*
etwas bedauern / Enttäuschung ausdrücken	*It's a pity that … /* *I'm disappointed that … /* *I was deeply disappointed by …*
an etwas erinnern	*Please remember to …*
Überraschung äußern	*I was surprised that …*
eine Bitte äußern	*Could / Would you …, please?*

einen Wunsch äußern	*I'd like to .../I'd love to ...*
einen Entschluss mitteilen	*I've decided to .../I'm going to .../ I've made up my mind to ...*
eine Absicht mitteilen	*I intend to .../I will .../I want to .../ I'm planning to ...*
Interesse ausdrücken	*I'm interested in ...*
Freude ausdrücken	*I'm happy/glad about ...*
Überzeugung ausdrücken	*I'm convinced that .../I'm sure that ...*
nach dem Preis fragen	*How much is it?/... does it cost?*
Ich hoffe, dir hat ... gefallen.	*I hope you liked/enjoyed ...*
Ich muss jetzt ...	*I have to ... now.*
Ich denke, es ist besser ...	*I think it's better to ...*

Auskunft geben über sich selbst

Ich wohne in ...	*I live in ...*
Ich wurde am ... in ... geboren.	*I was born in ... on (17th June 2005).*
Ich interessiere mich für ...	*I'm interested in ...*
Ich war schon in ...	*I've (already) been in .../to ...*
Ich möchte gerne ... werden.	*I'd like to be a/an ...*
Mir geht es gut.	*I'm fine.*
Mir geht es nicht gut.	*I'm not well./I don't feel well.*
Ich mag ...	*I like .../I enjoy ...*
Ich mag ... lieber (als ...)	*I prefer ... to .../I like ... better (than ...)*
Ich weiß ... noch nicht genau.	*I still don't know exactly ...*
Ich plane, ... zu tun.	*I plan to ...*
Ich freue mich (sehr) auf ...	*I'm (very much) looking forward to ... I'm (very) excited about ...*
Ich konnte nicht ...	*I wasn't able to .../I couldn't ...*
In meiner Freizeit ...	*In my free time/spare time ...*
Ich nehme regelmäßig an ... teil.	*I take part in ... regularly.*

Formulierungshilfen zur Strukturierung von Texten (z. B. für eine persönliche Stellungnahme oder einen Artikel)

einen Text einleiten	*To begin with, ... First of all, ...*
einen Text abschließen	*To sum up, .../In summary, .../ All in all, ... To conclude, .../In conclusion, ...*

Argumente aufzählen	*Firstly, ... Secondly, ... Thirdly, ... Finally, ...*
Argumente gegeneinander abwägen	*On the one hand ... On the other hand ...*
auf Widersprüche hinweisen/ etwas einräumen	*but* *however* *yet* *although* *despite/in spite of* *in contrast to* *otherwise* *nevertheless*
zusätzliche Aspekte anführen	*In addition, ...* *Moreover, ...* *Furthermore, ...* *Not only that, but ...* *Another important point/aspect (to mention) is ...*
Beispiele geben	*for example/e.g.* *for instance* *like* *such as*
Gründe anführen	*Due to ...* *Thanks to ...* *The reason for this is that ...* *because (of)* *as* *since* *therefore*
auf die Folgen von etwas hinweisen	*As a result, ...* *Consequently, ...*
die eigene Meinung ausdrücken	*In my opinion/view, ...* *Personally, I think/believe that ...* *To my mind, ...* *As far as I am concerned, ...* *As for me, ...*
Zweifel/Sorge ausdrücken	*I am not quite sure whether ...* *I doubt that ...* *I am concerned/worried that ...*
Zustimmung ausdrücken	*I think so too.* *I agree with this statement.* *That is right/correct.* *I am of the same opinion.*

Ablehnung ausdrücken	*I do not think so.* *I do not agree./I disagree.* *That is wrong/not correct.* *I am not of the same opinion.*

Verben des Sagens (z. B. für Fantasiegeschichten)

sagen	*to say sth/to tell sb sth*
fragen	*to ask*
sich fragen	*to ask oneself/to wonder*
antworten/erwidern	*to answer/to reply/to respond*
flüstern	*to whisper*
murmeln	*to murmur/to mutter/to mumble*
schreien	*to call (out)/to yell/to scream/ to shout*
erwähnen	*to mention*

4.3 Häufige Aufgabenstellungen zum Bereich „Writing"

Die Texte, die du in deiner Abschlussprüfung verfassen sollst, sind unterschiedlich lang. Halte dich beim Schreiben in etwa an die vorgegebene Textlänge.
In der Regel wird in der Aufgabenstellung eine ganz bestimmte Art von Text von dir verlangt. Die **Textsorten**, die in der Abschlussprüfung vorkommen können, sind **vielfältig**: Du musst z. B. in der Lage sein, kurze Nachrichten, Notizen, Einladungen oder Einträge in sozialen Netzwerken zu verfassen, Reviews oder Inserate zu formulieren, Fragen zu stellen, Empfehlungen auszusprechen oder Vergleiche anzustellen. Wichtig ist, dass du deine **Meinung ausdrücken** und zu einem Thema **Stellung nehmen** kannst. Außerdem wird von dir verlangt, **unterschiedliche Perspektiven einzunehmen**. Das bedeutet, dass du immer überlegen musst, in welche Rolle du jeweils schlüpfen sollst, wenn du einen Text schreibst.
Auch die **Themenbereiche sind vielfältig**. Häufig geht es in den Texten um „Urlaub" oder weitläufig um „Schule", aber auch kreative Schreibaufgaben, bei denen du deiner Fantasie freien Lauf lassen kannst, kommen immer wieder vor.
In der Regel sind **mehrere Aspekte vorgegeben**, die unbedingt in deiner Lösung enthalten sein müssen. Oftmals erhältst du zusätzliche Informationen, die du in deinen Text einbeziehen musst. Diese Informationen können dir in Form einer Grafik, eines Bildes oder auch eines Textes (z.B. eine E-Mail, eine Nachricht oder ein Zeitungsartikel) vorliegen. Gelegentlich wird dir auch der Anfang des Textes vorgegeben, den du fortsetzen sollst.
Im Folgenden werden die Textsorten, die am häufigsten in der Prüfung vorkommen, näher vorgestellt.

Formulare

Manchmal erhältst du ein Formular, das du ausfüllen musst. Es kann sich z. B. um eine Buchungsanfrage, ein Bewerbungsformular oder eine Registrierung für einen Onlineshop handeln. Bereits in der Arbeitsanweisung erfährst du, ob du ganze Sätze schreiben sollst oder ob Kurzantworten / Einzelwörter ausreichen. Lies also die Aufgabenstellung aufmerksam durch. Meist reichen bei dieser „Writing"-Aufgabe Stichpunkte aus.

E-Mail / Brief / Nachricht

Hier musst du entweder ein offizielles Schreiben verfassen oder eine persönliche E-Mail, einen persönlichen Brief bzw. eine Nachricht über eine „messaging app" auf deinem Smartphone schreiben. Sieh dir die Aufgabenstellung genau an und analysiere im ersten Schritt, an wen sich dein Text richtet: Sollst du eine förmliche Anfrage, z. B. an eine Firma, oder eine persönliche Nachricht an Freunde oder Verwandte formulieren? Oft musst du als „fiktive", also erfundene, Person einem fiktiven Adressaten schreiben. In welchem Stil dein Text geschrieben sein sollte, hängt von all diesen Faktoren ab.

- **Formelle(r) E-Mail / Brief:** Typische Beispiele für formelle E-Mails und Briefe sind Bewerbungen auf eine Stellenanzeige oder Kundenbeschwerden bzw. -anfragen. Bei dieser Art von Schreiben ist es wichtig, einen eher sachlichen Sprachstil zu verwenden. Vermeide Kurzformen wie „you're" oder „I'd" und verwende stattdessen die Langformen (also z. B. „you are" und „I would"). Achte auch auf eine passende Anfangs- und Schlussformel. Welche Wendungen sich hierfür eignen, erfährst du in Kapitel 4.2 – dort findest du auch weitere nützliche Formulierungshilfen.
- **Persönliche(r) E-Mail / Brief:** Bei einer persönlichen E-Mail oder einem persönlichen Brief an einen Freund / eine Freundin kann dein Tonfall ruhig etwas lockerer sein – auch Kurzformen oder eher umgangssprachliche Ausdrücke sind erlaubt. Oft ist in der Aufgabenstellung bereits eine E-Mail eines Freundes / einer Freundin vorgegeben, auf die du reagieren sollst. Lies dir den Text dann genau durch und versuche, auf die Aussagen oder Fragen darin einzugehen und deinen Text so zu formulieren, dass er zum Tonfall der vorgegebenen E-Mail passt.
- **Persönliche Nachricht:** Oftmals wird von dir verlangt, dass du eine knappe „message" formulierst. In deiner Abschlussprüfung wird in der Regel eine Situation in der Arbeitsanweisung vorgegeben, auf die du reagieren sollst. Manchmal enthält die Aufgabenstellung auch ein Bild, auf das du Bezug nehmen sollst. Auch hier solltest du an die Anrede zu Beginn denken und am Ende (d)einen Namen ergänzen.

Artikel

Häufig sollst du in der Abschlussprüfung einen Artikel schreiben. Es kann sich dabei z.B. um einen Beitrag für eine englischsprachige Schülerzeitung oder für eine Jugendzeitschrift handeln, in dem du eine bestimmte Fragestellung bzw. Problematik besprichst und ggf. dazu Stellung nimmst. Manchmal sollst du auch einen Artikel für einen Schreibwettbewerb verfassen. Achte auch hier wieder darauf, was genau von dir verlangt wird. Artikel für die Schülerzeitung sollten sachlich, aber trotzdem lebendig geschrieben sein; bei einem Beitrag für einen offiziellen Wettbewerb kann ein eher förmlicher Stil erforderlich sein, usw.

Geschichte

Auch das Verfassen einer Geschichte ist eine beliebte Aufgabenstellung. Hier gibt es viele verschiedene Möglichkeiten, wie die Aufgabe gestaltet sein kann. Vielleicht ist dir ein **Bild** vorgegeben und du sollst dazu eine Geschichte erfinden, vielleicht liegt dir aber auch der **Anfang einer Geschichte** vor und du sollst die „story" (mithilfe von weiteren Vorgaben) zu Ende führen. Besonders bei dieser Textsorte ist es wichtig, den Spannungsbogen aufrecht zu erhalten und den Leser oder die Leserin „bei der Stange zu halten". Dies funktioniert in der Regel nur, wenn du dir vor dem Schreiben die Zeit nimmst und eine ausführliche Ideensammlung machst. Wichtig ist auch, dass du dir klar machst, aus welcher Perspektive die Geschichte erzählt werden soll. Manchmal ist die Perspektive vorgegeben, aber gelegentlich kannst du auch frei entscheiden, ob du als Ich-Erzähler auftreten willst oder ob die „story" in der 3. Person erzählt werden soll.

Tagebuch- oder Blogeintrag

Manchmal wird auch von dir verlangt, über bestimmte Erfahrungen oder Erlebnisse zu berichten, z. B. in Form eines Tagebuch- oder Blogeintrags. Diese Texte sind oft in einem eher informellen, lockeren Stil gehalten. Sie sind in der 1. Person Singular verfasst und greifen meist ein besonderes oder einschneidendes Erlebnis auf, d.h., es bietet sich häufig an, auch auf Gefühle einzugehen.

In Kapitel 4.4 hast du Gelegenheit, einige der typischen Aufgabenformate der Abschlussprüfung gezielt zu trainieren. Darüber hinaus enthält das Kapitel auch mehrere vorbereitende Übungen, mit denen du dich langsam an das Schreiben längerer Texte herantasten kannst.

4.4 Übungsaufgaben zum Bereich „Writing“

1. **Gap sentences**
   Choose the best word from the box to improve the sentences below.

   dark – horror – loud – narrow – old – sandy – seafood –
   small – so – summer – terrible – quickly – young

   a) The ________________ house was at the end of the ________________ street.
   b) Jane likes listening to ________________ music in her ________________ bedroom.
   c) The ________________ boy ran away ________________.
   d) We had a ________________ meal in the ________________ restaurant.
   e) I didn't like the ________________ film because it was ________________ boring.
   f) My ________________ holiday was great.
   g) There was a long, ________________ beach with no one on it.
   h) The sky was very ________________ before the storm.

2. **Picture description – Taking notes**
   Look at the photograph. What can you say about it? Take some notes.

____

____

____

____

3. Picture description – Looking at details

Look at the photo from Task 2 again. Answer the following questions in complete sentences.

a) Where does the scene take place?

It takes place in front of a building.

b) Describe who you can see …

- in the foreground: ______
- in the background: ______

c) Describe …

- the boy's face: ______
- what he is holding: ______
- where he is in relation to the others: ______

d) Describe …

- the other people's clothes: ______
- what they are doing: ______

4. Picture description – Improving sentences

Look at your answers to Task 3. Improve each answer by adding more information – an adjective, an adverb or an additional phrase.

a) Where does the scene take place?

Answer in Task 3 a: It takes place in front of a building. ➡ It takes place in front of a **big white/grey** building – **probably outside a school.**

b) Describe who you can see …

- in the foreground: ______
- in the background: ______

c) Describe …

- the boy's face: ______
- what he is holding: ______
- where he is in relation to the others: ______

d) Describe …

- the other people's clothes: ______________________________
- what they are doing: ______________________________

5. **Questions – The story behind the picture**

Think of five questions you could ask about the picture.

- ______________________________
- ______________________________
- ______________________________
- ______________________________
- ______________________________

6. **A story about a picture – Bullying?**

Imagine what is going on between the boy in the foreground and the other teenagers. Think of answers to the questions you asked in Task 5 and write a short story in about 120 words.

____

7. **A story – A special flight**

What is the story behind the picture? Write a story in about 150 words. In your text, include three of the following aspects and tick (✓) them:

☐ Who took the photo?

☐ Where was the photographer travelling?

☐ When was the photo taken?

☐ Why was the photographer allowed into the cockpit?

☐ What did the pilot explain?

8. **A form – A school exchange programme**

Your school has got students from China coming to visit for 10 days. You would like a Chinese guest. Your teacher has asked you to fill in the form in English so that the Chinese teacher can match you with one of her students.

- Complete all parts of the form.
- Answer in words or numbers – you do not have to write in full sentences.

Name			
Class			
Age		Sex	
Nationality			
Your interests			
Describe yourself in three words:			
What do you really dislike?			

9. **A form – A holiday questionnaire**

Some pupils are doing a project about holidays and they have asked your class to complete a questionnaire.

- Complete all parts of the questionnaire. Write keywords only.
- You can use your imagination in your answers. But remember that your answers must sound real.

When was your last holiday?	__________
Where did you go to?	__________
How did you travel?	__________
How many people went with you?	__________
What two things did you enjoy the most?	__________
	__________
Describe your accommodation.	__________
	__________
Describe the weather during your holiday.	__________
	__________

Would you recommend where you went to other people?
Explain your answer using three or four words or phrases.

____

____

10. **Questions – Talking to a tour guide**
Imagine you and your family are on holiday in Canada. You meet your tour guide, Melissa Anderson from Ontario, who is an expert on everything about Canada. Ask her five questions about Canada's history, geography and/or tourist attractions.
Questions like "Are you married?" or "How long have you been working as a tour guide?" will not be accepted.

▸ ____________________

▸ ____________________

▸ ____________________

▸ ____________________

▸ ____________________

11. **Questions – Talking to a famous musician**
Imagine you have won a competition organised by a local radio station. The prize is an exclusive meeting with your favourite musician, who is performing at an open air festival tonight. You want to be prepared for the meeting, because you only have 15 minutes to talk to him/her. Write down five suitable questions you can ask.
Questions like "What's your name?", "How old are you?" or "Why aren't you in a serious relationship?" will not be accepted.

▸ ____________________

▸ ____________________

▸ ____________________

▸ ____________________

▸ ____________________

12. **A message – Party rules**

You are taking part in a school exchange programme with a school in Galway, Ireland. Your Irish "family" have agreed to host the farewell party for the German guests in their garden. The parents will not be there during the party, but they leave a note for their son, who is your exchange partner, and you. Write the note from the mother's perspective in about 50 words.

In your text, name three things the guests are not allowed to do.

13. **A note – A surprise**

Imagine you are visiting your Scottish aunt. Your aunt works at the local hospital and today her shift ends around noon. As she is always hungry when she gets home, you have prepared something for her to eat . However, you won't be home when she gets there, so you write her a note.

In your note, tell her

- where you have gone and with who,
- when you will be back,
- what you have prepared for her.

a) Keep your note as short as possible. Write about 50 words.

b) Now try to expand on your ideas. Write about 80 words. You can include additional details too.

14. A message – The lost guidebook

You are visiting a friend in the north of England. You have gone to London for the weekend, but your friend couldn't go with you. He lent you his London guidebook. Unfortunately, you cannot find it anymore.
Send your friend a message.

In your text,
- apologise,
- explain why you lost the guidebook,
- tell your friend what you would like to do to make up for it.

a) Keep your message short and write about 80 words.

b) Now write the same message in about 100 words. Try to make your text more interesting. You can add more details if you want to.

15. Notes – For and against

Read the following statements and imagine they are from your contacts on a social networking site. Do you like them or not? Collect ideas for possible answers and fill in this grid:

Statements	Arguments for 👍	Arguments against 👎
❶ Action films are only for boys.		
❷ In times of climate change flying should be at least twice as expensive as it is today.		
❸ People who eat meat are killers.		
❹ Living in a small village is the most boring thing I can imagine.		

16. A post – Give your opinion on a social networking site

Choose either statement ❶, ❷ or ❸ from Task 15 and give your opinion. Write an answer to the statement for a social networking site in about 80–100 words.

Topic	

17. **An e-mail – City or country?**

Your friend Katie has sent you the following e-mail:

Hi there,

You won't believe it: my father has found a new job at last! I'm so glad – I really couldn't bear to see his sad face much longer.
But the bad news is that his new company is in Exeter, more than 80 miles away from Bristol. Now we're discussing whether we should move to Exeter or to a small village between Exeter and Bristol. I wouldn't have to change schools if we moved to this place in the country; I could take a bus to school. But I don't know, can you imagine living in a small village? What do you think the better choice is?

Hugs,
Katie

Answer Katie's e-mail. In your e-mail, include the following aspects:

- what the news means for Katie's family
- possible advantages and disadvantages of moving either to Exeter or to a small village
- the option you think is the best choice for Katie

Write about 120 words. A suitable beginning and ending to the e-mail has already been written for you.

Hi Katie,

It's so good to hear that …

So in my opinion, ______ would be the best choice for you.

Take care,

(your first name)

18. In Task 17, a **suitable beginning** for the e-mail is already given. Think about the following situations and choose the correct address yourself.

a) In a letter to Carlos Fernandez, your pen friend in South America:

☐ Dear Mr Fernandez,
☐ Sir,
☐ Hi Carlos,

b) In an e-mail to Diana Watson, the manager of a hotel you stayed at (you only know her name and have never met her in person):

☐ Dear Ms Watson,
☐ Dear Mrs Watson,
☐ Dear Sir / Madam,

c) In a letter of application to the personnel manager of a company:

☐ Dear lady or gentleman,
☐ Dear Sir or Madam,
☐ Dear everyone,

d) In an e-mail to Linda Evans, your grandmother:

☐ Dear Granny,
☐ Hi Evans,
☐ Dear Mrs Evans,

19. Choose the **correct ending** for each situation.

a) In a letter to Carlos Fernandez, Mike's new pen friend in South America:

☐ Love, Mike
☐ Best wishes, Mike
☐ Yours sincerely, Mike

b) In an e-mail to Diana Watson, the manager of a hotel you stayed at (you only know her name and have never met her in person):

☐ Yours sincerely,
☐ Love,
☐ Best wishes,

c) In a letter of application to the personnel manager of a company:

☐ Regards,
☐ Yours faithfully,
☐ All the best,

d) In an e-mail to Linda Evans, your grandmother:

☐ Yours sincerely,
☐ Yours faithfully,
☐ Love,

20. Put the information below into a good **letter layout**. Think of the right punctuation and remember that some words have to be written with a capital letter.

yesterday, I saw your advertisement in the newspaper for ...

31 Appletree Lane, Norwich, NR67 2ST

yours faithfully

dear

(for) Computer City, 19 Park Road, Bath, BA2 7FD

John Stuart

sir / madam

(today's date)

21. A formal message – City break

You see an advertisement for a holiday in Britain online and you want some more information.

Treat yourself to a city break!

London – Birmingham – Liverpool – Edinburgh – Glasgow – Cardiff

From £ 50 per night

- 3-star or 4-star hotels
- breakfast included
- a place for everyone: single, double or family rooms
- optional: sightseeing tour package
- airport shuttle possible
- ticket service

Any questions? Just get in touch –
Write an email to info@citybreak.co.uk **or use our** **contact** form

Use the contact form below to write a formal message in about 120 words.

In your message …

- mention which city you have chosen.
- say when you would like to go and what type of room you need.
- ask about the prices, hotel locations and facilities (e. g. gym, spa, Wi-Fi).
- arrange at least one activity during your stay.

Contact us

Name

Email

Subject

Your message

Send

22. A formal e-mail – Camping in the Rocky Mountains

You and your friend are planning to go camping in the Rocky Mountains in Colorado in the summer. Although you have found useful information on the internet, you still need some advice.

Write an e-mail to the local tourist information office and ask for help. Include the following three points:

- say who you are and what you want to do in the summer,
- ask for some advice on accommodation,
- ask whether there are guided (hiking) tours.

Write 120 to 150 words.

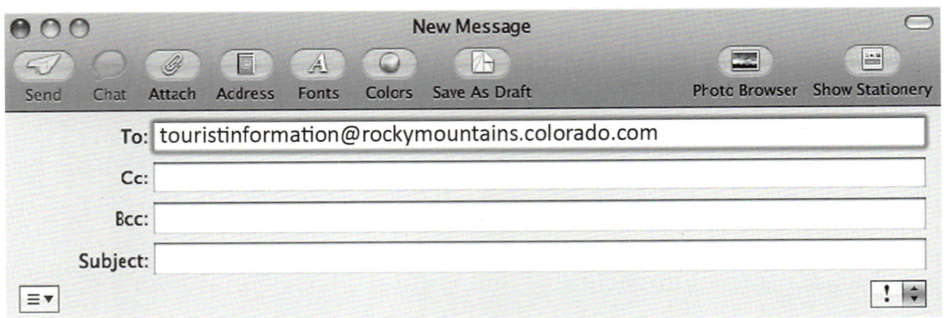

23. A formal e-mail/complaint – A holiday nightmare

You are back from a holiday in Britain. Unfortunately, your accommodation turned out to be a real nightmare.

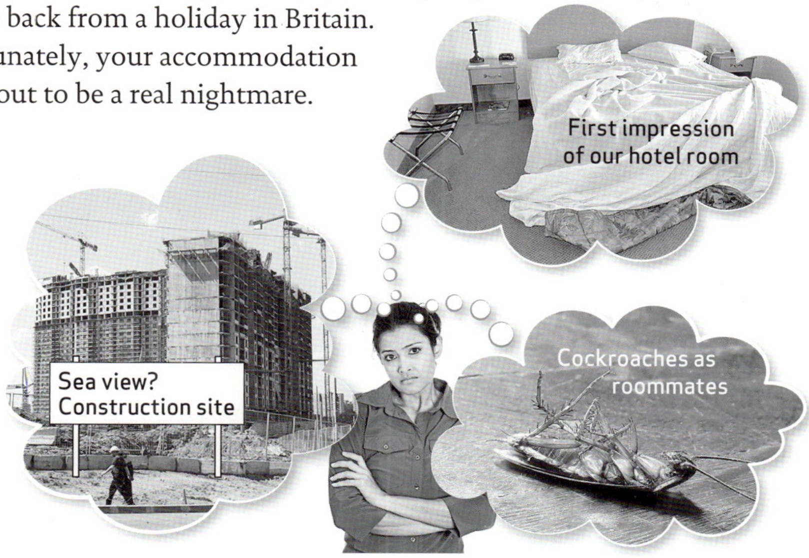

Write an e-mail and complain to the English travel agency. Write about 150 words.

Include the following aspects:

- the promises made on the agency's website
- what the hotel was like in reality
- what you expect the company to do next

Find a suitable beginning and ending.

24. Read the following job advertisement on a company's website.

HOLIDAY JOBS AT ICSD LIMITED –
FANTASTIC OPPORTUNITY FOR STUDENTS

Have you done some work experience and would now like to gain more practical knowledge as well as make some good money during your holidays? Apply to ICSD.

What we are looking for:
upbeat[1] and organised 16 plus students to add to our successful customer service team for a period of at least four weeks

What you have to do:
record phone or postal orders from German- or English-speaking customers, and update the database

What you need:
- excellent phone manner
- knowledge of Word and Excel
- good standard of German and English, both written and oral

You will be given two days' training before you start work.

Please send in a letter of application and your CV to:
Julia Weston, Personnel Manager (ICSD Ltd.), Coopers Row, London, W1A 2JQ, United Kingdom.

1 upbeat – *fröhlich, optimistisch*

Before you write a **letter of application**, look at the following list of ideas. Choose ten ideas you could use in your letter.

- ☐ I found the advertisement on your company's website.
- ☐ My teacher told me to apply for a job to improve my language skills.
- ☐ I could start work in July and stay for six weeks.
- ☐ I have good computer skills and like working with people.
- ☐ I like sports and working with small children.
- ☐ I am a very creative and outgoing person and would like to work in education.
- ☐ I am good at organising things.
- ☐ I am fluent in English and German.
- ☐ I would like to gain some work experience abroad.
- ☐ I am very good at languages, but have never worked with Excel.
- ☐ How many days off would I have if I worked for the company for six weeks?
- ☐ Enclosed: CV and certificates
- ☐ Enclosed: school reports and sports diploma
- ☐ Please give me the job – I'll do my best.
- ☐ I did work experience with a German company last year.

☐ I would like to be a member of your team.

☐ Please call me as soon as possible.

☐ I'm sure the job will be fun.

☐ I look forward to hearing from you.

☐ I'll do the job, but only if you can arrange a place for me to stay.

25. **A letter of application – Applying for a holiday job**

Now write a formal letter of application in answer to the job advertisement (see Task 24). In your letter, …

- introduce yourself and give reasons for applying,
- describe your personal qualifications,
- explain why you are suitable for the position.

Write about 150 words.

26. A personal e-mail – A language course in San Francisco

In the summer holidays, you are going to attend a language course in San Francisco. You are travelling together with an Italian friend you met on your last holiday.

Here's your friend's e-mail:

Hi there,

So cool – only a few more weeks and we'll be in San Francisco together!
OK, we've got English lessons in the morning, but we'll have plenty of time to explore the city, too. Have you got any special plans? I've attached two nice pictures to give you some ideas ☺.
Did you also get an e-mail from the language school today? They want to know whether we would like to stay with a host family or share an apartment with other students from the language course.
What do you think? I think it would be fun if we could stay at the same place.

Best wishes,
Fabio

Write an answer to Fabio. In your e-mail, include the following aspects:

- at least one activity you would like to do in San Francisco
- advantages of sharing an apartment with other students and/or of staying in a host family
- which of the two options you would prefer and why

Find a suitable beginning and ending. Write about 120 words.

a) Make a table and collect ideas for your e-mail.

b) Write the e-mail to Fabio.

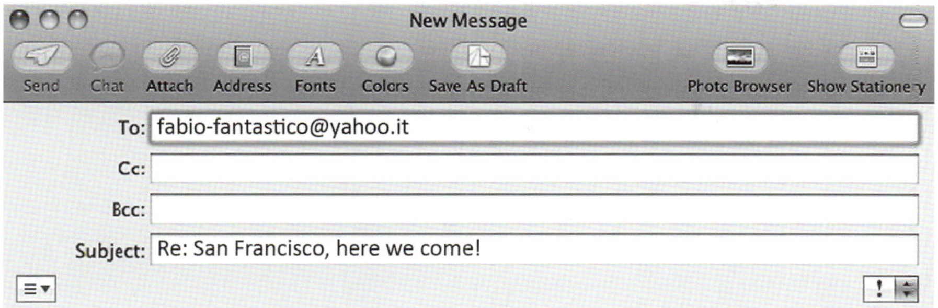

27. **A blog entry – A holiday abroad**

Imagine you are spending a fantastic holiday with other young people in an English-speaking country. While travelling you keep a **blog** about your experiences for your friends around the globe – in English.

In your blog entry, write about …

- the kind of trip you are on,
- the location,
- special people you met,
- an extraordinary experience during your trip.

a) Make a mind map to collect some ideas for your blog. Some questions have been included to help you.

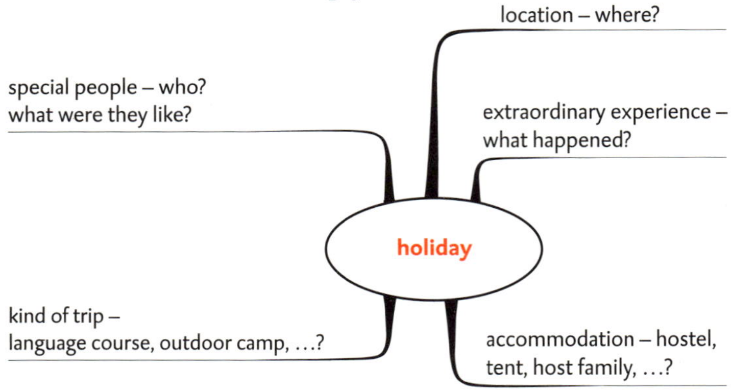

b) Choose your best ideas and write the blog entry.
Write at least 120 words.

28. A chat message – A visit from England

A friend of yours from England has sent you the following message:

Hi there,

You know what? My parents have said that if I pass my GCSEs, we are going to travel to Lower Saxony in the holidays and maybe we could visit you or meet at some place near you. Isn't that great? They told me to ask you if you've got any tips about what we could visit. Are there any places or sights that you could recommend?

See you soon,
Holly

Answer your friend's message. Include the following aspects:
- if / where you could meet
- one sight or place in Lower Saxony that you would recommend and why
- how to get there

Find a suitable beginning and ending. Write about 150 words.

29. **A diary entry – A special day**

Your parents have given you a special present for your birthday – an activity / event that you will always remember.

Write a diary entry in about 120 words. In your text, …
- describe your special day,
- say who was with you during the activity / event and
- describe how you felt during the activity / event.

30. A diary entry – An awful holiday

Imagine you have spent an awful holiday with your parents in an English-speaking country. After returning home, you write a diary entry of about 150 words.

Write the text and include at least four of the following aspects:

- Where did you spend your holiday?
- What did you do?
- What was so awful about the holiday? / What went wrong?

31. A diary entry – A frightening event

Continue the diary entry in about 150 words and …

- describe the frightening event,
- say where it happened and
- explain what you did.

Find a good ending to your text.

Sunday, 24 June

I'm still shaking while I'm writing these lines.

32. **A film review – Your favourite film**

You want to take part in an English writing competition. Its title is "Your favourite film". You are allowed to write 120–150 words.

In your text, include what the film is about and all of the following aspects:

- Which actor(s) play(s) the main role(s)?
- Where did you see the film?
- Why do you like the film?

33. **An article – Popular leisure activities among teenagers**

An online youth magazine is trying to find out what young people would like to do in their free time that they have not tried yet.

Write an article of about 120 words. In your text, …

- describe the type of leisure activity you would like to try,
- explain why you would like to try it,
- say when and where you would like to try it.

34. An article – No social networks for a week

For a school project you and your classmates have decided to live without social networks for one week. Write an article for your English school magazine about your experiences during this week.

Include the following aspects:

- the initial idea for the project
- advantages and disadvantages of social networks
- what you learnt from the experience

Write about 150 words.

35. **An article – School will be over soon: now what?**

You are a reporter for your English school magazine. As you are planning to go abroad for one year after finishing school, you write an article about taking a gap year.
Write at least 150 words.

In your text, include three of the following aspects and tick (✓) them:

- ☐ the reasons why you want to take a gap year,
- ☐ possible disadvantage(s) of taking a gap year,
- ☐ where you are planning to go,
- ☐ what you are planning to do,
- ☐ if you are planning to travel on your own or who you are planning to travel with and why.

36. **A story – A crazy day**

Think about who is telling the story. Then continue the story in about 120 to 150 words.
Write about the following aspects:

- What was crazy about the day?
- What was the message on the phone and what happened afterwards?
- How did the day end?

That day was just crazy. It all started with a message on my / his / her phone …

37. **A story – My first day on planet Earth**

Think about who is telling the story. Finish the story in about 150 words and write about …

- what X23 experiences / experienced on Earth,
- what he / she / it finds / found strange,
- a surprising or funny ending.

Hi, I'm X23 and it's my first day on planet Earth. …

5 Speaking

Immer wieder wird im Unterricht deine mündliche Kommunikationsfähigkeit überprüft. Auch im Rahmen der Realschulabschlussprüfung gibt es einen mündlichen Prüfungsteil. Das sogenannte „oral exam" findet ein paar Wochen vor der schriftlichen Prüfung statt; die mündliche Note fließt mit einem Drittel in das Gesamtergebnis der Abschlussprüfung ein.

5.1 Strategien zum Bereich „Speaking"

Langfristige Vorbereitung

Sich in einer Fremdsprache mündlich auszudrücken, ist nicht einfach. Man kann sich auch nicht kurzfristig – quasi über Nacht – auf diesen Prüfungsbereich vorbereiten. Will man in einer mündlichen Prüfung gut abschneiden, dann muss man **langfristig** und **nachhaltig** an der Sprechfertigkeit arbeiten.
Übungsmöglichkeiten bietet dir dein Englischunterricht. Nimm aktiv am Unterrichtsgeschehen teil, d. h., melde dich so oft wie möglich und sprich auf Englisch. So gewinnst du mit der Zeit Routine und wirst nach und nach gelassener. Wenn du dabei künftig auch noch die folgenden grundsätzlichen Tipps und Hinweise berücksichtigst, klappt das mit der Zeit sicherlich recht gut.

TIPP

- Nutze die Übungsphasen im Unterricht.
- Sprich deutlich und nicht zu schnell.
- Frage nach, wenn du etwas nicht verstanden hast.
- Vermeide einfache, kurze Antworten wie „yes" oder „no". Mit solchen Antworten kannst du keine Gespräche in Gang halten und auch deine mündliche Ausdrucksfähigkeit nicht unter Beweis stellen. Wenn es passend ist, begründe deine Meinung oder füge ein Beispiel an.
- Wenn du unsicher oder nervös bist, bilde lieber kürzere Sätze.
- Lerne die hilfreichen Wendungen (siehe 5.3) auswendig und wende sie immer wieder an. Auf diese Weise werden sie Teil deines aktiven Wortschatzes und es wird dir leichtfallen, sie auch in der mündlichen Prüfung zu benutzen.
- Bemühe dich, Sachverhalte auf unterschiedliche Weise auszudrücken, um zu zeigen, dass du einen vielfältigen Wortschatz hast. Beschränke dich also z. B. nicht auf „I think", um deine Meinung auszudrücken.
- Versuche, dich auch in deiner Freizeit mit der englischen Sprache zu beschäftigen. Du kannst z. B. englische Zeitschriften oder Bücher lesen, Fernsehsendungen oder Filme auf Englisch ansehen, ein Tagebuch auf Englisch führen oder die Grundeinstellung deines Handys auf die Fremdsprache ändern. Auf diese Weise wirst du immer vertrauter und sicherer im Gebrauch des Englischen.

5.2 Das „oral exam“

Ablauf der Prüfung

- Es werden immer zwei oder drei Schüler*innen gleichzeitig geprüft. Wer mit wem zusammen geprüft wird, wird einige Tage vor der Prüfung per Los entschieden. Du brauchst aber keine Angst zu haben, denn auch wenn dein Partner oder deine Partnerin vielleicht nicht so gut in Englisch ist, kannst du trotzdem die volle Punktzahl bekommen, denn deine Leistung wird unabhängig von der der anderen Prüflinge bewertet.
- Es sind immer zwei Lehrkräfte dabei. In der Regel sind das dein Englischlehrer bzw. deine Englischlehrerin und noch eine zweite Fachlehrkraft, die das Protokoll schreibt. Dein Lehrer oder deine Lehrerin führt das Prüfungsgespräch.
- Das „oral exam“ dauert etwa 12–15 Minuten.

Prüfungsteile

Das „oral exam“ besteht aus drei Teilen mit jeweils verschiedenen Aufgabenstellungen. Beachte, dass zwar die Bestandteile der Prüfung vom Ministerium festgelegt sind, dass jedoch die genaue Ausarbeitung der Prüfung an deiner Schule stattfindet. Höre also genau zu, wenn du im Unterricht wichtige Informationen zur Prüfung erhältst.

Part I

- **Warm-up / Speaking about yourself**
  Die Prüfung beginnt mit einer kurzen Begrüßung und Vorstellung der zweiten Lehrkraft. Häufig folgt dann die Frage, wie es dir geht. Danach werden dir Fragen gestellt, bei denen du etwas über dich selbst bzw. deine Lebensumstände erzählen kannst. Es kann sein, dass du z. B. auch deinen Namen oder deine Straße buchstabieren musst. Wiederhole also unbedingt noch einmal das Buchstabieren.
  Die Fragen können im Allgemeinen vier Bereichen zugeordnet werden:
  - *my family*
  - *my city/village*
  - *my hobbies/my free-time/activities*
  - *my school/my class/my course/my career*

TIPP

Diesen Teil kannst du schon langfristig vor der Prüfung vorbereiten und intensiv üben, indem du dir Aussagen zu deiner Familie, deinem Wohnort, deinen Hobbys etc. überlegst. Bereite z. B. „mind maps“ vor, in denen du verschiedene Aspekte notierst. Du kannst sie im Laufe der Zeit immer wieder ergänzen. Übe regelmäßig und am besten mit jemandem, der dir Rückmeldung geben und dich verbessern kann. Dadurch, dass du dir nur Stichpunkte notierst, bleibst du sprachlich flexibler und kannst in der mündlichen Prüfung besser auf die Fragen, die dir gestellt werden, reagieren.

▶ Responding to visual prompts / Bildbeschreibung

Part II

Hier musst du ein Bild bzw. Foto beschreiben und näher analysieren. Abschließend ist es deine Aufgabe, die dargestellte Situation auf dich selbst zu beziehen und z. B. über deine Vorlieben für und Abneigungen gegen die abgebildete Gegebenheit oder Aktivität (wie z. B. eine bestimmte Sportart) zu sprechen. Du kannst alles sagen, was dir zu deinem Bild einfällt. Wichtig ist, dass du englisch sprichst. Kleinere Grammatikfehler sind nicht so gravierend. Du kannst trotz einiger Grammatikfehler immer noch die volle Punktzahl erhalten. Entscheidend ist, dass der Inhalt deiner Äußerungen verständlich ist. Du sollst in etwa zwei Minuten über das Bild sprechen. Danach können sich Fragen anschließen, die du beantworten sollst.

TIPP

Sieh dir das Foto genau an und beschreibe es im Detail. Nutze die dir zur Verfügung stehende Zeit und sage alles, was dir zu dem Bild einfällt. Du brauchst keine Panik zu bekommen, wenn dir ein wichtiges Wort fehlt. Konzentriere dich dann einfach bei deiner Beschreibung auf andere Aspekte.

Folgende Fragen können dir dabei helfen, deine Antwort zu strukturieren:

- *What is happening?*
  Denk daran, das *present progressive* zu verwenden, wenn du beschreibst, was auf dem Bild gerade passiert.
- *How many people are in the picture? How old are they? Where are they? What do they look like? What are they wearing? What is their relationship to each other?*
- *When or where was the photo taken? Why are these people in this place?*
- *What is the main theme or message?*
- *What else can you say about it?*
- *What do you think about the picture? Why do / don't you like it? …*

▶ Paired discussion

Part III

Hier wird dir und dem anderen Prüfling eine bestimmte Situation anhand von Stichpunkten und / oder Bildmaterial vorgestellt, in die ihr euch hineinversetzen müsst. Ihr sollt euch nun miteinander unterhalten und gemäß euren Rollenvorgaben Informationen austauschen und eure Meinungen und Gefühle ausdrücken. Am Ende sollt ihr dann zu einer Entscheidung gelangen. Wichtig ist, dass ihr gegenseitig auf eure Äußerungen eingeht, sodass ein echter Dialog entsteht. Rückfragen eignen sich hierfür auch sehr gut. Insgesamt soll ein richtiges Gespräch entstehen, d. h., ihr könnt nicht einfach etwas sagen, das nicht zum vorangegangenen Redebeitrag passt.

TIPP

- Übe immer wieder mit verschiedenen Mitschüler*innen.
- Sieh dir das ausgehändigte Material in Ruhe an und nimm dir die Zeit, die Vorgaben genau durchzulesen.
- Höre im Gespräch aufmerksam zu. Wenn du eine Aussage oder Frage nicht verstanden hast, traue dich, nachzufragen. Nur so kannst du angemessen auf Redebeiträge anderer reagieren.

Speaking

5.3 Hilfreiche Wendungen

Die folgenden Wörter und Ausdrücke helfen dir in Gesprächen. Du solltest sie auswendig lernen. Die Wendungen sind übrigens auch als digitale „MindCards“ verfügbar, mit denen du am Smartphone oder Tablet üben kannst.

Bildbeschreibung *(Describing pictures)*

In the picture I / we can see …	*In dem Bild kann ich/können wir … sehen.*
The photo shows …	*Das Foto zeigt …*
It was taken in …	*Es wurde in … aufgenommen.*
In the background / foreground there is / there are …	*Im Hintergrund/Vordergrund ist/ sind …*
In the centre / middle of the picture …	*Im Bildmittelpunkt …*
On the left / right of the photo …	*Links/Rechts im Foto …*
The person in the top left-hand / bottom right-hand corner …	*Die Person in der linken oberen/ rechten unteren Ecke …*
At the top / bottom you can see …	*Oben/Unten kann man … sehen.*
Next to / Near …	*Neben/In der Nähe …*
Behind / In front of …	*Hinter/Vor …*
On top of / Under …	*Auf/Unter …*
Between … and …	*Zwischen … und …*

Mit folgenden Ausdrücken kannst du Vermutungen anstellen und deine Meinung über das Bild ausdrücken:

It seems as if …	*Es scheint als ob …*
The boy seems to …	*Der Junge scheint zu …*
Maybe …	*Vielleicht …*
The atmosphere is happy/sad/…	*Die Stimmung ist glücklich/ traurig …*
I (don’t) like the photo, because …	*Ich mag das Foto (nicht), weil …*
The photo makes me think of/ reminds me of …	*Das Foto erinnert mich an …*

Eine eigene Meinung ausdrücken *(Expressing an opinion)*

I (don’t) think / believe / expect / imagine / suppose (that) …	*Ich glaube (nicht), (dass) …*
In my opinion / view …	*Meiner Meinung nach …*
That’s not my opinion.	*Das ist nicht meine Meinung.*
I’m (not) sure / certain …	*Ich bin (nicht) sicher …*
I (don’t) doubt (that) …	*Ich bezweifle (nicht), (dass) …*

I would / wouldn't ...	*Ich würde (nicht) ...*
I would like / I'd like ...	*Ich würde / möchte gern ...*
I don't like / I dislike ...	*Ich mag ... nicht.*
I would / wouldn't prefer ...	*Ich würde lieber / würde lieber nicht ...*
I'm for ...	*Ich bin für ... / dafür, dass ...*
I'm against ...	*Ich bin gegen ... / dagegen, dass ...*

Andere nach ihrer Meinung fragen *(Asking other people for an opinion)*

What do you think about ... ?	*Was denkst du über ... ?*
What's your opinion on / view on / reaction to ... ?	*Was ist deine Meinung zu ... ? / Was denkst du über ... ?*
How do you see / view the situation / this?	*Wie siehst du die Situation / das?*
What would you say about ... ?	*Was würdest du über / zum Thema ... sagen?*
How do you (personally) feel about ... ?	*Was hältst du (persönlich) von ... ?*
Could you explain something to me?	*Könntest du mir etwas erklären?*
What about (the prohibition of drinking alcohol in public places)? Do you think that's right?	*Was denkst du über (das Verbot, Alkohol in der Öffentlichkeit zu trinken)? Glaubst du, dass das richtig / in Ordnung ist?*
I don't suppose you'll agree, will you? / ... you would agree, would you? *(eine Antwort fordernd)*	*Du wirst sicher nicht zustimmen, oder?*

Du kannst auch Fragen mit Verneinungen stellen, um deinen Gesprächspartner zu einer Meinungsäußerung zu bringen:

Don't you think that ... ?	*Glaubst du nicht, dass ... ?*
Wouldn't you like to see ... ?	*Hättest du nicht auch lieber ... ?*
Shouldn't we ... ?	*Sollten wir nicht ... ?*

Zustimmen und widersprechen *(Agreeing and disagreeing)*

This is / That's true.	*Das stimmt.*
I agree (with you).	*Ich bin deiner Meinung.*
(I'm sorry but) I disagree (with you).	*Ich bin nicht deiner Meinung.*
Yes, of course.	*Ja, natürlich.*
No, not at all.	*Nein, ganz und gar nicht.*
That's a good / great / fantastic idea.	*Das ist ein guter / großartiger / fantastischer Vorschlag.*

Excuse me but I think that's a bad idea / That's a bad idea.	*Das ist kein guter Gedanke/keine gute Idee.*
You're right (about / that ...)	*Du hast recht (mit/wenn du sagst, dass ...).*
I'm sorry, but you're wrong (about ... / about that).	*Das stimmt nicht.*

Wenn du entsprechende Adverbien vor „right", „wrong" und „understand" stellst, wird deine Antwort sehr deutlich.

You're absolutely right.	*Du hast völlig recht.*
You're totally wrong.	*Du liegst völlig falsch.*
I think you don't really understand (the problem).	*Ich glaube, du verstehst (das Problem) überhaupt nicht.*

Wenn du dir mit deiner Meinung nicht sicher bist, verwende Ausdrücke wie:

I'm not sure / certain.	*Ich bin (mir) nicht sicher.*

Jemanden unterbrechen *(Interrupting someone)*

Can I ask you something?	*Kann ich dich etwas fragen?*
Can / May I (just) say something, please?	*Kann ich bitte etwas sagen?*
Excuse me, but ...	*Entschuldigung, aber ...*
I don't wish to stop you but / I'm sorry to interrupt but ...	*Ich möchte dich nicht unterbrechen, aber ... /Ich unterbreche dich ungern, aber ...*
I'm sorry, I don't agree with ...	*Ich bin anderer Meinung (als) ...*
I'm sorry, that's not right / fair.	*Das ist nicht richtig/fair.*
I'm sorry, but (I'd just like to say) ...	*Es tut mir leid, aber (ich möchte kurz anmerken) ...*
You're wrong there. *(nachdrücklich)*	*Du hast nicht Recht./Da hast du mit Sicherheit nicht Recht.*
I don't think you're right.	*Ich glaube, dass du nicht Recht hast.*
Oh, come on! You don't really believe that. *(wütend)*	*Das glaubst du doch selber nicht.*
How can you say that?	*Wie kannst du das sagen?*

Darum bitten, dass etwas wiederholt wird *(Asking for something to be repeated)*

Excuse me, could you say that again, please?	*Kannst du das bitte noch einmal sagen?*
Sorry, could you repeat that / what you said about ... ?	*Kannst du das bitte wiederholen?*

I'm sorry / I'm afraid I didn't quite hear / catch / understand what you said. Could you say it again / repeat it, please?	*Es tut mir leid, aber ich habe nicht genau verstanden, was du meinst/ gesagt hast. Kannst du das bitte noch einmal sagen?*
I'm sorry / I'm afraid, I missed / forgot what you were saying (about ...). Could you explain it again / once more, please?	*Es tut mir leid, ich habe nicht verstanden/ich habe vergessen, was du (über ...) gesagt hast. Kannst du das bitte noch einmal erklären?*
I'm sorry / I'm afraid, you were talking a bit too fast for me – could you say it again a little bit more slowly / would you mind repeating what you said, please?	*Es tut mir leid, du hast für mich etwas zu schnell gesprochen. Könntest du das bitte etwas langsamer wiederholen?/Es tut mir leid, das war ein wenig zu schnell für mich. Könntest du es bitte etwas langsamer wiederholen?*

Ein bereits behandeltes Thema aufgreifen *(Returning to an earlier topic)*

You said earlier ...	*Du hast vorhin gesagt ...*
You mentioned / talked about ...	*Du hast ... erwähnt.*
A few minutes ago you said ...	*Vor ein paar Minuten hast du gesagt ...*
As you said before ...	*Wie du vorhin/schon gesagt hast, ...*
Can we go back to ... for a minute?	*Können wir noch einmal auf ... zurückkommen?*

Das Thema wechseln *(Changing the subject)*

We've talked a lot about ... Could we look at ... now?	*Wir haben viel über ... geredet. Könnten wir jetzt über ... sprechen?*
Can we move on and talk about ... ?	*Können wir weitermachen und über ... reden?*
We should really talk about ... too.	*Wir sollten wirklich auch über ... reden.*
That's my opinion about (tennis). But what about (football)? What do you think about it?	*So denke ich über (Tennis). Aber was meinst du zu (Fußball)/hältst du von (Fußball)?*
Can we talk about ... now?	*Können wir jetzt über ... sprechen?*
Perhaps we should also talk about ...	*Vielleicht sollten wir auch über ... reden.*
Can / May I say something at this point?	*Kann ich an dieser Stelle etwas sagen?*

Andere zum Reden bringen (*Making people talk*)

Direkte Fragen mit Fragewörtern wie „what", „why", „where", „when", „who", „which", „how":

What do you think, (Anne)?	*Was meinst du, (Anne)?*
Why do/don't you think so?	*Warum glaubst du das (nicht)?*
Can we find a solution together?	*Können wir zusammen eine Lösung finden?*

Entscheidungsfragen:

Are you interested in … ?	*Interessierst du dich für … ?*
Do you want … ?	*Willst du … ?*

Bestätigungsfragen:

The weather is terrible today, isn't it?	*Das Wetter ist schrecklich, oder?*
It isn't cold outside, is it?	*Es ist nicht kalt draußen, oder?*

TIPP

Manchmal musst du kurz überlegen, bis du weißt, was du sagen möchtest. Damit das Gespräch dennoch nicht unterbrochen wird, kannst du folgende Füllwörter benutzen:

- *Well, …*
- *Let me see … / I see …*
- *I'm not sure, but …*
- *What I'm trying to say is …*
- *Actually, I think …*
- *I guess …*

Lerne diese Ausdrücke auswendig und versuche, sie bereits während des Unterrichts im Gespräch anzuwenden.

Wenn einer von euch nicht mehr weiter weiß, kann der andere mit solchen Fragen helfen:

- *Are you saying that …?*
- *What do you think about … ? / Don't you think that … ?*

5.4 Übungsaufgaben zum Bereich „Speaking“

Oral exam – Part I

In diesem Teil musst du etwas über dich selbst erzählen. In der folgenden Übung sollst du in Vorbereitung auf ein mögliches Prüfungsthema eine Mindmap erstellen. Hinweis

1. Make a mind map of your family. The following aspects might help you. Feel free to add other details, too.
   - your family members' names
   - their ages
   - your parents' jobs
   - your family members' hobbies
   - your house / your flat
   - the activities you do together
   - where you have gone on holiday / are planning to go on holiday
   - what you like / don't like about your family
   - your grandparents / aunts / uncles …
   - your pet
   - …

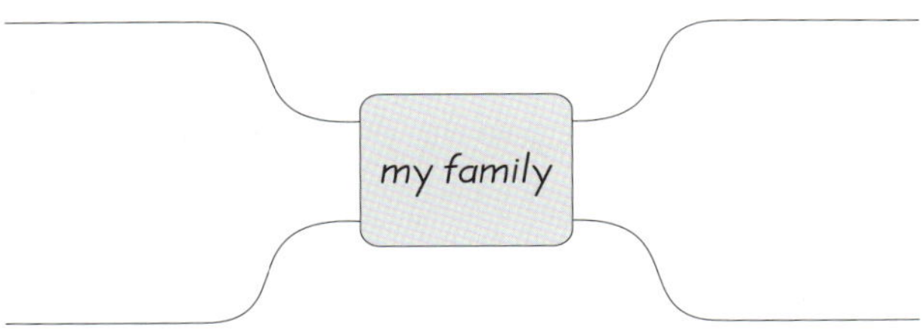

In einem zweiten Schritt übst du deine Präsentation, indem du versuchst, mithilfe deiner Mindmap eine zusammenhängende und gut strukturierte Antwort auf die Frage deines Lehrers oder deiner Lehrerin zu geben. Hinweis

2. **Teacher:** Tell me something about your family.
   You: Well, in my family, there are …

Oral exam – Part II

Hinweis

In diesem zweiten Prüfungsteil legt man dir ein Bild vor. Du musst zunächst im Detail beschreiben, was du auf dem Bild siehst, und dann ein paar persönliche Gedanken äußern. Du hast rund zwei Minuten Zeit, alles über das Bild zu sagen, was dir einfällt. Wenn du jedoch ins Stocken gerätst, wird dir dein Lehrer oder deine Lehrerin Fragen stellen, die dir helfen, deine Redezeit zu nutzen.

3. **Teacher (to Candidate A):** Describe the picture, please.

Hinweis

Die Fragen, die sich an deine Bildbeschreibung anschließen können, hängen natürlich davon ab, auf welche Aspekte du bereits eingegangen bist. Mögliche „prompts" (Hilfestellungen) könnten z. B. sein:

Teacher:
- What has happened? / What will happen next?
- What could be the problem?
- Why are they sitting at the computer?

4. **Teacher (to Candidate B):** Describe the picture, please.

Possible prompts:

Teacher:
- What could the children be talking about?
- How is the girl feeling?
- What could happen next?
- Do you know anyone who has been in a situation like this?

Oral exam – Part III

Hinweis

Im letzten Teil des „oral exam" führst du mit einem anderen Prüfling ein Gespräch zu einem vorgegebenen Thema. Es kann sein, dass ihr Rollenkarten erhaltet, die unterschiedliche Informationen enthalten. Die Stichpunkte auf euren Rollenkarten führen euch als roter Faden durch das Gespräch. Dabei kann es sich z.B. um ein Verkaufsgespräch im Supermarkt oder an der Kinokasse, um ein Gespräch mit einem Austauschschüler/einer Austauschschülerin oder um die Organisation einer Party bzw. Schulveranstaltung handeln (Aufgabe 5).
Es ist aber auch möglich, dass ihr beide dieselbe Collage/dieselben Stichpunkte erhaltet und euch in Bezug auf die Fragestellung einigen sollt (Aufgabe 6).

5. "At the cinema"

Teacher: In this part of the test you are going to talk to each other. One of you wants to buy cinema tickets, the other one works at the ticket office. When you have read your prompts, you can start with your dialogue.

Rollenkarte A

You are on a trip through Great Britain and want to go to a cinema. You go to the ticket office to buy tickets for yourself and two of your friends. It is now 6.30 p.m.

Here are some prompts you can use:
- tickets for "The Royal Family"?
- number of tickets: 3
- time film ends?
- where to buy popcorn, something to drink?

Rollenkarte B

You sell tickets at the cinema in Birmingham. You are talking to the customer. It is now 6.30 p.m.

Here are some prompts you can use:
- how many tickets?
- £ 6 back rows, £ 4 front rows
- student ID? Ticket £ 1 cheaper
- end: 8.45 p.m.
- interested in film poster? → cinema shop

6. "Money for charity"

   Teacher: At our summer party last year the school raised €2,500 to give to a charity. Which charity do you think we should give it to? Here are some we have selected, but of course you may have other ideas, too. Discuss carefully the reasons for and against each charity and try to come to a decision about what to do with the money.

6 Anhang: Hörverstehenstexte

Listening Test 1: Short dialogues

Text 1: What must Rob buy?

Penny: Hi.

Rob: Hi, Penny, it's Rob. I've got a problem with your shopping list.

Penny: Okay, what's the problem?

Rob: Well, I've almost finished shopping but I can't read what you've written next to Parmesan cheese. Is it 25 grams, two 50-gram packets or 250 grams?

Penny: Unless you want Parmesan on everything, including your cornflakes, I think 250 grams sounds a lot, don't you? Get the two packets.

Rob: Two 50-gram ones or two 25 grams?

Penny: Weren't you listening? The two 50 ones.

Text 2: What time does Tom arrive in school?

Mrs West: Hello, Tom. Late again.

Tom: I'm sorry, Mrs West. I forgot my pencil case, so I went home for it – and I'm only 15 minutes late.

Mrs West: Yes, Tom – ONLY! School starts at ten to nine!

Tom: I'm sorry, Mrs West.

Mrs West: And Tom, you should remember to put everything in your bag before you go to bed. So you're ready for school the next morning.

Tom: Yes, Mrs West.

Mrs West: And another thing, Tom.

Tom: Yes, Mrs West?

Mrs West: Do you normally come to school in your socks?

Text 3: Which poster do Vicky and Pete put on the school wall?

Vicky: Pete, you and I have got to organise the party for the fifth year this week.

Pete: Yes, I know. Have you got any ideas what we can do for them?

Vicky: Lots really. They always like party games, so we've just got to think of three or four, and then we can have some music – a disco – something like that. We can also have a talent contest, and, of course, we need food and drink. What do you think? Have you got any other ideas?

Pete: It all sounds great, but not the disco! You know fifth year kids don't dance, especially the boys! Should we have a theme for the party this year, too, like … 'monsters' or … 'ghosts'?

Vicky: Yeah, you're right about the disco. I like the theme idea … but monsters and ghosts? What about kings and queens?

Pete: That's okay. I suppose some kings were monsters as well, weren't they?

Text 4: Where does Mary post the letter?

Paul: Can you do something for me on your way to work?

Mary: Yes, of course, if I've got the time.

Paul: Could you post my letter for me? It's very important.

Mary: That's no problem. I'll post it in the village.

Paul: No, don't post it there. The letters aren't collected until 6 o'clock. Can you take it to the postbox near the chemist's? The letters are collected in the morning there.

Mary: Which chemist's?

Paul: The one opposite the station.

Mary: I think I should go five minutes earlier then – it's always busy near there and I don't want to be late for work.

Text 5: Which present doesn't June buy for her nephew?

Trevor: Hello, June. What are you doing looking in the toyshop window?

June: Looking for a good idea for my nephew. It's his birthday on Saturday. I've got him a T-shirt but I want another present, too.

Trevor: How old is he?

June: He'll be nine. What do you get 9-year-old boys?

Trevor: They're no problem. Buy him a football.

June: He doesn't like football, or tennis. Actually, he doesn't like sport at all; he's more the reading sort of person. That's funny, really, because his dad is sport mad and hates books, unless they're about football, of course.

Trevor: What about a computer game? There are lots of good ones for young people.

June: His mum won't allow it. She says he's too young for computer games.

Trevor: I think you should go to the bookshop then – you'll get something there for him.

June: I'll do that. Thanks, Trevor.

Text 6: Where will John and Lynn go on holiday this year?

Lynn: Where should we go on holiday this year, John?

John: I've been thinking about that, too. Last year, we went to Spain, so I don't want to go there again. I'd love to go to Africa, though.

Lynn: So would I. Africa would be super, but it's expensive.

John: Perhaps one year we'll have enough money for that. I'd like to go to Paris or Rome, or maybe Switzerland.

Lynn: I don't like mountains and I've been to Paris before. Rome isn't too expensive – let's go there and then next year we can go to Africa. Oooh, I'd love to go there – all those wild animals and that fantastic countryside and those super people.

John: Let's book this year's holiday first, Lynn.

Listening Test 2: Short texts

Text 1: Which group of people get onto the plane second?

I'm pleased to tell you that flight TA 3654 to Toronto is now ready for boarding.
Unfortunately, we can only use the front door of the plane today, due to a faulty walkway to the rear one. This means that boarding will take a little longer than normal. Please listen carefully to the boarding procedure and have your boarding card and passport ready.
First class, business class and adults with small children may now start to board the plane. The next group of passengers to get on the plane are those in Economy – rows 25 to 35. Please look at your ticket to see which row you are seated in. Once these passengers have boarded, rows 10–24 may follow.
We would like to apologise for any inconvenience this may cause.

Text 2: How will Daniel get home if his mum can't meet him?

Oh … Hi, Mum … um … so, you're busy at work or doing something … OK, I'll leave a message. I'm still at Paddington Station – the train's late again. There's a bad storm near London and it's causing a lot of problems – trees blown down and things like that. I'll probably be in Exeter about 6.30 now – no guarantees about that, though, since there might be more disruption. Can you wait for me outside the station? If you can't make it, can you text me, please? I'll then get a taxi. It shouldn't be too expensive and it's quicker than the bus. See you later.

Text 3: Which is the correct way to the hotel?

Tourist: Excuse me, I'm looking for the Castle Hotel.
Passer-by: Oh, I know where that is – it's in the marketplace.
Tourist: How do I get there?
Passer-by: Go straight ahead and turn left at the end of the road. Then … take the second road on your right. It'll take you straight to the marketplace. In the marketplace, go right. The hotel is about 50 metres further on your right but the entrance to it is just round the first corner.
Tourist: It sounds rather hard to find.
Passer-by: No, it's not – it just sounds difficult. You'll find it easily enough.
Tourist: Thank you.

Text 4: What is Tom going to do now on Saturday?

Tom: Do you know what the weather is going to be like this weekend, Clara?

Clara: It isn't going to be great, Tom. There's heavy rain coming in from the Atlantic. The weather forecast on the radio also said it would be a wet start tomorrow for everyone. But in the South it should be sunny on Sunday.

Tom: Well, that's spoilt my plans. I was going to take the dogs for a long walk on the beach on Saturday but I won't bother now. They can have a quick run about in the park instead. What are you doing at the weekend?

Clara: I'm driving down to London on Saturday to see my sister. I'll be back on Monday.

Tom: So you'll have the nice weather on Sunday and me and my dogs will be getting very wet.

Clara: It looks that way, doesn't it?

Text 5: Where will each group of friends wait?

Anna: Rosie's had a great idea for my birthday, Mum.

Mum: What's that?

Anna: Rosie said her dad would take us flying. His friend has got a four-seater plane he can fly and he'll take Rosie, me and four of our friends with him.

Mum: How's that going to work? That's six people.

Anna: He said that there's a small café at the airport where we can buy pizzas or sandwiches and sit outside to eat them. So he'll take three of us up in his plane for half an hour while the other three are eating. Then he'll land and we'll swap over.

Mum: That's really nice of him. How are you all going to get to the airport?

Anna: Mum's 7-seater taxi?

Text 6: Where was Lilly when she found out that she'd lost her camera?

Harvey: Hi Lilly. How was your holiday?

Lilly: I had a great time but I lost my camera on the second day.

Harvey: That wasn't a very good start to your holiday. What happened?

Lilly: It was my own fault. I'd been walking around San Francisco for hours and saw a really nice bench. I sat down and after a while I saw a taxi – so I waved to it and the driver stopped. He took me back to my hotel. The next morning after breakfast I realised I'd left my camera on the bench!

Harvey: Didn't you go back for it?

Lilly: Do you really think it would still have been there? I don't.

Harvey: It might have.

Lilly: No way. But I had my smartphone with me so I could still take some holiday photos.

Listening Test 3: The German exchange

Aiden: Miss, have you got a little bit of time to talk to me?

Mrs Jackson: Of course, Aiden. What can I do for you?

Aiden: I was ill when you talked about the German exchange. I think I'd like to go but could you tell me more about it, please?

Mrs Jackson: Sure. The school is in the south of Germany. It's got about 800 pupils. We'll visit it first; normally we go in January when it's cold – and the German pupils come to us in March. We won't have the exact dates until we book the plane.

Aiden: My friend said maybe not everyone could go.

Mrs Jackson: No, he got that wrong. Not all the pupils from Germany can come to us – we've only got fifteen people in our German group so the Germans can only send 15 people, too.

Aiden: That's good to know. Will our partners be boys or girls?

Mrs Jackson: We always try to match a boy with a boy and a girl with a girl, but that doesn't always happen. And their English is good! But you must try to speak German in Germany.

Aiden: OK, I can do that. What do we do on the exchange?

Mrs Jackson: This is the fifth year we've had the exchange and we do similar things every year. When we get to Germany, you'll go with your partner to school and join your partner's lessons.

Aiden: You mean I'll have to do Maths in German? – I can't do that! I can't do Maths in English.

Mrs Jackson: Don't worry – we arrive on Wednesday, so your first day in school is on Thursday. In the afternoon we all go ice-skating so everyone gets to know each other. On Friday, we go into the town and we'll show you all the sights – your partners have to go to school in the morning but they finish at 1 o'clock. So they'll meet us there later.

Aiden: What happens at the weekend?

Mrs Jackson: We don't have a programme for the weekend. Your partner organises that. On Monday afternoon and Tuesday, though, we've some trips to different places planned.

Aiden: How do we travel and how much will the exchange cost?

Mrs Jackson: We'll get the train to Manchester airport and then fly to Germany from there. In Germany, a minibus will collect us at the airport and take us to the school. The exchange costs £270 – but that includes everything: the travel, the trips in Germany and England, all the extras like insurance, and two evening meals – on the last night in Germany and in England we always go to an Italian restaurant together. Look, I've got a handout here – read it and if you want to come, give me the form on Friday.

Aiden: Thanks – it sounds fun, but I'll have to talk to my parents about it.

Listening Test 4: Off the sofa and do it!

Sam: Hi Beth. I saw you in town yesterday, but I don't think you saw me.

Beth: No, I didn't, I'm sorry. Did you buy anything?

Sam: Actually I wasn't buying anything. I just wanted some information and brochures.

Beth: Sounds interesting. Information about what?

Sam: I've always wanted to learn windsurfing and I thought I'd do something about it instead of just sitting at home saying to myself, "I'd like to go windsurfing".

Beth: I know that feeling. But don't you have to be an excellent swimmer to do that?

Sam: Not really. The main thing is that you *can* swim! Anyway, this morning I thought I'd get some information. I know I could get most of it off SeaSports' website but I wanted to talk to someone, too.

Beth: Where are the courses?

Sam: Do you know where Snettisham Beach is?

Beth: Of course. We often went there as little kids to have a picnic.

Sam: Well, … there's a narrow road going left just before the beach car park. And if you go about one mile down it, you come to the sailing club. Behind the club, there's a big lake. The courses are done on the lake but once you've learnt all the basics, you can go on the sea, too.

Beth: I can imagine it's quite difficult. You must need hundreds of lessons before you can do it.

Sam: No, not at all. That's what's really interesting. The guy in the shop told me that after a one-day course most people can go windsurfing on the sea if it's not too windy.

Beth: I thought it'd take much longer.

Sam: No, it doesn't. At first you don't go on the lake. They've got a windsurfing board on land balanced on something so it moves about. You learn to control this board and try not to fall off it – there're two footprints on it, too, so you know exactly where to stand. Once you can do this, you go onto the water. The guy said that I'd fall in a lot but I'd learn very quickly how to get across the lake by myself.

Beth: What about turning around?

Sam: It's quite easy apparently. But what is very difficult is getting going again after you've fallen in. The sail is wet and heavy and you have to pull it out of the water – that's tiring and you can fall off the board again doing this.

Beth: So, in one day you can learn how to windsurf?

Sam: Yes, but you're still only a beginner.

Beth: I'd love to come, too. Can I? How much does it cost?

Sam: It's £60 for the day – that's three hours in the morning and two in the afternoon.

Listening Test 5: My Norfolk

John Watson: One of my favourite counties in Britain is Norfolk. Not only has it got a lot of wild coast, it's also got many large country houses. In my area there are three I'd like to tell you about.

The first is Sandringham House. King Edward VII bought it in 1862 when he was Prince of Wales and it's been one of the private homes of the Royal Family ever since. You can go into the house and the gardens most times of the year, but not at Christmas, when the members of the Royal Family use it.

My next favourite house is Holkham Hall. The house is very, very big and was built in the 1700s. It sits in the middle of a huge park full of deer. It's still owned by the same family but they have to think of exciting ways for the house to earn money. Tourism brings a lot and so does the only car park to the fantastic beach there. In recent years, though, the owners have started having open air concerts; sometimes classical ones where people bring picnics, sit in the park and listen to the music, or they have concerts by well-known people in the music industry.

My final house is Houghton Hall and it's not far from Sandringham House. It was built originally for the first British Prime Minister in the 1720s but in 1797 it was inherited by the family who continue to own it today. It's not as big as Holkham Hall, but the owners have a similar problem: the house needs to pay for itself. The house is open to the public but not every day throughout the year. However, in recent years they've found a colourful way for it to earn money. The house becomes an art gallery for famous artists such as Damien Hirst, who once exhibited a dead shark in a glass case.

Listening Test 6: Things you didn't know about London

Speaker: Everyone knows London, don't they? But I wonder how many of you know some of the facts I'm going to tell you.

There are over eight million people who live in London and these people speak 300 different languages. And every year, London gets an average of 17 million visitors – perhaps you were one of them? If you were, then maybe you know that every year Oslo, the capital of Norway, gives London a big Christmas tree for Trafalgar Square.

You've heard of Big Ben and you'll know it's not really the name of the tower but only of the bell inside it. However, only few people know that the Houses of Parliament still have a strange law: you're not allowed to enter the building wearing a suit of armour. I can just imagine people doing that today, can't you?

Have you heard of Peter Pan? Of course there have been lots of books and films about him. But did you know that all the royalties from the books and the films go to a children's hospital in London called Great Ormond Street? Royalties are a percentage of the book price or the ticket price to see a film or a play. The author, James Matthew Barrie, didn't have any children himself, so when he died, he gave the hospital this present, which has made it quite rich.

London had the very first underground railway in the world, but there were some unexpected surprises for the workers when building it. At Aldgate Station, for example, they discovered a huge grave with 1,000 dead bodies in it from the plague of 1665. They decided to continue building the station above the bodies rather than removing them all! They're still there!

London is slowly growing upwards rather than outwards and you only have to look at its skyline to see this. One of the most interesting buildings is the Shard. You can't miss it because it's 310 metres high. Many of London's high-rise buildings have been given fun names such as the Gherkin, the Cheese Grater or the Walkie-Talkie. Look out for them next time you're in London.

Listening Test 7: The California Gold Rush

Speaker: In 1847, California became a US territory. Most Americans at the time lived on the East Coast. But thousands traveled west to California after a settler reported finding gold there.

James Marshall found the gold nugget in January 1848. Mr Marshall was building a sawmill near the American River in central California. When he looked in the water, he saw shiny pieces of metal. One of them was about the size of a fingernail. Mr Marshall took the piece and put it in his mouth. Paul Johnston is curator of Maritime History at the Smithsonian's Museum of American History here in Washington, D.C. The museum displays the gold nugget Mr Marshall found.

Paul Johnston: And you can see Mr Marshall actually bit down on it. You can see the molar marks, his bite mark on it as well as a little chip taken out of the upper left hand corner for assaying, or testing the purity of the gold.

Speaker: Mr Marshall knew he found gold because the metal was soft. He and his boss gave the nugget to the US government to prove they found gold on the land. News of James Marshall's discovery traveled to the East Coast. But communication was slow in the middle of the 19th century. People in the big eastern cities of New York and Boston heard only rumors about gold in California. It was not until December 1848, almost a year after Mr Marshall's discovery, that President James Polk told Congress the rumors were true. During the next weeks and months, thousands of young men from the Northeast left their homes and families to seek great riches in California.

Paul Johnston: You didn't really have to work for it, as far as they knew. You just had to lean over and pick it up and you were rich.

Speaker: One of those young men was Benjamin Buckley. His records suggest he found thousands of dollars' worth of gold. Buckley put some money in banks and sent some to family members. Alexander Van Valen, however, was not as successful. The Smithsonian's Museum of American History has letters he wrote to his wife and daughters in New York.

Paul Johnston: His wife tried to make a living by sewing and by borrowing money from the financiers against her husband's future profits. But it was not any easier for her than it was for her husband 3,000 miles away in California.

Speaker: In two years, Alexander Van Valen earned only $ 500. Most people who traveled to California to find gold were like Van Valen – they did not get rich. But Paul Johnston says the California Gold Rush was important for other reasons.

Paul Johnston: The Gold Rush really put California on the map. It made it desirable. It made the East Coast want California to become part of the United States. So, it was huge.

Speaker: In 1850, California became the country's 31st state.

Adapted from: https://learningenglish.voanews.com/a/california-gold-rush-1849/1969067.html

Listening Test 8: The Stolen Generations

Greg: This is *TopFM*, my name is Greg and I'd like to welcome you to our special programme on the history of Australia. Jenny Green has come into the studio today to talk about the so-called Stolen Generations. Jenny, could you explain to our listeners what happened to these people?

Jenny: Sure. From the late nineteenth century to about 1970, various Australian governments took Aboriginal children – or children who had at least one Aboriginal parent – away from their families. Their aim was to make them adopt white culture.

Greg: What was the idea behind that?

Jenny: Well, basically, the governments were trying to get rid of Aboriginal peoples and their traditions. They thought that if Aboriginal children were forced to adopt white culture, the Aboriginal way of life would soon die out.

Greg: But Aboriginal peoples had been there long before the first Europeans arrived.

Jenny: That's true, of course, but many whites thought their culture was better than that of the Aboriginal peoples.

Greg: What happened to the children?

Jenny: The children were separated from their parents – their families – and often taken thousands of miles away, so they would never see each other again. You can imagine how awful this was for them. Many children were also told that their parents had died or just left them. These children were then put into homes run by the church or the state. Some were also adopted from the homes by white families. Most were given "white" names and the only language they were allowed to use was English, not their own – that was forbidden. They were taught to reject their Aboriginal past.

Greg: Sounds like something out of a bad film ...

Jenny: But, sadly, it was for real. In some areas, one in three children were taken away – nearly every Aboriginal family lost children in this way. In the homes, children were badly treated and often left cold and hungry. They were given an education, but usually a rather poor one – one just enough to allow them to do basic work, for example as household servants or shepherds.

Greg: Things must have got better since then, though.

Jenny: Yes, but it's taken a long time. In 1997, there was a critical report of what happened to the Stolen Generations. One of its suggestions was to have an annual National Sorry Day for all Australians to remember this part of their country's history – it was later renamed the National Day of Healing. In 2000, during the Olympic Games in Sydney, an Aboriginal runner was chosen to light the Olympic fire. After winning a gold medal, she ran around the track carrying both the Aboriginal flag and the Australian one – a powerful symbol of reconciliation. But it wasn't until 2008 that an Australian prime minister officially apologised to the Stolen Generations.

Greg: So has the sad history of the Stolen Generations finally come to an end?

Jenny: Unfortunately, not completely. Many Aboriginal people still suffer from how they were treated by the whites. And apparently, the number of children who are taken away from their parents is still much higher for Aboriginal people than for white people. Even today, governments seem to spend a lot more money on putting Aboriginal children into state-run homes than on helping them to stay with their parents.

Greg: These aren't very happy facts, are they? Well thanks for now, Jenny, and we'll talk some more after the break …

Listening Test 9: What can be done?

Harry Jacks: Welcome to our programme. With me today is Gerri Hartwell, who works with young people in Birmingham. We're going to talk about some of the problems she deals with every day. Ms Hartwell, can you give our listeners a picture of the main problems that affect young people?

Gerri Hartwell: Call me Gerri, Harry – everyone I work with does. It's difficult to explain all the problems and why they happen, but as most people know, the main ones are drugs, smoking, alcohol, computer game and smartphone addiction. Drugs and smoking are under control – our statistics show that drug use is less than five years ago and not as many young people are smoking.

Harry: That's good news.

Gerri: Yes, it is. We've had a very strong anti-drug campaign which sports organisations, such as football clubs, and many pop stars have supported. The anti-smoking campaign has also been successful. There's now no advertising for cigarettes, and there's not much smoking in television programmes and films. You see, if young people don't see smoking as the cool thing to do, they don't do it. The government has banned smoking inside all public places – such as pubs, discos, train stations and so on – which has also helped. But perhaps the biggest factor has been to hugely increase the price of a packet of cigarettes to about £ 11, with talks of that price increasing even more.

Harry: That's a lot of money! But the other big problem is alcohol, isn't it?

Gerri: Sadly, yes. Young people have always found alcohol interesting but the problem is now out of control. Many teenagers, even at the age of 13, get drunk every week ... and there's a lot of binge drinking.

Harry: Can you explain what binge drinking is exactly for our listeners?

Gerri: Yes, of course. Many young people are drinking a lot of alcohol very quickly. They're doing this just to get drunk. If teenagers thought about this more, they'd see that boasting about how drunk they got is not exactly cool – actually, it's the opposite.

Harry: So what's happening about this problem?

Gerri: Well, like smoking, we're making adverts to show young people how and why drinking too much is bad for you. We've got pictures of people lying drunk on the floor in the streets, girlfriends getting angry at their boyfriends and leaving them, or the other way around, friends not wanting to go out with other friends – accidents, of course, and illnesses. We also want the government to make it more difficult for young people to buy alcohol and make it more expensive, too. In America, you have to be 21 years old before you can drink, so why not here, as well? We also want ID cards, like the "Ausweise" in Germany and in other countries. Then pubs, discos and supermarkets can check the ages of their customers.

Harry: So there's lots of work to be done here.

Gerri: Yes, there is. And then we've got the computer games problem. Many young people play games for more than four hours a day. Can you imagine that? And the games these people play are often the ones that should be banned.

Harry: Before we go on to talk more about this, let's have a short break with some music. Any wishes, Gerri?

Gerri: An unusual one, maybe. I'd like 'Say it's not true' by Queen – there's a message in it for us all – 'think about what you're doing before it's too late'.

Listening Test 10: Environment views

Presenter: Hi. I've invited Grace and Lewis to come on my programme today so we can hear their views about the environment. Grace, do you want to start?

Grace: Sure. Everyone knows we're making a mess of our planet but there never seems to be anything really done about it.

Lewis: That frustrates me, too. There's lots of talking, but where's the action?

Grace: Exactly. And when something is suggested, like wind farms, then people start complaining about how ugly they look and that they spoil the view! Or when a solar farm is planned, suddenly that area is special for the lesser-spotted, black-headed butterfly that no one has seen for the last 60 years! So part of the problem is *us*.

Presenter: I certainly agree with you there. But what about our daily lives? Would you like to see any changes there?

Lewis: Yes. I keep telling my parents to walk more. My mum uses her car to take her letters to the post office in the village. It only takes five minutes to walk there! But, no, she has to take the car – find her keys, open the garage, get the car out, close the garage door and then drive to the post office; all that takes more than five minutes anyway.

Grace: My parents are much the same. They could walk or use their bikes but somehow they don't. If petrol was made more expensive, they probably would for short journeys – and that means other people might, too.

Lewis: But it isn't just car owners to blame. My grandad was saying that when he was a kid, there were buses every seven minutes into the town. If I miss the bus, I have to wait an hour for the next one.

Grace: That's the point. If there were more buses, people would use their cars less and that would mean less pollution and cleaner air. And if there were more car-free routes for bikes, more people would cycle.

Presenter: I would, definitely. What else gets you angry?

Grace: Us again! I watched a programme about the effects of tourism yesterday, which was really interesting. Planes pollute, we know that. But many areas in the world have very little water, so when large hotels with swimming pools and golf courses are built and their guests use showers every day, the water situation becomes even worse.

Presenter: I've never really thought about that – and I guess a lot of water is then also used for washing towels and sheets. With the world having so many environmental problems, is there anything you'd particularly like to see happen?

Lewis: It would be nice to think that people in the developing countries won't do the same terrible things that we've done for centuries, but I can't see how. Okay, new factories will probably be cleaner, but will people care about using plastic bags, for example? And I think the first thing many people will do as soon as they can afford it is to buy an old car, which means the car problem starts again, only in a different country.

Grace: What I'd like to see are the industrial nations helping the poorer ones to develop in a green way. It would be nice if the world could work together, just for once, on an issue that affects everyone.

Presenter: I think that's a good place to stop for a moment and listen to some music.

Listening Test 11: Five-star hotel or wilderness?

Reporter: I'm Marc White from CBC Radio 1. We're doing a short survey on how people in Vancouver like to spend their holidays. Could you tell me your first name and say what you usually do when you're on holiday?

John: I'm in a bit of a hurry, but that's an easy question to answer. My name's John and I'm 35. I've got a very stressful job, and I hardly ever go on holiday, but when I find the time, I only want to relax, so my wife and I usually go to a luxurious boutique hotel on Vancouver Island that doesn't allow small children. We go for long walks in the woods, get massages, go to the sauna and enjoy the fantastic food there.

Olivia: Hi, I'm Olivia and I'm a student at the University of British Columbia. I'm 21 and I love travelling, but I don't want to be seen as a tourist. Since I don't have much money, I usually go couchsurfing when I'm abroad. It's a great and cheap way to meet locals, make new friends and explore places far away from the typical tourist paths.

Hailey: I'm Hailey and I'm 25 years old. I wouldn't like to go couchsurfing. I think it's dangerous to stay at the house of someone you don't know. I love travelling, but I don't earn much money, so I always stay at youth hostels. I always choose a small hostel so that there's a cosy atmosphere and travellers get in touch with each other easily.

Carter: Hello, my name's Carter and I'm 16. In my summer vacation I usually go camping with my friends. I love hiking and fishing and being outside 24/7, so I wouldn't like to spend my holidays in any other way. My parents, in contrast, usually go on city trips together with their friends from the golf club.

Josh: Camping is great, isn't it? I'm Josh and I'm 15. My parents bought a large mobile home five years ago, so we always go camping. I like sleeping in the comfy bed of the mobile home, whereas my younger brother always sleeps in a tent. We always go to the same campsite, which is great, because we meet the same people every year.

Sara: Hi, I'm Sara and I'm a mum. When we go on holiday, we usually rent an apartment at the coast. Staying at a hotel's just too expensive for a family of six and a dog, although I'd really love to not have to cook. We tried camping once, but it rained for a week, so that wasn't much fun.

Lara: My name's Lara and I'm from Germany. My family moved to BC three years ago. I've got some really nice friends here, but my best friend Lisa still lives in Frankfurt, so when I go on holiday, I always visit her.

Reporter: Thanks everyone for sharing all this with me and our listeners. I hope you have a great time on your next holiday.

Listening Test 12: What's on your plate?

Reporter: Hello. My name's Allison Hill of BBC London. I'm reporting live from busy Oxford Street on this rainy Saturday morning, where I'll be interviewing people about what is usually on their plates.
Excuse me, sir, do you have a minute? Could you give me your first name and tell me a bit about your eating habits?

Henry: Of course. I'm Henry and I must admit that I'm a bit lazy when it comes to cooking. I'm single and I think it's too much work to cook just for myself, so I usually go to the pub with my colleagues after work. There's the "King's Head" next to the office and they usually have great specials.

Reporter: And what's on your plate?

Liam: Hi, I'm Liam and I'd love to be a good cook, but unfortunately I'm not. This means that my freezer's full of ready-made meals, which I simply pop into the microwave. At the weekend, I sometimes eat a fresh salad or some raw vegetables. However, my girlfriend gave me a cookery course as a Christmas present, so my cooking skills will hopefully improve …

Clare: My name's Clare and I've been a vegan for two years. My diet is plant-based and I avoid all animal foods, such as meat, dairy products, honey and eggs. I also love Indian food, so I usually have a vegetarian curry for dinner. Vegan food is not as boring as many people think.

Finn: Vegan food? Not for me, thank you! There's nothing I enjoy more than a big chunk of steak. All my family love meat, no matter what: pork, beef, veal, lamb, chicken – I could go on forever. We also like to try exotic types, such as crocodile. In the summer, we have a barbecue at least once a week. I'm Finn by the way.

Colin: You should really consider your health, Finn! I'm Colin and I'm a vegetarian. Since I don't have a garden of my own and can't afford to buy organic food all the time, I got involved in a community garden last year. We share a garden and grow all kinds of fruit and vegetables, which is great fun and really rewarding.

Hanna: My name's Hanna. What a great idea to join a community garden – I moved to London two months ago and I find it very difficult to make friends. I bet being part of a project like this would help me meet nice people who are on the same wavelength. I consider myself a part-time vegetarian, because I usually eat vegetarian meals, but when I go out for dinner, I sometimes order fish or chicken.

Tessa: Hi there, I'm Tessa. One of my new year resolutions is to lose some weight. That's why I'm trying to cut down on sugar and carbohydrates. I recently read an article about animal transports, so I decided not to eat any more meat for ethical reasons.

Original-Aufgaben der Abschlussprüfung an Realschulen in Niedersachsen

Realschulabschlussprüfung in Niedersachsen
Englisch 2020

I. Listening

Part 1 – Questions 1–5

5 Punkte

Listen to five short recordings. For each recording, there is a question with three pictures. Choose the correct picture and put a tick (✓) in the box A, B or C below it.

Example

0. What is the man going to buy?

A ☐ B ☐ C ☑

1. When does the drama group meet?

A ☐ B ☐ C ☐

2. Who is going to do the dishes?

A ☐ B ☐ C ☐

3. Which room does the guest get?

A ☐ B ☐ C ☐

4. How does Kevin get to his job interview?

A ☐

B ☐

C ☐

5. Where do the tourists go first?

A ☐

B ☐

C ☐

Part 2 – Questions 6–12: A Job Interview

7 Punkte

Listen to Kevin being interviewed for a job at a clothes shop.
For each question, tick (✓) the correct box a, b or c.
The first question is an example.

0. The applicant's name is ...
   - a) Sandy Burns. ☐
   - b) Kevin Grant. ☑
   - c) Kevin Burns. ☐

6. Kevin learned about the job offer ...
   - a) on the Internet. ☐
   - b) at a job fair. ☐
   - c) from a friend. ☐

7. Kevin has heard that ...
   - a) the shop offers good quality. ☐
   - b) the shop's advertising is attractive. ☐
   - c) the working conditions are good. ☐

8. Kevin thinks his ... is his weakness.
   - a) motivation ☐
   - b) persuasiveness ☐
   - c) honesty ☐

9. He recommends that a female applicant could wear …
   a) jeans. ☐
   b) trainers. ☐
   c) a fancy blazer. ☐

10. In Costa Rica, Kevin …
   a) sold coffee. ☐
   b) guided tourists. ☐
   c) worked in a national park. ☐

11. Kevin speaks … best.
   a) Spanish ☐
   b) French ☐
   c) Polish ☐

12. In the beginning, on weekdays, Kevin would earn … pounds per hour.
   a) six ☐
   b) eight ☐
   c) ten ☐

Part 3 – Questions 13–18: Phone Repair

6 Punkte

The display of your smartphone is broken. You call the hotline of a repair shop to find out about their services. Listen to the recorded message and fill in the missing information. The first question is an example.

Name of the shop	0. Phone Hospital
Opening times	13. ______________
Where	14. ______________
Cost of your repair	15. ______________
How long it takes	16. ______________
Guarantee	17. ______________
Additional services	18. ______________

Part 4 – Questions 19–24: Polyglot

6 Punkte

You will hear a radio interview with Leyla Skovekolá, who speaks many different languages. Decide whether each statement is true *or* false.
Put a tick (✓) in the correct box true *or* false.
The first question is an example.

	Statement	true	false
0.	Leyla Skovekolá is a polyglot.	✓	☐
19.	Steven is fluent in French.	☐	☐
20.	Leyla did most of her language learning in class.	☐	☐
21.	She used her own choice of books to learn English.	☐	☐
22.	Learning lists of words is useful for learning a language.	☐	☐
23.	Leyla sees digital media as a good source for language learning.	☐	☐
24.	You can do other things while learning a language.	☐	☐

II. Reading

Part 1 – Questions 1–5: Short texts

5 Punkte

Read the texts (1–5) below and the statements a, b and c next to them.
Decide which of the statements is the correct one for each text.
Put a tick (✓) in the correct box.

a) Children should be left on the ground. ☐
b) You should run away. ☐
c) You should turn your face towards the lion. ☐

All Service Moving

LOCAL RESIDENTIAL MOVING RATES: Less than 50 miles from our local office

The rate for 2 movers + 1 truck is $140 / hour. Each additional mover is $55 / hour. We bill with a 1-hour minimum on weekdays and a 4-hour minimum on weekends / holidays. Time starts and ends at our office. Time to and from our office is a fixed cost based on mapped time without traffic.

** Long distance rates vary

(206) 508-5855
www.allservicemoving.org

a) Additional movers are free of charge. ☐

b) If you live far away, you have to expect different rates for moving. ☐

c) The billed time begins at your house. ☐

Lovely luggage

I ordered this luggage after reading positive reviews about it, and I must say most reviews were correct. The luggage is even better than some of the more expensive brands. Quality is great and sturdy, colour is lovely and no need for a separate lock. Absolutely delighted, I hope that it lasts for many trips. Very happy with my new luggage.

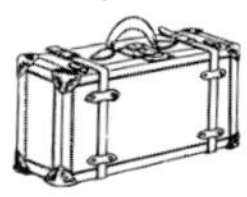

luca w.

a) The reviewer recommends buying an extra lock. ☐

b) The buyer prefers more expensive brands. ☐

c) Luca bought the product on the basis of other reviews. ☐

Romeo and Juliet tickets (London)

Desperately seeking Romeo and Juliet Ballet tickets for May 29, or June 1, matinee or evening.

Looking for five tickets but could live with just two!

Coming into town from the United States with my son who loves ballet dancing.

a) They would be OK with tickets on May 30. ☐

b) Two tickets would be enough. ☐

c) Their son is taking part in the London performance. ☐

UNDERGROUND TRAVEL INFORMATION

Please carry water with you at all times!

Don't get on a train if you feel unwell.
If you feel unwell while on a train, please get off at the next stop and seek help from a member of staff.

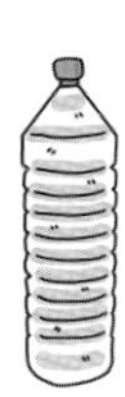

a) Drinks are forbidden on underground trains. ☐

b) Water is sold on the trains. ☐

c) You should only ride the train if you feel well. ☐

Part 2 – Questions 6–11: An Interview with Emma Watson

6 Punkte

Read the answers actress Emma Watson has given in an interview. Below the answers there are eight questions. Decide which question is most suitable for each answer.
For texts 6–11 write the correct letter A–H in the box next to the number. There are more questions than answers. Each letter can only be used once.

6. ☐ I was not 100 percent sure. I only really knew that when I did *The Perks of Being a Wallflower* and took some time off and went to university and really thought about what it meant. There are also other aspects of myself that I like to explore. I really love to paint and draw and to make art. Maybe at some point I will do something with that.

7. ☐ In *The Perks of Being a Wallflower* I was specifically playing one character. It was really weird, because I was much more experienced than any of the other actors on the set, but I was the most nervous of all of them. It was funny.

8. ☐ Now that I know that acting is the thing I want to do, that's more where my passion is and my focus is. I still find clothes very interesting, but I am finding more and more that I don't want to wear a dress and heavy makeup. I want to wear jeans more. It's quite intense to do it all the time.

9. ☐ They help me to keep me grounded. They definitely don't let me off the hook, as they are quite strict. They were very disciplined with me and they are quite serious; they make me take learning and education very seriously.

10. ☐ Especially animals. They have real human personalities. For me getting to hang out with my dog makes me smile, and in New York I have two cats who are so hilarious. One of my cats definitely thinks she is a human being and wants to do human things. Animals are a huge sort of comfort. And then just being able to see the funny side of life and to laugh at yourself is very important. Comedy is what can get you through trying situations.

11. ☐ It sounds like a cliché, but I would like to be able to be still. I would like to find a way to be content with myself and where I am. And I am not good at being still. I am always moving and doing different things. I am very driven, but I would like to find a way to be happy on my own.

A How important have your parents been for your personal development?

B You have so much moviemaking experience. Do you still have moments when you get insecure?

C Is there something that you wish for in life?

D How have your siblings reacted to your success?

E What makes you laugh and puts you in a good mood?

F What did you dream of as a child?

G Did you always know that you wanted to become an actress?

H You have been involved with fashion brands. Why have you lost interest in that?

New interview of Emma Watson with Savoir Flaire, November 07, 2012, https://watsonuncensored.blogspot.com/2012/11/new-interview-of-emma-watson-with.html?m=1

Part 3 – Questions 12–17: Zero Hour – Climate Crisis

Read the following text about environmental teenage activist Jamie Margolin. For questions 12–17, tick (✓) the correct box a, b or c. For each question there is only one correct answer.

6 Punkte

Zero Hour – Climate Crisis

Last year, Jamie Margolin was shocked by news alerts flashing on her phone: mudslides in Colombia, Hurricane Harvey, Hurricane Maria and, closer to home, "the thick smog that covered Seattle thanks to stronger-than-usual wildfires in Canada." Instead of simply swiping them away, Jamie decided to do something about it.

"It was already in the back of my mind to start a youth mobilisation movement," she says. "I was nervous to go there, especially since I'm so young. But last summer I realised I have to take action, even if it's going to be a lot of action." After messaging friends on Instagram Jamie founded Zero Hour, a youth organisation mobilising around the climate crisis.

"We are not a movement that happened overnight," says Jamie, who connected with adult mentors from the Women's March as well as young people who protested the Dakota Access Pipeline at Standing Rock. "It took hours and hours every day of slow but gradual movement building, and it still does."

This July, Zero Hour will host a weekend of youth action in Washington D.C. The core 25 members – who collaborate online from across the States and are mostly still at school – want to influence politicians in giving up on fossil fuels and to protest in a march.

The goal is to show how youth are affected by climate change. "It's not about a sad polar bear on an ice cap. It's about people's lives and kids and futures. People say 'Climate change? We'll deal with that later.' But it's urgent: it's zero hour."

Jamie calls climate change the "most urgent issue of our time," as it will affect young people's future and will disadvantage people, especially in poorer regions. She has relatives in Colombia, where her mother is from, who live near fracking sites and are worried about the drinking water.

"People are always asking me to plan for my future," she says. "But my generation is inheriting a totally uninhabitable planet. Within the next couple of years, we have to turn this around, or else my generation will really suffer."

Rosalie Chan: These teenage activists are shaping our future – Agents of change, Jamie Margolin – Zero Hour – 16 – climate crisis – Seattle, 1st June, 2018. https://www.huckmag.com/perspectives/activism-2/teenage-activists-protest-worldwide-agents-of-change

12. The news alerts on Jamie's phone were about …
    a) usual Canadian wildfires. ☐
    b) natural catastrophes. ☐
    c) mudslides in Seattle. ☐

13. She …
    a) wanted to start a youth organisation. ☐
    b) thought she was too young to do anything. ☐
    c) wanted to join an activist group. ☐

14. Zero Hour …
    a) started overnight. ☐
    b) is part of the Standing Rock protest. ☐
    c) took time and patience to form. ☐

15. Zero Hour members …
    a) plan to protest in March. ☐
    b) are all from the State of Washington. ☐
    c) want politicians to ban fossil fuels. ☐

16. Their goal is to …
    a) protect young people's future. ☐
    b) deal with climate change later. ☐
    c) save polar bears on ice caps. ☐

17. Jamie believes that climate change …
    a) will affect poorer people less. ☐
    b) causes fracking in Colombia. ☐
    c) might make our planet unliveable. ☐

Part 4 – Questions 18–23: Dead Whale Washed Up in Philippines Had 40 kg of Plastic Bags in Its Stomach

6 Punkte

Read the text about dead whales below.
For questions 18–23, tick (✓) the correct box true *or* false *<u>and</u> give the line(s) of reference in the text.*
The first question is an example.

A young whale that washed up in the Philippines died from 40 kg of plastic bags in its stomach. Marine biologists and volunteers from the D' Bone Collector Museum in Davao City, on the Philippine island of Mindanao, were shocked to discover the brutal cause of death for the young whale.

After conducting an autopsy, the museum stated on their Facebook page that they had uncovered "40 kilos of plastic bags, including 16 rice sacks, 4 banana plantation style bags and multiple shopping bags" in the whale's stomach.

Images from the autopsy showed endless piles of rubbish being taken out of the animal, which was said to have died from "gastric shock" after swallowing all the plastic.

The D' Bone Collector Museum biologists who conducted the autopsy said it was "the most plastic we have ever seen in a whale".

"It's disgusting," they added. "Action must be taken by the government against those who continue to treat the waterways and oceans as dumpsters."

The use of single-use plastic is especially excessive in south-east Asia. A 2017 report by Ocean Conservancy stated that countries like Indonesia, the Philippines, Thailand, and Vietnam have been dumping more plastic into the ocean than most other nations.

Marine biologist Darrell Blatchley, who also owns the D' Bone Collector Museum, said that in the 10 years they have examined dead whales and dolphins, 57 of them were found to have died because of rubbish and plastic in their stomachs.

In June last year, a whale died in southern Thailand after swallowing more than 80 plastic bags, which weighed up to 8 kg in the creature's stomach. Marine biologists estimate around 300 marine animals including pilot whales, sea turtles and dolphins, are killed by plastic each year in Thai waters.

Hannah Ellis-Petersen: Dead whale washed up in Philippines had 40kg of plastic bags in its stomach, Guardian 18 Mar 2019; https://www.theguardian.com/environment/2019/mar/18/dead-whale-washed-up-in-philippines-had-40kg-of-plastic-bags-in-its-stomach

	true	false	line(s)
0. 40 kg of plastic were in the stomach of a young whale.	✓	☐	1/2
18. The young whale died peacefully.	☐	☐	
19. The museum went public with the results of the autopsy.	☐	☐	
20. This amount of plastic in a whale is normal nowadays.	☐	☐	
21. According to the text, the government uses the oceans to get rid of waste.	☐	☐	
22. South-east Asian nations are responsible for large amounts of plastic trash in the oceans.	☐	☐	
23. Every year, around three hundred large marine animals die from swallowing plastic waste worldwide.	☐	☐	

III. Mediating

8 Punkte

Repair Café

Evin ist vor kurzem mit ihrem Bruder aus Syrien nach Deutschland gekommen und ist neu in deiner Klasse. Sie sucht Kontakte und ist technisch interessiert. Da ihre Deutschkenntnisse noch gering sind, hilfst du ihr, die Informationen auf der Website über ein örtliches Repair Café zu verstehen, damit sie dort Reparaturdienste anbieten kann. Sie schreibt dich in einem Chat an.

Wegwerfen? Denkste!

An jedem ersten Samstag im Monat findet im Gemeindehaus zwischen 14 und 17 Uhr eine lockere Zusammenkunft von Nachbarn mit reparaturbedürftigen Dingen, Neugierigen und freiwilligen Helfern statt. Die Aktivitäten werden kostenlos und auf ehrenamtlicher Basis von den Reparaturexperten vor Ort ausgeführt.

Ziel ist es neben dem Vermeiden von Müll, Erhalt von Werten und Verbreiten von Wissen auch Kontakte und den sozialen Zusammenhalt der Gemeinschaft zu fördern. Ebenfalls bieten wir Beratung zu Neuanschaffungen oder für die weitere Verwendung von Geräten, die veraltet zu sein scheinen, wie so manches Notebook oder Smartphone.

Die Initiative der „Repair-Cafés" geht auf die niederländische Journalistin Martine Postma zurück, die bereits 2009 das erste Repair-Café in Amsterdam eröffnete.

Wer mehr über die Initiative und die Ideen dahinter erfahren möchte: https://repaircafe.org/de/

Wir freuen uns über zahlreiches Erscheinen und Unterstützen dieser Initiative. Wir möchten darum bitten bzw. darauf hinweisen, dass:

- Reparaturen, soweit es möglich ist, von den Besuchern unter Anleitung selbst ausgeführt werden
- eine Reparatur nicht garantiert oder gar verlangt werden kann
- Ersatzteile nicht kostenlos sein können (der Materialwert sollte erstattet werden)
- die Besucher für die Entsorgung ausgetauschter Teile oder nicht zu reparierender Geräte selbst zuständig sind

Natürlich freuen wir uns auch über eine freiwillige Spende. Der Verein schafft Werkzeuge an und finanziert Ersatzteile vor. Das kostet alles Geld. Zudem sind laufende Kosten zu begleichen. Aber auch ein Päckchen Kaffee oder ein Kuchen sind willkommen.

Wer als freiwilliger Helfer mitmachen oder Sachspenden mitbringen möchte, soll bitte vorher mit uns Kontakt aufnehmen.

Für alle Fragen stehen wir gern zur Verfügung:

repaircafe@hilfsverein-niedersachsen.de

Reparatur-Café: Wegwerfen? Denkste!, https://hölderlin-eins.de/vereine-gruppen

09:15: Connected with Evin

Evin: Hey! Thanks for offering your help. I've found this website about a repair café. I think I could help people who have problems with their bikes. Can you tell me where and when the repair café takes place?

Me (1): ______________________________

____

Evin: Great, that should work. If I do some repairs, will I get paid?

Me (2): ______________________________

Evin: For me it's about helping others anyway. What about tools? Do I have to bring or buy them myself?

Me (3): ______________________________

____

Evin: I see. And how does it work? Would I repair the bikes on my own?

Me (4): ______________________________

____

Evin: Oh, that's cool. But what if I can't help them?

Me (5): ______________________________

____

Evin: Can I just go to the next meeting if I want to help?

Me (6): ______________________________

____

Evin: All right. Unfortunately, my German writing is not very good yet. Can you contact them for me and ask if they need someone who can repair bikes? And could you ask them if they think it would be a problem that my German isn't that good yet? Thanks so much.

Me (7/8): Du schreibst dem Repair Café eine E-Mail, um Evins Anliegen in Erfahrung zu bringen.

An: repaircafe@hilfsverein-niedersachsen.de

Betreff: Anfrage

IV. Writing – Set I

Part 1 – A Review: Bad Restaurant

10 Punkte

The picture on the right shows a restaurant where you ate a few days ago. Write a review of the restaurant for traveladvisor.com.

Write about 100 words.

Include:

- *when you went there and what you ate*
- *a description of the conditions and the food you were served there*
- *how many stars you give this restaurant and why*

traveladvisor.com

☆☆☆☆☆

Enter your review here:

Part 2 – A Diary Entry: To Your Future Self

Inhalt: 7,5 Punkte
Sprache: 7,5 Punkte
Gesamt: 15 Punkte

Write a diary entry to your future self in 10 years from now.
Write about 150 words.

Include:
- *what hopes and dreams you have for your future (e.g. how you live, your family, your job etc.)*
- *what goals you would like to achieve*
- *what you think the world will be like*

Dear future me,

IV. Writing – Set II

Part 1 – An E-Mail: Shared Flat for Work and Travel

10 Punkte

You want to work and travel around Spain and are looking for a shared flat in Barcelona. You find the following ad and decide to write an e-mail in order to apply.

Write about 100 words.

Looking for a shared flat? We're three international students looking for a flatmate. We offer: 15 sqm room and a shared bathroom for only 350 EUR a month.

Please let us know:
- who you are and why you would like to stay with us
- what you can contribute to our group
- questions about the flat

TO:

SUBJECT:

Part 2 – An Article: Stay at Home – Online Distance Learning

Inhalt: 7,5 Punkte
Sprache: 7,5 Punkte
Gesamt: 15 Punkte

In a teen magazine you find the competition below. You decide to write an article. Write about 150 words.

We use technology for everything these days – so isn't it strange that you still have to go to school? Why can't you stay at home and study via video chat with your teacher and other students?
Sounds great! Or is it?

Tell us about:

- advantages and disadvantages of this kind of learning
- if studying via video conference would be useful and possible at your school
- your opinion

We will publish the three best articles on our website.

Anhang: Hörverstehenstexte

This is the listening part of the final examination 2020 level B 1 for schools in Lower Saxony. There are four parts to the test. You will hear each recording twice. For each part of the test there will be time for you to look through the questions. You must not speak during the test.

Part 1

Now look at part 1, questions 1 to 5. Listen to five short recordings. For each recording, there is a question with three pictures. Choose the correct picture and put a tick in the box A, B or C below it. Before we start, here is an example.

Example

What is the man going to buy?

Man: I'm going shopping now. Anything else we need for our holiday?
Woman: The sunscreen from our last trip should still work. I haven't got any sunglasses, but I can borrow some of yours, can't I? Hm, maybe something to kill the time at the airport.
Man: Yes. That's a good idea. I'll stop by the newsagent's.

The third picture with the magazine is correct. So there is a tick in box C.

Text 1

Look at the three pictures for question 1 now.
Now we are ready to start. Listen carefully. You will hear each recording twice.

When does the drama group meet?

Good morning, students. The drama group would like to remind you that their new play, *Romeo and Juliet,* will premiere today at 5:00. There are still tickets available. The drama group gathers in the assembly hall at 4:00 instead of 3:30, as initially planned. The Spanish club will not take place today because …

Now listen again.

Text 2

Who is going to do the dishes?

Dad: That was yummy. So, who is going to do the washing-up today?
Boy: Not me. I have cooked, so I'm out.
Girl: And I have done the shopping. So, Dad, you know who it is!
Dad: OK. You won.

Now listen again.

Text 3

Which room does the guest get?

Receptionist: Well, here is your key. Your room number is 105.

Woman: Thank you. Oh, erm, it is a double bed, right?

Receptionist: Oh, I'm afraid it isn't. Let's see, I could give you room 306 instead, which is a very small one, or 510 on the fifth floor, but I have to warn you – our elevator is currently out of order.

Women: Well, I think separate beds are fine then.

Now listen again.

Text 4

How does Kevin get to his job interview?

Mother: Today is your job interview, right? How are you gonna get there?

Kevin: I think I'll take the tram. It's the cheapest.

Mother: Haven't you heard? Trams still don't operate because of the construction at the station.

Kevin: Oh no! Can you give me a ride?

Mother: Honey, I've got errands to run. Take your bike!

Kevin: Mum! I don't want to arrive there being all sweaty.

Mother: OK then. I can go to the city centre first anyway.

Now listen again.

Text 5

Where do the tourists go first?

Man: So, how should we start the day today?

Woman: I'd love to go for a ride on the London Eye today.

Man: Great idea, but I kind of want to do that to watch the sunset. How about starting with St Paul's Cathedral or Buckingham Palace?

Woman: Alright. Let's head for the palace and make a stop at the cathedral on our way there.

Now listen again.

This is the end of part 1.

Part 2

Now turn to part 2, questions 6 to 12 – A job interview. Listen to Kevin being interviewed for a job at a clothes shop. For each question tick the correct box, a, b or c. The first question is an example. Now you have 30 seconds to look at part 2. Now we are ready to start. Listen carefully. You will hear the recording twice.

Sandy: Good morning, I'm Sandy Burns. Mr … Grant?

Kevin: Yes, I'm Kevin Grant. Good morning, how are you?

Sandy: I'm excellent, thanks. First of all, I'd like to know, how did you hear about the job? On the Internet?

Kevin: Well, I went to a job fair with a friend of mine and came across your stand. It looked really interesting.

Sandy: I see! So, what caught your interest in our shop?

Kevin: Actually, I love coming here to shop for clothes myself. And I usually buy something because you offer such great quality at good prices. And I find your advertising very attractive, especially for young people like me. Also, the people I talked to at the fair only said good things about the working conditions.

Sandy: *(Laughs)* That's true, of course. So, why would you be a good shop assistant, and do you have any weaknesses?

Kevin: I've got to say, I don't like working on my own. I need people around me and then I'm really motivated. Friends tell me that I'm very persuasive and think that I could sell them anything, but I think I might be a little bit too honest for that. I could never trick anyone into buying something. I would want the people to be happy with what they buy and not regret it, because if they aren't happy, they probably won't come back.

Sandy: Fair enough. What about your sense of fashion? Let's say I was your customer. What kind of outfit would you recommend for a job interview?

Kevin: Of course, that would depend on what you apply for, but a smart, casual outfit probably works in most cases. Navy blue denim trousers, a white blouse combined with a plain blazer would look nice. Maybe no trainers. Rather simple, low-heeled shoes, nothing too fancy.

Sandy: OK, thank you. In your CV, you say that after school you spent some time travelling and working abroad. Where did you go and what did you do?

Kevin: I was in Central America, mostly in Costa Rica. I worked for a fair trade organisation there for around two months. I sold coffee and traditional clothes to tourists close to one of the national parks. It was great fun.

Sandy: So, do you speak Spanish or any other foreign languages?

Kevin: Yeah, I learned enough Spanish to get by and talk to customers in the shop. At school I had French, but I can't really speak it too well. But my mother is Polish and raised me bilingually. That's why I'm fairly fluent in that language.

Sandy: Brilliant! Now, do you have any questions for me?

Kevin: I couldn't find any information about the pay. What could I expect?

Sandy: Well, during your probation period, which is three months, you'd earn £ 6 per hour during the week and eight at the weekend. After your probation you'd get a raise every year of around £ 1. The current limit is £ 10 an hour on weekdays and we'd expect you to work 42 hours per week. Alright, Mr Grant, if you have no further questions, I'd like to thank you for coming. And we will call you shortly and let you know about our choice.

Kevin: Thank you. I hope to see you soon.

Now listen again.

This is the end of part 2.

Part 3

Now turn to part 3, questions 13 to 18 – Phone repair. The display of your smartphone is broken. You call the hotline of a repair shop to find out about their services. Listen to the recorded message and fill in the missing information. The first question is an example. You have 20 seconds to look at part 3. Now we are ready to start. Listen carefully. You will hear the recording twice.

You have reached the Phone Hospital. Unfortunately, you are calling out of office hours. Our shop is open from 8:00 to 6:00 on weekdays and from 10:00 to 3:00 on Saturdays. During these hours you can also reach us by phone. If you are calling for general information, we hope to be able to answer your questions with this announcement. The phone hospital is now located in the Metro Shopping Center. We have closed our shop in Winchester Street. We offer several services, including battery and screen replacements. Before starting the service operation, we perform a thorough check-up procedure with your device and then make a transparent offer for you without any hidden costs. Screen repairs range from 25 to 149 dollars depending on your model. If you need the battery to be replaced, you can expect prices ranging from 29 to 79 dollars. In most cases you can pick up your repaired phone within a short period of time. We repair 99 percent of the phones we receive within a day. The repair may take up to 48 hours if the needed parts are not in stock. All repairs are carried out by our expert technicians. We only use certified high-quality parts for replacement. All our repairs come with a 12-month warranty, so you have nothing to worry about. If you don't live nearby, you can use our pick-up and delivery service starting at $ 19, depending on where you live. For any further questions, please contact us during our office hours. Thank you for calling.

Now listen again.

This is the end of part 3.

Part 4

Now turn to part 4, questions 19 to 24 – Polyglot. You will hear a radio interview with Leyla Skovekolá, who speaks many different languages. Decide whether each statement is true or false. Put a tick in the correct box "true" or "false". The first question is an example. You now have 30 seconds to look at part 4.
Now we are ready to start. Listen carefully. You will hear the recording twice.

Steven: Good morning, listeners, and a good morning to Leyla Skovekolá. She's a polyglot, and … what that is, she's going to tell us now.

Leyla: Good morning, Steven, thanks for having me on the show today. Well, a polyglot is someone who speaks and learns many foreign languages.

Steven: I've got to say – I don't speak any foreign languages, although I took French at school. What languages do you speak, and how did you manage to learn them successfully?

Leyla: I'm a native speaker of Croatian, and, well, obviously I do speak English, which I had at school, but that's not where I actually learned it. I learned it outside of school on my own, with my own methods. That's the way I also acquired Spanish, French, German, Arabic, Japanese, Mandarin and Russian.

Steven: That's impressive! Erm, what do you mean by 'your own methods'? Are schools using the wrong ones?

Leyla: It's hard to say they are wrong, but personally, I've always been bored with the textbooks. My favourite book was 'Harry Potter', so I started to read it in English. At the beginning, I hardly understood anything, but I kept on reading and by the end of the book I was able to follow it with hardly any problems.

Steven: So, you're saying: read what you're interested in. Mm, I'm not a big reader. What should I try to learn a new language? Memorise lists of words?

Leyla: *(Laughs)* If you try to memorise a list of words, for example for a test on the following day, the words will be stored in your short-term memory and you'll forget them after a few days. To learn a language, however, you want to keep words long-term, so you need to revise them in the course of a few days repeatedly. Talk to other people and actually use the words. And if you have no one to talk to, talk to yourself. Also, surround yourself with the language you want to learn. Find content on YouTube that you are interested in. Or watch a series. Of course, you will not understand everything right away, but be a little bit patient – you will see the success and noticing that success motivates me and you to continue learning.

Steven: That sounds useful, but I'm afraid I simply don't have the time to learn a new language.

Leyla: Yes, we're all very busy and no one really has the time to learn languages today, but if we just plan ahead a little bit, we can create that time. Listen to a podcast on your way to work while driving or while you're doing your household chores. In fact, doing chores is suddenly fun and the time flies by.

Steven: Leyla, thank you very much. That was truly inspiring. I also think that some language teachers can learn from that.
And on our show tomorrow, we're talking to Kevin – an adventurer who spent several months working in Costa Rica. Tune in!

Now listen again.

This is the end of the listening part. Good luck for the rest of your examination!

Realschulabschlussprüfung in Niedersachsen
Englisch 2021

I. Listening

Part 1 – Questions 1–7

7 Punkte

Listen to seven short recordings. For each recording, there is a question with three pictures. Choose the correct picture and put a tick (✓) in the box A, B or C below it.

Example

0. What is the man going to buy?

A ☐

B ☐

C ☑

1. Which road should you take into London?

A ☐

B ☐

C ☐

2. What does the guest order?

A ☐

B ☐

C ☐

3. Which app is Casey looking for?

A ☐

B ☐

C ☐

4. What type of transportation does the couple choose?

A ☐

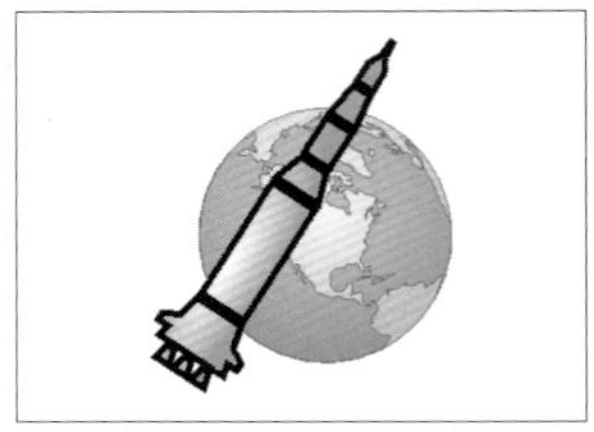

B ☐

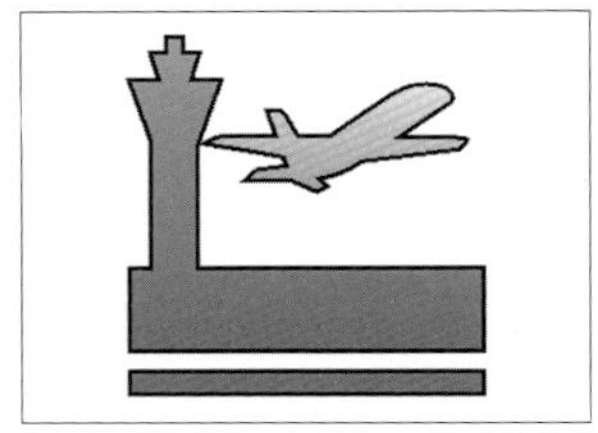

C ☐

5. How does the customer pay?

A ☐

B ☐

C ☐

6. Which stamp does the woman buy?

A ☐

B ☐

C ☐

7. What is their plan for the weekend?

A ☐

B ☐

C ☐

Part 2 – Questions 8–13: Apartment Viewing

Listen to Peter Schmidt talking to a real-estate agent while looking at an apartment. For each question, tick (✓) the correct box a, b or c.

6 Punkte

8. The kitchen is ...
   a) a separate room. ☐
   b) old-fashioned. ☐
   c) fully equipped. ☐

9. Peter Schmidt would ...
   a) need to bring his own furniture. ☐
   b) be able to move in with his own couch. ☐
   c) be allowed to use the apartment's TV. ☐

10. The apartment has ...
   a) two bedrooms that share a closet. ☐
   b) more than one kitchen. ☐
   c) a room with a washing machine. ☐

11. The rent ...
   a) is paid every three months. ☐
   b) covers no additional costs. ☐
   c) includes the cost of the Internet. ☐

12. Peter Schmidt might move in ...
   a) if the landlord chooses him. ☐
   b) in two weeks. ☐
   c) after completing his renovation work. ☐

13. The application form must ...
   a) include a reference. ☐
   b) be sent to Peter Schmidt's employer. ☐
   c) reach the office before the weekend. ☐

Part 3 – Questions 14–20: Power Skates

7 Punkte

You are interested in a pair of Power Skates.
You listen to a commercial to find out more about them.
Fill in the missing information.
The first question is an example.

Name of the product:	0. Power Skates
Powered by:	14. ______
Max. range:	15. ______
How to learn:	16. ______
Max. speed:	17. ______
How to control speed:	18. ______
Discount price:	19. ______
Coupon code:	20. ______

Part 4 – Questions 21–26: Returning from Germany

6 Punkte

You will hear a radio interview with Noah Clarkson, an American teenager who has just returned from spending a year in Germany as an exchange student. Decide whether each statement is true or false and put a tick (✓) in the correct box. The first question is an example.

	Statement	true	false
0.	Emily Sanders spent a year in Germany.	☐	✓
21.	Noah's great-grandfather lives in Germany.	☐	☐
22.	Noah disliked public transportation in Germany.	☐	☐
23.	Noah travelled to cities outside of Germany.	☐	☐
24.	Noah thinks American food is less healthy than European food.	☐	☐
25.	Noah thinks most Germans are reserved when you first meet them.	☐	☐
26.	Noah is going to visit some German friends this summer.	☐	☐

II. Reading

Part 1 – Questions 1–6: Short texts

Read the texts below and read the statements 1–6.
Decide whether the statements are true or false. Then tick (✓) the correct box.

6 Punkte

1.

Teacher for extracurricular activities at Triangle Lake Elementary School

We are looking for teachers, counselors, and coaches, who offer musical, creative, academic or athletic programs and clubs for our students.

Pay: up to $30 per hour depending on qualifications
Working hours: 3–5 p.m. Mon–Thu during school weeks

Experience and qualifications favored, but not needed.

Applications to school office:
TLS, School Road, Blachly

2.

Youth Service Office London

Due to water damage our office is closed indefinitely!!!

In urgent cases we will arrange appointments in the family centre in Zach Street.

Please contact us by email or phone! (contact below).

Our letter box is still cleared daily.

Phone: 020-39 34 89
Email: ysol@london.co.uk

3.

Do you need help running your errands?

I am George, a sixteen-year-old student, trying to save money for a year abroad. Very reliable and motivated.

I offer:
Grocery shopping
Walking your dog
Office courses
Help in the garden
And much more

Available times:
Weekdays from 5–7 pm,
Saturdays from 10 am – 4 pm

From £7 depending on job.

4.

Band members wanted for Indie Rock project: "Aim 42"

Looking for bassist and drummer!

Bassist: Strong riffy bass that can fill some space. Ability to chord progression is a must.

Drummer: Must know when slow and simple is appropriate while still being able to play accurately at higher speeds.

Rehearsals: Every Wednesday at 9 pm at basement of Cedar Creek public swimming pools.

Understanding of music theory required.

Contact us on Insta if interested: @Aim_42

		true	false
1.	On Tuesdays George can walk your dog in the morning and in the afternoon.	☐	☐
2.	The elementary school is looking for experienced teachers only.	☐	☐
3.	As a new band member, you have to be able to read music.	☐	☐
4.	The Youth Service Office can still be reached by post.	☐	☐
5.	The band meets once a week to practice.	☐	☐
6.	The teaching wage is the same for everybody.	☐	☐

Part 2 – Questions 7–13: Charlene Rocha – A Teen Activist

7 Punkte

Read the answers teen activist Charlene Rocha has given in an interview. Below the answers there are eight questions. Decide which question is most suitable for each answer. For texts 7–13 write the correct letter A–H in the box next to the number. There are more questions than answers. Each letter can only be used once.

7. ☐ There are so many more components to it than people think! I'm currently working with a committee called Break the Chains and we are fighting against anti-Black racism. We held a protest in Pickering, Ontario that was about two hours long, but behind-the-scenes there were many more hours of emailing, discussions, writing, and researching!

8. ☐ The first time I learned about it was through a speaker that came to my school. She told us about the effects climate change was causing in poorer countries. I was completely in shock that we could have such a huge problem in the world and have governments still refusing to act. I felt motivated to do something.

9. ☐ I enjoy celebrating the world we are saving! I go on hikes with my friends, rollerblade with my sister, take my dog for long walks, and swim at the beach. Activism isn't supposed to be super stressful – it's a fun thing to do!

10. ☐ Find a cause that you are passionate about and research it! Knowing the facts is an important factor to effective activism. Whether it's reading a book, or listening to the news, knowing about these issues is a great way to get involved and inspire other people around you too.

11. ☐ It was a rush of emotions. I did a speech completely on the spot and it definitely was spontaneous. I was a pretty quiet person before I became an activist, so this was definitely something that shocked my friends, family, and me!

12. ☐ Sometimes I get nervous, forget what to say, and make mistakes. But that is completely okay! The way that I've learned to handle speeches is by reminding myself that it's just a speech. Even if I do seem nervous, I will learn and grow from it.

13. ☐ Everything is connected. For example, Black and Indigenous people are affected the most by climate change in Canada. This means that in addressing one issue, you are fighting for another one as well.

A What did it feel like speaking at a *FridaysForFuture* event when you were 13?

B How do you handle speaking in front of a large crowd?

C When did you first become aware of environmental activism?

D Besides protests and giving speeches, what else is there to activism?

E What do you do to relax and wind down?

F Why do you fight for so many things at once?

G What is your next big project?

H What is a great first step for kids to make activism a part of their lives?

Adapted from: Teen activist Charlene Rocha/OWLconnected, 02. 07. 2020, http://owlconnected.com/archives/interview-charlene-rocha

Part 3 – Questions 14–19: Why Teenagers Really Do Need an Extra Hour in Bed

6 Punkte

Read the following article about the sleep needs of adolescents.
For questions 14–19, tick (✓) the correct box a, b or c.
For each question there is only one correct answer.

The biology of human sleep timing changes as we age. As puberty begins, bedtimes and waking times get later. This trend continues until 19.5 years in women and 21 in men. Then it reverses. At 55 we wake at about the time we woke prior to puberty. On average this is two hours earlier than adolescents. This means that for a teenager, a 7 am alarm call is the equivalent of a 5 am start for a person in their 50s.

However, biology is only part of the problem. Additional factors include a more relaxed attitude to bedtimes by parents, a general disregard for the importance of sleep, and access to electronic devices, which keep teenagers awake. The amount of sleep teenagers get varies between countries, geographic region and social class, but all studies show they are going to bed later and not getting as much sleep as they need because of early school starts.

Sleep scientists have shown that teenagers need about nine hours a night to maintain full alertness and academic performance. But in reality, many were getting just five hours of sleep on school days. Unsurprisingly, teachers reported students being tired in class.

In the US, the observation that teenagers have biologically delayed sleep patterns compared to adults prompted several schools to put back the start of the school day. An analysis found that academic performance was enhanced, as was attendance. In the UK, Monkseaton High School near Newcastle instituted a 10 am start in 2009 and saw an uptick in academic performance.

However, a later start by itself is not enough. Society in general, and teenagers in particular, must start to take sleep seriously.

If you are dependent upon an alarm clock, or parent, to get you out of bed; if you take a long time to wake up; if you feel sleepy and irritable during the day; if your behaviour is overly impulsive, it means you are probably not getting enough sleep. Take control. Ensure the bedroom is a place that promotes sleep – dark and not warm – don't look at electric screens for at least half an hour before trying to sleep and avoid bright lights. Seek out natural light in the morning to adjust the body clock and sleep patterns to an earlier time.

Adapted from: Russell Foster: Why teenagers really do need an extra hour in bed, New Scientist, 17. 04. 2013, https://www.newscientist.com/article/mg21829130-100-why-teenagers-really-do-need-an-extra-hour-in-bed/#ixzz6aGjzT0Wf

14. Sleeping time …
    a) is consistent through life. ☐
    b) starts later with puberty. ☐
    c) ends later for seniors. ☐

15. For teenagers an alarm at 7 am feels …
    a) later than for 50-year-olds. ☐
    b) the same as for 50-year-olds. ☐
    c) like a 5 am alarm for 50-year-olds. ☐

16. According to the article, teenagers often get too little sleep because …
    a) their parents go to bed too late as well. ☐
    b) they think sleep is unimportant. ☐
    c) they are often woken by their smartphones. ☐

17. To realize their full potential at school, teenagers should …
    a) sleep around nine hours per night. ☐
    b) set an early alarm. ☐
    c) rest for five hours after school. ☐

18. After starting times were delayed at some schools …
    a) students' performance got worse. ☐
    b) more students were present in class. ☐
    c) students began to take sleep more seriously. ☐

19. For better sleep …
    a) your bedroom should be warm and dark. ☐
    b) avoid looking at your smartphone before bedtime. ☐
    c) seek out natural light right before going to bed. ☐

Part 4 – Questions 20–26:
Dutee Chand – An Indian Sprint Star's Rapid Rise

7 Punkte

Read the article about the Indian athlete Dutee Chand. For questions 20–26, tick (✓) the correct box true *or* false *<u>and</u> give the line(s) of reference in the text. The first question is an example.*

Sprinter Dutee Chand is India's national champion at 100 m and at Rio 2016 became only the third Indian woman to qualify for the women's Olympic 100 m. The 23-year-old talks about her financial hardship as an aspiring athlete and the controversy she has had to overcome in her eventful career: "People around the world see me running for just 10–12 seconds. But no one knows that to run these seconds, I have to train 365 days a year." Dutee Chand is one of South Asia's fastest running female sprinters competing in the 100 m. "If you don't win, people will forget you. So, you always have to win. And you have to work very hard for it. I train six times a day. During our workout we have to do repetitions of 100–500 m sprints." Last year, Dutee clocked her career-best time at 11.22 seconds.

She was inspired by her sister who was a state-level runner. "I never dreamt of becoming an internationally successful runner. But then my sister told me that if I took up running, I would be able to support my education. So, to keep my studies going I started running. But I faced a lot of problems. I had no running shoes and no money to buy any. There were no proper running tracks to practise on. No good coaches. So I started running alone in my village, barefoot, on the river bank and on the road. My diet consisted of whatever was cooked at home."

Dutee Chand had to overcome many financial hardships to succeed. Sometimes she even spent the nights on railway platforms because she had no money to pay for a hotel. Then, in 2014, she was accused of doping because the level of male hormones in her blood was higher than normal. Therefore, she was excluded from participating in the Commonwealth Games. But she appealed to an international court. "Everyone has hormones", she says, "some have more and some have less. Was it my fault?" Eventually, she won the case and was allowed to participate.

The ban affected her preparations for the 2016 Olympic Games. At the 2017 Asian Championship, Chand won two bronze medals. But her biggest success so far came in 2018 during the Asian Games when Dutee won two silver medals in the 100 and 200 meters. She is currently aiming at a podium finish in the 2021 Tokyo Olympics.

Adapted from: BBC Indian Sportswoman of the Year: Dutee Chand, Reporter: Rakhee Sharma, 03. 02. 2020, https://www.bbc.com/sport/av/51107178

	true	false	line(s)
0. Dutee Chand is a national sprint champion from India.	✓	☐	1
20. She was the first Indian woman to qualify for the Olympics.	☐	☐	
21. Dutee trains several times a day.	☐	☐	
22. She completed her fastest 100 m run in under eleven seconds.	☐	☐	
23. Her sister was internationally successful as a runner.	☐	☐	
24. Dutee used to train barefoot because she was too poor to buy running shoes.	☐	☐	
25. She was banned from the Commonwealth Games for possible doping in 2014.	☐	☐	
26. In 2018, Dutee won two silver medals at the Asian Games.	☐	☐	

III. Writing – Set I

Part 1 – Feedback: London City Tour

10 Punkte

You have just finished a guided city tour of London. You rated the tour and the guide in five categories as seen in the table.

Leave feedback in which you explain your ratings.

Write about 80 words.

Friendliness	★★★★
Entertainment	★★★☆
Interesting information	★★★★
Selection of sights	★★☆☆
Overall impression	★★★☆

Part 2 – An E-Mail: International School Competition

Inhalt: 9 Punkte
Sprache: 9 Punkte
Gesamt: 18 Punkte

You have found the following competition on the website of Schools United. Write an entry for the competition in about 150 words.

Tell us what $ 50,000 could do for your school.
You can win the money for your school if you convince us!

Include these aspects:

- *a short introduction to your school*
- *what needs to be better*
- *how you would spend the money*

TO: competition@schoolsunited.com

SUBJECT: $ 50,000 for my school

Dear Schools United,

III. Writing – Set II

Part 1 – A Report: Stolen Bike

10 Punkte

Your bike was stolen, and you reported the theft to the police. The police asked you to write a short report including the following:

- *Where and when you left your bike*
- *A detailed description of your bike*
- *Whether your bike was registered and locked*

Write about 80 words.

Part 2 – A Blog Entry: My Trip to Mars

Inhalt: 9 Punkte
Sprache: 9 Punkte
Gesamt: 18 Punkte

Imagine you live in the year 2050. You have just returned from a trip to planet Mars. Write a blog entry about the trip.

In your text include:

- *How you travelled and what the journey was like*
- *What life is like on Mars*
- *What you missed there and what you are now missing on Earth*

Write about 150 words.

Anhang: Hörverstehenstexte

This is the listening part of the final examination 2021 level B 1 for schools in Lower Saxony. There are four parts to the test. You will hear each recording twice. For each part of the test there will be time for you to look through the questions. You must not speak during the test.

Part 1

Now look at part 1, questions 1 to 7. Listen to seven short recordings. For each recording, there is a question with three pictures. Choose the correct picture and put a tick in the box A, B or C below it. Before we start, here is an example.

Example

What is the man going to buy?

Man: I'm going shopping now. Anything else we need for our holiday?
Woman: The sunscreen from our last trip should still work. I haven't got any sunglasses, but I can borrow some of yours, can't I? Hm, maybe something to kill the time at the airport.
Man: Yes. That's a good idea. I'll stop by the newsagent's.

The picture with the magazine is correct. So there is a tick in box C.

Text 1

Look at the three pictures for question 1 now.
Now we are ready to start. Listen carefully.

Which road should you take into London?

Traffic is crazy this morning. Here's an update for all drivers trying to get into the city. There's serious congestion on the M1 southbound at junction four at Elstree. You have to expect delays of at least an hour if you're on the M1. Our advice is to get off at junction five and take the A41. The A1 is also quite busy. It's not an alternative today. Have a safe journey.

Now listen again.

Text 2

What does the guest order?

Waiter: So, have you made up your mind? Let me tell you, the ribeye steak is awesome.
Woman: Well, I was just looking at the Caesar salad. Does it come with chicken?
Waiter: We can do that. Is that what you want? That'd be three dollars extra.
Woman: You know what? I think I'm going for your recommendation.
Waiter: Good call, ma'am.

Now listen again.

Text 3

Which app is Casey looking for?

Casey: Hey, Jeff, what was that app called that you told me about the other day?
Jeff: Hey, Casey, do you mean "Find My Lover"? That's a nifty dating app.
Casey: Hmm. I think it had to do with sharing your calendar with others.
Jeff: Share your calendar? You can share events with the default calendar app.
Casey: Yeah, I know that.
Jeff: Well, with "Cal-Export", you can print your calendar so that you put it on your wall old-fashioned style.
Casey: Or give it to others. That's what I was thinking of. Thanks.

Now listen again.

Text 4

What type of transportation does the couple choose?

Man: Honey, we've never been on a cruise. It's always been my dream to cross the pond on one.
Woman: That's because I get seasick, honey. Huh. But how would you feel about city hopping across Europe?
Man: Only if we get there on a cruise or by rocket. That's a thing now, isn't it?
Woman: Oh, come on. Very funny. Like I wouldn't get sick on a rocket.
Man: All right, then. But I'll tell the pilot to try and fly as fast as one.
Woman: It's gonna be awesome.

Now listen again.

Text 5

How does the customer pay?

Sales clerk: All right, that's 4.99, please.
Customer: Ah, there you go.
Sales clerk: Oh, I'm sorry, we're cash free.
Customer: Oh, OK. Shoot, I don't have a card with me. Oh, well, then this should work.
Sales clerk: Thank you very much. Have a great day.

Text 6

Which stamp does the woman buy?

Woman: I need a stamp, please.
Man: Sure. Which one do you need? 60, 75 or 90?
Woman: It's for a postcard to Germany. So 90, I guess.
Man: 60 is for national, 75 for international postcards and 90 is for letters. Here's the one you need.

Text 7

What is their plan for the weekend?

Mother: Hey, it's our family weekend coming up. What would you like to do?

Boy: Mom, let's go to the Mighty Midland's Park. There's a new crazy roller coaster.

Mother: Hm. Crazy idea, but it's also crazy expensive.

Boy: Why don't we go for a walk in the forest then?

Mother: Really? I'd love that.

Boy: I was just kidding. It's the last chance to see *In the Dark Light* on the big screen. So we don't actually have a choice, Mom.

Now listen again.

This is the end of part 1.

Part 2

Now turn to part 2, questions 8 to 13. Listen to Peter Schmidt talking to a real estate agent while looking at an apartment. For each question tick the correct box, a, b or c.
Now you have 30 seconds to look at part 2.
Now we are ready to start. Listen carefully.

Woman: Hi, Peter Schmidt from Germany, how are you doing?

Peter: I'm fine, thanks. Yes, that's correct. I'm interested in the apartment.

Woman: Awesome. Well, let's go right in. And here we are. This is the spacious living area with a modern open kitchen to our left. It has all the latest appliances. The fridge has a built-in screen to show you recipes and what groceries you need.

Peter: Uh huh. That's nice. Oh, and there's a sofa. Does it belong to the apartment?

Woman: Yes, the apartment is furnished. Everything you see here is included. If you want to bring your own couch, you'd have to store this one away. You bring your own TV set, computer and stuff. But there are loads of power outlets for all your devices.

Peter: I see it all looks very nice and is in good condition. So how many rooms are there overall?

Woman: Well, it's a two-bedroom apartment. Both bedrooms have their own closet. Then there's one bathroom with a shower bath and the kitchen has a pantry attached. And over there is a laundry room for your clothes. It has a dryer, too.

Peter: What about the rent?

Woman: The rent for the apartment is 210 dollars per week. You pay at the beginning of the month. Then there are the additional costs for maintenance, electricity and so on. This is paid quarterly and it's currently around three hundred dollars. Internet and cable are not included.

Peter: OK, and when is the apartment available?

Woman: Very soon. The landlord wants to choose his new tenant in about two weeks, depending on the renovation work that will be done in the first week of June. I would say that end of June should be possible.

Peter: OK, great. I'm interested. How do I apply?

Woman: All you have to do is fill in this application form. Of course it can help to show a reference from your current employer or someone like that, but please make sure to get your form to our office by Friday.

Peter: All right, I can do that. Thank you very much.

Woman: I'm keeping my fingers crossed for you. Good-bye, Peter.

Now listen again.

This is the end of part 2.

Part 3

Now turn to part 3, questions 14 to 20 – Power Skates. You are interested in a pair of Power Skates. You listen to a commercial to find out more about them. Fill in the missing information. The first question is an example. You have 20 seconds to look at part 3.
Now we are ready to start. Listen carefully.

(Jingle: Power Skates) Have you ever dreamed of gliding along the street without any physical effort? Then this dream is about to come true with Power Skates *(Jingle)*. You don't only get to your destination quickly, it's fun too. Power Skates are skates powered by a rechargeable battery. Charge them anywhere. Just hook them up to your household outlet. In only 20 minutes, your Power Skates are charged enough for you to glide two miles and your Power Skates are fully charged in sixty minutes. You can go up to six miles on a single charge. *(Jingle)*

Is it difficult to ride them? Not at all. It's super easy and super safe. Our free app offers a great video tutorial for you to learn how to ride your Power Skates safely. For the first 20 miles your speed is limited to five miles an hour to start slowly and safely. As soon as you're more experienced, you are able to go full speed at 15 miles an hour. What do you get when you purchase Power Skates today? Your super sleek Power Skates come with a powerful charger and with a super precise remote control. That's what you use to control your Power Skates: speed and light. That's right. You can make your Power Skates light up in a variety of great colors. If you think Power Skates are expensive, you're wrong. You can get your Powers Skates for only 399 dollars at your local store. But wait, if you buy your pair on our website www.powerskates.com today, you'll get a 50 dollar discount. All you have to do is enter our voucher code when you check out. That's right. You'll get your Power Skates for only 349 dollars.

The voucher code is "safeandfun21". I'll say it again: "safeandfun21". Your Power Skates are waiting for you. Order them now. *(Jingle)*

Due to occasional shortages, some sizes may not be in stock.

Now listen again. [...] This is the end of part 3.

Part 4

Now turn to part 4, questions 21 to 26. You will hear a radio interview with Noah Clarkson, an American teenager who has just returned from spending a year in Germany as an exchange student. Decide whether each statement is true or false and put a tick in the correct box. The first question is an example. You now have 30 seconds to look at part 4.
Now we are ready to start. Listen carefully. You will hear the recording twice.

Radio host: Good morning, listeners. My name is Emily Sanders, and with me today is Noah Clarkson. He's 18 years old and he just returned from a year in Germany as an exchange student. Noah, why did you choose to go to Germany? And was it a good decision?

Noah: Hey, thanks for having me on the show. Oh, it was the best decision of my life. Well, so far *(laughs)*. I absolutely loved it in Germany. And I'll definitely go back. I decided to go to Germany because my great-grandfather immigrated from there. So, I've always been curious what life's like there.

Radio host: And what is it like? And what is it that you like about Germany?

Noah: There are many things that Germany seems to do right and that make living awesome there. First, I love public transportation there. Here in the States, everyone uses their cars and you hardly ever see buses or trains. Kind of sad! In Germany, public transportation is such a big thing. You're able to skip the traffic and five or six minutes later, you're at the stop where you want to be. And on the bus or the train, you can just relax. It's insane. It's super clean, super chill.

Radio host: And obviously it's good for the environment. Did you travel around a lot?

Noah: Yeah, that's another cool thing. Germany is right in the middle of where you want to be in Europe. You hop on a plane or train and within a few hours you're in another great place in Europe. I went to Lisbon in two and a half hours or so. You're in another great country. You can use the same money and everything's so easy.

Radio host: I see. What about the food? How did you like that in Germany?

Noah: The food is superb. Every one in Europe. They're all mixed into Germany. You have Mediterranean food, Italian food, Turkish food, and it all tastes so original, the best that it can. Here in America, the food is so oily and has chemicals in it, I think. In Germany, I eat and I feel fit afterwards.

Radio host: I'm sure you made some friends over there. Do you keep in touch?

Noah: Yes, well, here's the thing about people in America and in Germany. I feel like people in America are more outgoing but at the same time more selfish maybe. Of course, this is stereotypes, but Germans seem kind of cold at first. But once you get past that first wall of cold, and you actually become friends with them, that's when you notice how loyal and respectful they are to you. It's likely that when you are friends with a German, you're going to be friends with them for a very, very long time. Of course, not all Germans are like that and not all Americans are superficial, but it's still an impression that I have. So, yeah, my host brother and a friend are coming to visit me over summer. I'm really looking forward to that.

Radio host: Noah, thank you for sharing your impressions with us. It's always interesting to hear about other countries. Now, coming up, some music from some of the … *(fade out)*

Now listen again.

This is the end of the listening part. Good luck for the rest of your examination!

Bildnachweis
2021-7: schlafendes Mädchen © StockSnap/Pixabay
2021-8: Dutee Chand © Picture: picture alliance/AP Photo | Vincent Thian
2021-13: Mars © Picture: KELLEPICS/Pixabay

Realschulabschlussprüfung in Niedersachsen
Englisch 2022

I. Listening

Part 1 – Questions 1–7

7 Punkte

Listen to seven short recordings. For each recording, there is a question with three pictures. Choose the correct picture and put a tick (✓) in the box A, B *or* C *below it.*

Example

0. What is the man going to buy?

A ☐

B ☐

C ☑

1. Where does the band meet for the final rehearsal?

A ☐

B ☐

C ☐

2. Which dog is missing?

A ☐

B ☐

C ☐

3. When does the main boarding start?

A ☐

B ☐

C ☐

4. Where will the party be?

A ☐

B ☐

C ☐

5. What's the weather forecast for Friday?

A ☐

B ☐

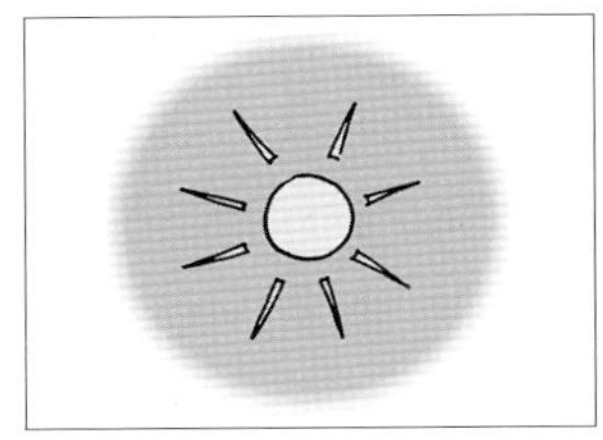

C ☐

6. How much flour are they adding to the pancake batter?

A ☐

B ☐

C ☐

7. Where is the couple going on holiday?

A ☐

B ☐

C ☐

Part 2 – Questions 8–13: Robin's New Life in New York City

Listen to Anne and Robin talking online about Robin's new life after he's moved from a small town in Oregon to New York City.
For each question, tick (✓) the correct box, a, b *or* c.

6 Punkte

8. Robin's new home …
   a) has a backyard. ☐
   b) is near a skatepark. ☐
   c) is across the street from his school. ☐

9. At the moment, Robin mostly …
   a) skates in the park. ☐
   b) explores New York City. ☐
   c) works on his basketball skills. ☐

10. Robin …
   a) loves the skyscrapers and sights. ☐
   b) enjoys the atmosphere of the city. ☐
   c) thinks the city is too noisy for him. ☐

11. Robin's new school …
   a) is smaller than his old school. ☐
   b) has a bad name in the city. ☐
   c) offers many activities. ☐

12. Rubio and Jalen have …
   a) played basketball with Robin. ☐
   b) skated with Robin. ☐
   c) shown Robin around the city. ☐

13. Anne is going to visit Robin …
   a) during spring break. ☐
   b) when school is out in June. ☐
   c) after her summer job. ☐

Part 3 – Questions 14–20: Staying at a Youth Hostel

7 Punkte

You are on a class trip in Copenhagen.
The youth hostel manager tells you what you have to know about your stay.
Fill in the missing information.
The first question is an example.

Name of the youth hostel?	0. Danhostel Copenhagen
Location of students' and teachers' rooms?	14. ____________
Where do I find my room number?	15. ____________
Breakfast time and location?	16. ____________
Who to inform in case of food allergies?	17. ____________
Consequence of smoking?	18. ____________
What should you do before going bowling?	19. ____________
Wi-Fi password?	20. ____________

Part 4 – Questions 21–26: Interview with an Influencer

6 Punkte

You will hear a radio interview with the social media influencer Emma D. Decide whether each statement is true or false and put a tick (✓) in the correct box.
The first question is an example.

Emma D. …	true	false
0. is like most other influencers.	☐	☑
21. is sponsored by brands.	☐	☐
22. creates new outfits.	☐	☐
23. says that fashion trends repeat themselves.	☐	☐
24. says that her followers start buying lots of new clothes.	☐	☐
25. already sells her clothes online.	☐	☐
26. sells clothes for men and women.	☐	☐

II. Reading

Part 1 – Questions 1–6: Short Texts

Read the texts (1–6) below and read statements a, b *and* c *next to them. Decide which of the statements is the correct one for each text. Put a tick (✓) in the correct box next to the statement.*

6 Punkte

1. Today | 9:21 AM

Miriam! My mom promised we can have our sleepover this weekend. Try to convince your dad that you can come on Friday. Then you can stay for two nights. Wouldn't that be awesome?!

😀 XOXO Kaddy

a) Miriam is allowed to spend two nights at Kaddy's place. ☐

b) Kaddy would like Miriam to stay longer. ☐

c) Kaddy has to convince her mom. ☐

2. Hey!

The bookshop phoned.

They've got the books you ordered but will only keep them till Thursday. Can you make it?

a) The books will be delivered to the shop on Thursday. ☐

b) The shop will order the books before Thursday. ☐

c) The books need to be collected by Thursday. ☐

3.

a) Cyclists must allow pedestrians to go first. ☐

b) Pedestrians must watch out for cyclists on this path. ☐

c) Cyclists must walk their bikes from here. ☐

4.

WAITER WANTED!

Standing on the front lines, our waiters are vital to the guest experience. Can you handle such responsibility?

Our waiters should:

- Always be friendly and attentive.
- Be flexible. Working hours are not 9 to 5.
- Be experienced but it's no requirement.

a) People skills are most important for the job. ☐

b) People work regular hours. ☐

c) Work experience is necessary for the job. ☐

5.

a) Only elderly and physically challenged people may sit here. ☐

b) This seat has to be offered to elderly or physically challenged people. ☐

c) Elderly and physically challenged people will vacate this seat for you. ☐

6. Today | 7:21 AM

Hey Sam! Do you remember the backpack I had yesterday? I don't know where it is. Did I leave it in your flat? 🤞 It's not mine. I borrowed it and gotta give it back today! 😱 Thx, Bob

a) Bob has to return a backpack. ☐

b) Bob is looking for a backpack he can borrow. ☐

b) Bob left the flat with the backpack. ☐

Part 2 – Questions 7–13: An Interview with a Londoner

7 Punkte

Read the answers Alexa has given in an interview about her home town, London. On the next page there are eight questions. Decide which question is most suitable for each answer.
For texts 7–13 write the correct letter (A–H) in the box next to the number. There are more questions than answers. Each letter can only be used once.

7. ☐ I don't think there's a language that isn't spoken here. No matter where you come from, you fit right in. The city is one big melting pot of different cultures, languages and accents. At first, I thought it was British accents everywhere, but it turns out I was wrong.

8. ☐ People are always in a rush, so when they bump into you, they won't always apologize. I'm not criticizing Londoners because technically this doesn't mean that Londoners are rude. It just means that everyone has their own business to get to. They don't want to be late for their business meeting or class. Personally, if I were in a hurry in such a big, crowded city, I would do the same.

9. ☐ It is as appetizing as it sounds and looks. The best thing about it is: it's cheap! Usually, London is an expensive place to live, but it's a matter of where you go. Of course, right in the city where all the tourists go, you can't save any money. I enjoy some of the great Indian places in the suburbs.

10. ☐ It really depends on the neighbourhood. Theatres are a big thing – not just cinemas, but theatres where they produce plays. But the places people go to a lot are London's parks. They are huge! People go there to hang out with their friends, have a picnic, or just go outside and enjoy the weather. You can also find a gym at every corner, but they're expensive.

11. ☐ They say the weirder the better! You could walk into a fancy restaurant in pyjamas and they would still serve you. People start their own trends all the time. So, at one point, you just give up on trying to follow them. You begin to become more creative with your choices. Store-wise you find a lot of designer brands. That's why tourists think clothes are expensive here.

12. ☐ Like in most countries in the western world, the majority of the population is Christian. With London being so international, there is a lot more variety in religions than in most other cities in the world. Overall, London isn't much of a religious place but Christmas is a very big deal.

13. ☐ This may come as a surprise, but it isn't as big as it may seem in London. Sure, it's offered in some restaurants in the afternoon. And there are a couple of parlours that celebrate this British tradition. Actually, the amount of coffee shops found around this city is triple the number of tea parlours.

A How do Londoners spend their leisure time?

B Londoners are known for being polite. Is this true?

C How do you feel about the fashion in London?

D Would you say that London is an international city?

E How do Londoners usually get around?

F Is religion important in London?

G Is teatime still a thing there?

H What do you think of the food in London?

Adapted from: https://www.theteenmagazine.com/interviewing-a-londoner-what-it-s-like-to-live-in-london

Part 3 – Questions 14–19: Who is Banksy?

6 Punkte

Read the following article about the artist "Banksy". For questions 14–19, tick (✓) the correct box, a, b *or* c. *For each question there is only one correct answer.*

Every time a piece by Banksy appears people get very excited. His work can sell for over £ 1 million and is known all over the world.
But what do we really know about the mysterious artist?
We don't exactly know who he is. Banksy is a famous – but anonymous – British graffiti artist. He keeps his identity a secret. It is assumed that he was born in Bristol around 1974. Although a lot of his art is produced in public places, he usually only reveals that it is his after it has appeared in his social media.
Banksy first got noticed for spray-painting trains and walls in his home city of Bristol during the early 1990s, before appearing in London. Street art and graffiti can be seen as criminal damage, so in the beginning it is thought the artist stayed anonymous to keep out of trouble. At first his pieces were mainly in Bristol, but in the 2000s his artworks started appearing all over the UK and other parts of the world.
A lot of his art is done in a particular style which people can easily recognise, because he chose to use a technique invented by the artist Blek le Rat to create his pieces: stencils – probably because it is a faster way to paint. However, Banksy does more than just street art: he has produced drawings, paintings and installation pieces. He even created his own theme park called Dismaland. Banksy's work is known for critical political messages, dealing with topics such as homelessness, racism or pollution.
Though regarded as mindless vandalism by some, the majority think his work is very valuable. As a result, his pieces can go for thousands of pounds.
Banksy has often made clear that he doesn't like to sell his work for so much money. In late 2018 *Girl with Balloon* (2006), a copy of one of Banksy's most popular wall paintings, partially destroyed itself with a hidden shredder at an auction just after being sold for $ 1.4 million. After that Banksy called the destroyed version *Love is in the Bin* and it was said to be the first work ever created

during a live auction. But its destruction most likely raised the value of the painting.
Since many people consider street art to be vandalism, some of his work was painted over as soon as it appeared. Sometimes graffiti artists put their own work over it. That's why the owner usually covers it up with plastic sheeting to protect it. There is a debate about why Banksy's work can be protected as 'art' when other graffiti artists are sometimes put in prison for doing the same thing

Adapted from: https://www.bbc.co.uk/newsround/51504255

14. We know …
    a) Banksy's real name. ☐
    b) that Banksy was born in Bristol. ☐
    c) that Banksy likes public places for painting. ☐

15. Banksy started his career …
    a) in the 2000s. ☐
    b) by spraying trains and walls. ☐
    c) in London. ☐

16. Banksy …
    a) creates street art called "Dismaland". ☐
    b) invented the stencil technique. ☐
    c) draws attention to political issues. ☐

17. Most people think that his art is …
    a) worth lots of money. ☐
    b) criminal damage. ☐
    c) pointless. ☐

18. Banksy's work "Girl with Balloon" …
    a) was sold just after its destruction. ☐
    b) probably lost value by its destruction. ☐
    c) was renamed after its destruction. ☐

19. Other street artists …
    a) have painted over Banksy's work. ☐
    b) protect Banksy's works with plastic covers. ☐
    c) criticise Banksy for vandalism. ☐

Part 4 – Questions 20–26: Long-Lost Sisters Find Each Other

7 Punkte

Read the article about two sisters, Victoria and Alyss. For questions 20–26, tick (✓) the correct box, true *or* false, *and give the line(s) of reference in the text. The first question is an example.*

27-year-old Victoria Voorhees knew she was adopted as a two-month-old girl. That's why she decided to take a WhoAmI-home DNA test to find out a bit more about her Hispanic background and genetic makeup.
She was astonished when the results revealed she had a sister and was sent a photo of a woman who looked very much like her.
As an adopted child, Victoria always dreamed of having an older sibling. But she couldn't believe her eyes when she first saw the photo of her sister. "At first, I was like: there's no way, that's impossible! Maybe they found someone that has some similarities to me? But I know now that's not how it works."
She sent her sister a message through the WhoAmI-app and rushed home to tell her parents.
28-year-old Alyss Ravae and Victoria chatted. Then they joined a video call with their biological mother for the first time. "I showed her some photos of me growing up with my adoptive parents," says Victoria, "and she was happy but crying!"
Alyss says of her sister, "We live very parallel lives even though we were placed in very different situations."
It's not just their mutual love of Halloween, of Stephen King, of *It* and *The Shining* that she was fascinated by; they both have bat tattoos on opposite feet but the same part of the ankle.
Alyss said: "When she sent me that picture of her tattoo, I literally just dropped my phone." They also both have cats and make and sell pet portraits online.
Victoria said: "We both like hiking trails as well. I'm going to show her all the cool ones around here in Chicago!" To show everyone their similarities, the two sisters created a video for social media in which they demonstrate all the things they have in common. If you didn't know better, you'd think that these two people have spent all their lives together. Whereas in fact they have yet to meet in person. They are now planning to meet up for the first time as soon as possible.

Adapted from: https://www.goodnewsnetwork.org/sisters-long-lost-matching-tattoos-victoria-chicago

According to the article, Victoria …	true	false	line(s)
0. was adopted as a child.	✓	☐	1
20. took a test to learn about her genes.	☐	☐	____
21. never wanted any siblings.	☐	☐	____
22. sent a message to her parents.	☐	☐	____
23. also got to know her biological mother.	☐	☐	____
24. was shown photos of her sister growing up.	☐	☐	____
25. and her sister have lived in similar circumstances.	☐	☐	____
26. and her sister have shared their similarities with the rest of the world.	☐	☐	____

III. Writing – Set I

Part 1 – A Complaint: Empty Box

10 Punkte

You ordered a pair of Bluetooth earphones online but all you got was an empty box. Write a complaint to the online shop.

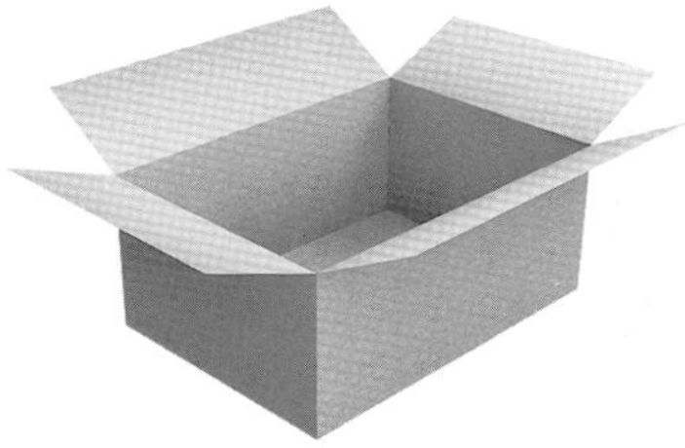

Include:

- *the reason for writing*
- *how you feel*
- *what you want the online shop to do*

Write about 80 words.

Part 2 – A Letter of Application: Au Pair Job

Inhalt: 9 Punkte
Sprache: 9 Punkte
Gesamt: 18 Punkte

You have found the following advert for an au pair job in Stockholm, Sweden, and decide to apply for it. Write about 150 words.

We are looking for an au pair that would enjoy spending time with our kids (boy and girl, aged 5 and 7), doing activities with them, speaking to them in English and fits in with the family.

Tell us about yourself:

- education, hobbies and interests
- work experience
- why you are the right person for this job

To: contact@aupair4u.com

Subject: Applying for an au pair job

III. Writing – Set II

Part 1 – A Comment: My Parents are Forcing Me into an Apprenticeship

You find the following post on a website and decide to leave a helpful comment. Write about 80 words.

10 Punkte

alex_06:

I'm just graduating from school and my parents are forcing me into an apprenticeship at their car dealership. I'd rather become a musician and don't care for cars at all. They say they're not going to support me in any other way. Can I make it without their support? What should I do?

97 reply share

Inhalt: 9 Punkte
Sprache: 9 Punkte
Gesamt: 18 Punkte

Part 2 – A Blog Entry: Time Travel into the Past

Imagine you had the chance to use a time machine and travel back in time for a day. Write a blog entry about that day.

In your text, include:

- *what time you decided to travel to and why*
- *what you experienced on that day*
- *whether or not you can imagine going back to that time again and explain why*

Write about 150 words.

Anhang: Hörverstehenstexte

This is the listening part of the final examination 2022 level B 1 for schools in Lower Saxony. There are four parts to the test. You will hear each recording twice. For each part of the test there will be time for you to look through the questions. You must not speak during the test.

Part 1

Now look at part 1, questions 1 to 7. Listen to seven short recordings. For each recording, there is a question with three pictures. Choose the correct picture and put a tick in the box A, B or C below it. Before we start, here is an example.

Example

What is the man going to buy?

Man: I'm going shopping now. Anything else we need for our holiday?

Woman: The sunscreen from our last trip should still work. I haven't got any sunglasses, but I can borrow some of yours, can't I? Hm, maybe something to kill the time at the airport.

Man: Yes. That's a good idea. I'll stop by the newsagent's.

The picture with the magazine is correct. So there is a tick in box C.

Text 1

Look at the three pictures for question 1 now.
Now we are ready to start. Listen carefully.

Where does the band meet for the final rehearsal?

Principal: Good morning, staff and students of Hillary High School. Our school band is ready to play at the school festival next Saturday. The rehearsal this Tuesday will not be in the music room as usual due to groundworks. The band meets in the gym on Tuesday and on Friday they meet in the assembly hall for the final rehearsal. I'm looking forward to the festival and music from our great school band.

Now listen again.

Text 2

Which dog is missing?

Woman: This is Loved And Lost Animals' Home. How can I help you?

Man: Hello. My name is Jack Austen. Our dog, Leo, ran off yesterday morning. Maybe someone brought him in to you?

Woman: Let's see. Could you describe your dog, please?

Man: It's a crossbreed with black fur and a white head, long, hanging ears and a short tail. He wears a collar around his neck.

Woman: Right. I'll check for you. Can you call back in 10 minutes?
Man: Yes, of course. Thank you.

Now listen again.

Text 3

When does the main boarding start?

Announcer: Good morning to all passengers for Kansas City. This is the boarding announcement for flight AA3421 to Kansas City. Your boarding starts at 9.20. For passengers with young children, as well as passengers requiring special assistance, boarding starts at nine. Priority boarding starts at 9.10. Please have your boarding pass and identification ready. Thank you for your attention.

Now listen again.

Text 4

Where will the party be?

Girl: You know what? I didn't get Ben's invite, but he told me I could come to his party. It's on Saturday, right? But where is it? At his house?

Boy: Yeah, it's at his place. I think he wanted to celebrate down by the river, but that didn't work out for some reason. He thought about renting a club, but … too expensive. And some folks would have been too young to get in.

Now listen again.

Text 5

What's the weather forecast for Friday?

Speaker: The weather forecast for this weekend doesn't look too promising, really. There's going to be some heavy rain and temperatures in the low sixties. If you're planning on having a barbecue, you might want to do that on Friday. It should still be dry. You shouldn't expect any sunshine, though.

Now listen again.

Text 6

How much flour are they adding to the pancake batter?

Boy: Okay, let's make pancakes. How much flour do we need?

Girl: The recipe says 200 grams, but I don't think that would be enough for the five of us.

Boy: That's true. Let's make it 300, then. That'll leave 700 grams for David's birthday cake on Saturday.

Girl: Brilliant. So let's add the eggs and the milk.

Now listen again.

Text 7

Where is the couple going on holiday?

Woman: Look, this website has some great holiday deals. You know, I've always wanted to go to a desert island.

Man: And I cannot think of anything more boring. How would you feel about going to the mountains? I believe it's not that hot there. Or how about going to a big city by the sea? Look, there's Rio and there's Sydney.

Woman: Cities are probably one of the hottest places of all. You know, I'd love to go hiking again.

Man: Me too. I think there's only one place where we can do that.

Now listen again.

This is the end of part 1.

Part 2

Now turn to part 2, questions 8 to 13. Listen to Anne and Robin talking online about Robin's new life after he's moved from a small town in Oregon to New York City. For each question, tick the correct box, a, b *or* c. *You now have 30 seconds to look at part two.*
Now we are ready to start. Listen carefully.

Anne: Hey, Robin, can you hear me?

Robin: Yeah. So nice to see you. How are you?

Anne: Good. How's life in New York?

Robin: It's crazy. You can't imagine.

Anne: Really? Hit me.

Robin: Well, we moved to the Upper West Side in Manhattan. So, we don't have our own house with a backyard anymore. Just an apartment. It felt kind of small at first, but now I got used to it. Cool thing is there's a skate park across the street and my new school is only two blocks away. So, no more endless bus rides twice a day.

Anne: A skate park. Nice. So, you still skate a lot?

Robin: Not really. I've just been there once so far. I haven't had the time to explore the city yet. I really want to get on the basketball team. Pretty much all I do is work on my shot. Tryouts are next week.

Anne: What? You're living in the most amazing city in the world and haven't even checked it out yet?

Robin: Well, of course, a little bit. This city is unbelievable. I mean, the skyscrapers and sights aren't bad, but it's the vibe of the city that really gets me. It's true what they say – this city never sleeps. There's always something going on in the streets. Everything's so loud here. It bothered me at first, but now I don't really notice it anymore.

Anne: Really? I don't know. I think I prefer the peace and quiet here in Oregon. So, how's school?

Robin: Everything is so different. Way bigger. Not like our tiny school back in Oregon, but still, the school has a good team spirit because there is a different assembly or team project every week. Also, it's supposed to be one of the better inner-city schools. You can choose classes that I had never heard of before. It's great.

Anne: That's nice. Have you met some cool people to hang out with?

Robin: Yeah, I met Rubio and Jalen on the basketball court in the park. Now we're practicing together for the tryouts, and they told me they also skate. After we've hopefully all made the team, they're going to show me all the nice spots to skate in the city.

Anne: Sounds nice. When am I going to meet them?

Robin: You want to come visit? That's great. Come right away!

Anne: Like New York's around the corner. But, yeah, I think I could come see you in spring break. Or wait, I'll come over in summer. We'll have much more time then. School's out in June, and I'll be counseling at a summer camp right after. But I'm free all of July and August.

Robin: Great. Book a flight. I can't wait to show you everything. Remember when I was so afraid of moving here? Now I really feel at home. You know, I definitely miss you guys, but we can always stay in touch and visit. So, tell me, what's up in T-Lake? Is Angie still with …

Now listen again.

This is the end of part 2.

Part 3

Now turn to part 3, questions 14 to 20. You are on a class trip in Copenhagen. The youth hostel manager tells you what you have to know about your stay. Fill in the missing information. The first question is an example. You now have 20 seconds to look at part three.
Now we are ready to start. Listen carefully.

Hello, everybody. Please listen up. Welcome to Danhostel, Copenhagen. I'm Ola. I'm the hostel manager. I'd like to give you some useful information on your stay, so please note down the most important things. Your teacher told me he's going to test you later tonight. First, your rooms are on the second floor, and your teachers' rooms are on the first floor. The rooms are right below yours, so your teachers are closer than you might think. You'd better watch out. You will all get one of these key cards. You can find your room numbers on them so that you don't accidentally knock on the wrong doors. Make sure you don't lose your card, as there is a € 10 deposit on it. I guess you'd like to get that back at the end of your stay. Breakfast is served on the top floor from 7 to 10. You can eat as much as you like, but do not smuggle anything out. If you want to get some supplies for your trips, you can buy a lunch bag for € 3 at the entrance to the dining hall. Dinner is from 6 to 8. You can choose between two different meals. Vegan and vegetarian. If you eat nothing but meat, you will go hungry. We are a meatless hostel. Please let the kitchen staff know if you're suffering from any intolerances or food allergies. Our chefs will be happy to provide you with tasty alternatives. For example, we offer some excellent gluten-free specials. In case you are still hungry at night, there's a snack machine on each floor. The quiet time starts at 11. That's when you have to stay in your rooms and also turn down the volume. Alcoholic drinks, smoking or other drugs are strictly prohibited. If you break this rule, you will be expelled immediately.

If you get bored in the evening, you can use the bowling alley in the basement. We've got six lanes. If you don't only want to watch other people bowl but have a go yourself, you should make a reservation in advance. Bowling is extremely popular at the moment. Maybe that's because it's free. The shoes, however, are not. The rent is € 5 for a pair, and you're not allowed to bowl without them. On departure day, make sure to clean your room. Remove the sheets from your bed and put them into the laundry container, which you will find on your floor on the day of your departure. Now enjoy your stay. And if you have any questions, let me know. All right. The Wi-Fi password: DHC – all in capital letters – 2022 – in numbers. So DHC2022. Have a great stay.

Now listen again.

This is the end of part 3.

Part 4

Now turn to part 4, questions 21 to 26. You will hear a radio interview with the social media influencer Emma D. Decide whether each statement is true or false and put a tick in the correct box. The first question is an example. You now have 30 seconds to look at part four.
Now we are ready to start. Listen carefully. You will hear the recording twice.

Radio host: Good morning, listeners. With me today is a person some of you might already know. If so, you've come across her photos and stories on Instapic. Her name is Emma D., and you can find her under her username at Emma – underscore – D. And perhaps you've noticed that she's unlike most other influencers. Hi, Emma. It's a pleasure to have you on the program today.

Emma: Good morning. Thanks for having me.

Radio host: For those who don't know you, what do you do differently than most other influencers out there?

Emma: Well, most other influencers are sponsored by brands. It's their job to promote their products, the latest fashion, the newest makeup, the coolest technology and all the stuff that people care about. I, on the other hand, like used clothes and accessories and want to show what you can do with them. For example, followers send me clothes they don't wear anymore, and I turn them into new outfits and post them on my site.

Radio host: I happen to be one of your followers, and I have to admit, it's really hard to believe that it's all second hand. What inspired you to completely focus on second hand?

Emma: The thing is trends are never completely new. Big sunglasses – that was a trend in the eighties and now people are wearing them again. So why buy new ones if it's all been there before? Many people throw their stuff away because they think it's not fashionable anymore. I think that's idiotic. I followed other influencers and thought that they're not sending the right message. We live in a throwaway society, and I really don't like that.

Radio host: I absolutely agree. What do you think: how did you become so successful and gain so many followers?

Emma: I think many people have realized that if we continue living the way we do at the moment, we will need more than one planet. Things have to change, and people know it. And it's a fact: following the latest trends and buying loads of new clothes is not something that makes you happy in the long run. It only satisfies you for a short while. But I show my followers how to be creative and make a lot out of a little, and they tell me that they find it inspiring. They begin to appreciate the things that they already have. It actually makes them happy, and that makes me happy in return. And last but not least, they're saving a lot of money.

Radio host: That's an interesting point. But speaking of money, can you actually make a living off of it?

Emma: Well, I can't live from my postings, but that's not my goal. I'm running a local second-hand shop. Many of my followers go there to buy what they see online or trade in their old clothes. Also, I want to start selling these clothes online too – at fair prices, of course.

Radio host: So, you're using and reselling clothes for women only?

Emma: Well, most of my followers and customers are women, but most clothes can be worn by men and women. It's just a matter of how you want to design your outfit. There's nothing gender-specific in what I do.

Radio host: Emma D., thank you for sharing your thoughts with us. I hope your ideas go viral and other influencers start listening and trying to make the world a better place, too. Coming up in our program is Stephen, who reads out children's books online. Stay tuned.

Now listen again.

This is the end of the listening part. Good luck for the rest of your examination!

Bildnachweis
2022-4 © Can Stock Photo/korvin79

Realschulabschlussprüfung in Niedersachsen
Englisch 2023

Um dir die Prüfung 2023 schnellstmöglich zur Verfügung stellen zu können, bringen wir sie in digitaler Form heraus.

Sobald die Original-Prüfungsaufgaben 2023 freigegeben sind, können sie als PDF auf der Plattform *MyStark* heruntergeladen werden (Zugangscode vgl. Umschlaginnenseite).

Aktuelle Prüfung

www.stark-verlag.de/mystark

7 Die Zeitformen des Verbs

Seite

8 Die Hilfsverben

9 Die infiniten Verbformen: Infinitiv, *Gerund* und Partizip

Anhang

Erster Teil: Satz und Text

Part One: Sentences and Texts

1 Wortstellung, Satzarten, Satzverknüpfung

Word Order, Sentence Types, Sentence Links

§ 1 Wortstellung im Aussagesatz und Vorsubjekt *there*

Word Order in Statements and Sentences Starting with *there*

F

Vorsubjekt	*be*-Form	(logisches) Subjekt	Verb	Ergänzung bzw. restlicher Satz
		The bus stop	is	round the corner.
		Lots of people	are waiting	at the bus stop.
There	is	a bus stop		round the corner.
There	are	lots of people	waiting	at the bus stop.

Die normale Wortstellung im englischen Aussagesatz lautet:

Subjekt — Verb — Ergänzung (Objekt)
Die Satzmelodie ist fallend.

Dem eigentlichen (logischen) Subjekt kann jedoch das Vorsubjekt *(introductory subject) there* vorangestellt werden. Die Satzmelodie steigt dann bis zum logischen Subjekt an und ist erst danach fallend.

V Wenn die Person oder Sache, um die es geht, zum ersten Mal genannt wird, beginnt man im Englischen den Satz häufig mit *there is/there are* (bzw. *there was, there'll be,* etc.), weil die Person oder Sache auf diese Weise besser hervorgehoben wird.

there is / there are zur Einführung einer Person oder Sache

there is / there are + Nomen

There are several discos in our part of the town.	In unserem Stadtteil gibt es ...
There's a dance in the church hall tonight.	Heute abend findet ... statt.
There's a good chance you'll meet a number of your friends.	Die Chancen, daß ... sind groß.
Last Saturday **there was** a big political meeting in the market place.	Letzten Samstag war ... .

There is/there are werden gern dem deutschen Ausdruck ‚es gibt' gleichgesetzt. Tatsächlich ist der Anwendungsbereich von *there is/there are* aber viel größer, und die Übersetzung mit ‚es gibt' ist nicht immer möglich.

there is/there are + Nomen + Partizip des Vollverbs

There is a bus service **connecting** the new shopping centre with the station.	Eine Buslinie verbindet ... .
There were lots of people **watching** when the mayor opened the new shopping centre.	Viele Leute schauten zu, als ... .
If they go on building supermarkets, **there'll** soon **be** no small shops **left** in our area.	... werden bald keine kleinen Läden ... übrig sein.

Diese Konstruktion kann meist nicht mit ‚es gibt' übertragen werden. Gewöhnlich entspricht ihr im Deutschen ein normaler Aussagesatz.

§ 2 Die Stellung der Objekte im Satz
The Position of Objects in a Sentence

F

Subjekt	**Verb**	**Objekt**
Mr Miller	bought	a diamond ring.

Enthält der Satz nur ein Objekt, so folgt dieses grundsätzlich dem Verb.

Subjekt	**Verb**	**indir. Obj.**	**direktes Objekt**	**indir. Obj.**
Mr Miller	gave	his wife	a diamond ring.	
Mr Miller	gave		the diamond ring	**to** his wife.

Bei zwei Objekten ergeben sich folgende Möglichkeiten:

1. Das indirekte Objekt geht dem direkten Objekt voraus.
2. Das indirekte Objekt steht hinter dem direkten Objekt. In diesem Fall wird es durch *to* angeschlossen.

V

Entscheidend für die Stellung der Objekte ist ihre Länge und Betonung.

Nachstellung des längeren oder des betonten Objekts

Beide Objekte gleich betont

The shop assistant showed [the customer] (indirektes Objekt) [lots of picture postcards and souvenirs.] (direktes Objekt)

He sold [twenty beermugs] (direktes Objekt) [**to** a party of American tourists from Kansas City.] (indirektes Objekt)

Sind beide Objekte in etwa gleich betont, so folgt das längere Objekt dem kürzeren. Dabei ist es gleichgültig, ob das indirekte Objekt (meist eine Person) oder das direkte Objekt (meist eine Sache) ans Ende rückt.

Ein Objekt besonders betont

Since she was so confused, Mrs Smith passed [her husband] (indir. Obj.) [the door key] (dir. Obj. (betont)) (and not the car key he had asked for).

When the Smiths were on holiday, the postman handed [all their letters, newspapers and parcels] (direktes Objekt) [**to** their neighbours.] (indir. Obj. (betont))

Ist ein Objekt stärker betont als das andere (z. B. weil es einen Gegensatz ausdrückt), so nimmt es die zweite Stelle ein, auch wenn es kürzer ist.

Pronomen als Objekte

Can you lend **me** 10 p? I'll give **it** back **to you** as soon as I get some change.
I've left my glasses in your flat. Could you give **them to my brother** when you see him at the office?

Wenn als direktes Objekt *it* oder *them* auftreten (meist zur Bezeichnung von Sachen), so wird das indirekte Objekt immer nachgestellt. Ansonsten gelten für Pronomen die selben Stellungsregeln wie für Nomen.

H

1. I've **asked you** a question, but you haven't answered it.

   Die Verben *ask, cost* und *forgive* erlauben keine Nachstellung des indirekten Objekts.
   Das indirekte Objekt kann also nicht mit *to* angeschlossen werden.

2. She **described** her pain **to the doctor** and the doctor **explained to her** why it was nothing serious.

   Describe und *explain* gehören zu einer Gruppe von Verben, bei denen das indirekte Objekt **immer** mit *to* angeschlossen und gewöhnlich nachgestellt wird.
   Weitere Verben dieser Gruppe sind:

announce	ankündigen	*distribute*	austeilen	*say*	sagen
deliver	liefern	*introduce*	vorstellen	*suggest*	vorschlagen
dictate	diktieren				

3. When you go to the shops **get me** an evening newspaper, and don't forget to **get** something **for the dog**.
   ... und vergiß nicht, etwas für den Hund mitzubringen.

   Bei einigen Verben wird das indirekte Objekt, wenn es nachgestellt wird, nicht mit *to*, sondern mit *for* angeschlossen, z. B. bei *buy, get (holen), make, order (bestellen).*
   Meist kann bei den deutschen Entsprechungen die Präposition *für* benutzt werden.

Don't throw away your old clothes, give them **to** the Salvation Army. ..., gib sie der Heilsarmee.

Im Gegensatz zum Deutschen wird ein nachgestelltes indirektes Objekt im Englischen immer mit einer Präposition angeschlossen (meist mit *to)*.

§ 3 Passivsätze
Passive Sentences

F

	indir. Objekt	**direktes Objekt**	
The other day somebody gave	me	a book on pollution.	
		A book on pollution	was given to me.
	I	was given a book on pollution.	

	Präpos.-objekt	
People often **talk about**	pollution	these days.
	Pollution	is often **talked about** these days.

Im Englischen lassen sich folgende Arten von Passivsätzen unterscheiden:

1. Wie im Deutschen kann das direkte Objekt des Aktivsatzes zum Subjekt des Passivsatzes werden.
2. Daneben kann das indirekte Objekt des Aktivsatzes (meist eine Person) Subjekt des Passivsatzes sein (keine direkte Entsprechung im Deutschen).
3. Auch ein Präpositionalobjekt des Aktivsatzes kann zum Subjekt des Passivsatzes werden. Die Präposition bleibt beim Verb.

   Zu den Zeitformen des Passivs vgl. § 75.

V Passivsätze werden verwendet, wenn nicht der Verursacher einer Handlung im Vordergrund steht, sondern der Betroffene oder das Geschehen an sich. Sie kommen deshalb vor allem in Zeitungsberichten und historischen oder technischen Beschreibungen vor. Passivsätze bieten zugleich die Möglichkeit, andere Satzteile als im Aktivsatz an das betonte Satzende zu rücken und somit hervorzuheben.

Passivsätze: Geschehen oder Betroffener im Vordergrund

a) As a post office spokesman revealed recently, more than a hundred telephone boxes **were damaged** last year in our area alone. Windows **were smashed,** wires **were pulled out** and telephone books **torn up.**

b) Every day millions of telephone calls **are made.** They **are** all **registered** and the bills **are printed out** automatically every month.

Passivsätze werden vor allem dann verwendet, wenn man den Verursacher einer Handlung nicht kennt (vgl. Text a) oder nicht nennen will, weil er z. B. unwichtig ist (vgl. Text b).

Passivsätze mit *by-agent*

The fire **was discovered** *by a passing taxidriver* who called the fire brigade.
When the fire brigade arrived most of the furniture **had** already **been moved out** *by the owners of the house.*
Their children **were looked after** *by the neighbours.*

Soll der Verursacher einer Handlung ausdrücklich erwähnt werden, so wird er durch *by* eingeführt. Er hat dann mehr Gewicht als im Aktivsatz.

Persönliches Passiv bevorzugt

After the accident I was taken to hospital where **I was given** a complete medical check. Later **I was shown** the X-rays and **I was told** that there was nothing wrong with me.

Nach dem Unfall wurde ich ins Krankenhaus gebracht, wo ich gründlich untersucht wurde. Später wurden mir die Röntgenaufnahmen gezeigt und man teilte mir mit, es sei alles in Ordnung.

Wo die Wahl zwischen zwei Passivkonstruktionen besteht, erscheint häufig die betroffene Person als Subjekt (‚persönliches Passiv'), vor allem bei Verben des Gebens und Übermittelns *(give, bring, offer, show, sell, send).* Diese Passivkonstruktion kann im Deutschen nicht nachvollzogen werden. Das Deutsche benutzt statt dessen, wie die Übersetzung zeigt, verschiedene andere Konstruktionen (z. B. mit ‚man').

H Twenty-five people **are reported to have been injured** when a bus left the road and hit a tree near Exeter.

Wie berichtet wird/Berichten zufolge wurden fünfundzwanzig Menschen verletzt, als . . .

All ships **are required to carry** a sufficient number of life-boats and life-jackets for their passengers.

Alle Schiffe müssen laut Vorschrift genügend Rettungsboote . . . mit sich führen.

Vor allem in der Zeitungs- und Amtssprache trifft man häufig auf Passivstrukturen, die aus einem Verb des Sagens und Meinens *(say, report, believe, think)* und einer Infinitivkonstruktion bestehen. Auch hier sind im Deutschen meist völlig andere Konstruktionen üblich.

§ 4 Die Stellung von Adverbien und anderen Umstandsangaben im Satz
The Position of Adverbs and Other Types of Adverbials in a Sentence

F Adverbien und andere Umstandsangaben *(adverbial phrases* vgl. § 52 V2) können im Satz grundsätzlich folgende Stellungen einnehmen:

1. **Anfangsstellung:**
   Am Satzanfang, bzw. vor dem Subjekt.
2. **Binnenstellung:**
   Vor dem Vollverb, bzw. wenn ein Hilfsverb vorhanden ist, zwischen Hilfsverb und Vollverb. (Zu Sätzen mit mehreren Hilfsverben vgl. H 1.)
3. **Endstellung:**
   Nach Verb + direktem Objekt (soweit vorhanden). Andere Satzteile wie Präpositionalergänzungen können dem Adverb folgen.

	Subjekt	Hilfsverb		Vollverb + Objekt	
Carefully	the doctor			examined the patient.	
	The doctor		carefully	examined the patient.	
	The doctor	has	carefully	examined the patient.	
	The doctor			examined the patient	carefully.
Anfangsstellung			Binnenstellung		Endstellung

H Zur Bildung von Adverbien aus Adjektiven s. § 52 F.

V Welche der möglichen Stellungen eine Umstandsangabe im einzelnen Fall einnimmt, hängt unter anderem von ihrer Länge ab: Zusammengesetzte Ausdrücke *(adverbial phrases)* kommen meist nicht in Binnenstellung vor. Außerdem spielt es eine Rolle, ob die Umstandsangabe normal betont oder besonders hervorgehoben werden soll.
Der wichtigste Gesichtspunkt für die Stellung einer Umstandsangabe ist jedoch, welchem Bedeutungstyp sie angehört (vgl. auch § 52 V 2).

Die Stellung von Orts- und Zeitangaben

Angaben des Ortes: Endstellung bevorzugt

Her new car was made **in Japan.**
He parked his car **in the no-parking area in front of the police station.**
Inside, the car was in perfect condition, but **outside** there was a lot of rust.

Die Endstellung wirkt neutral. Die ebenfalls mögliche Anfangsstellung hebt die Ortsangabe besonders hervor und wird vor allem zur Gegenüberstellung verwendet.

Angaben der bestimmten Zeit: Anfangs- oder Endstellung bevorzugt

During the rush hour there was a great deal of traffic in the city centre.
It took my Dad over an hour to get home from work **today.**

Anfangs- und Endstellung verleihen der Zeitangabe in etwa dasselbe Gewicht.

Die Stellung verschiedener Arten von Adverbien

Adverbien der unbestimmten Zeit oder Häufigkeit: Binnenstellung bevorzugt

Do you cycle to school **regularly?**
My brother and I **often** go for a long bike ride.
Sometimes the wind is so strong that cycling is no fun.

Neben der Binnenstellung ist vor allem bei längeren Adverbien (*regularly, occasionally,* etc.) auch die Endstellung möglich.
Die seltenere Anfangsstellung hebt das Adverb der unbestimmten Zeit besonders hervor.
(Bei *adverbial phrases* wie *several times a week* ist die Binnenstellung nicht möglich.)

Adverbien der Art und Weise: Binnen- und Endstellung bevorzugt

Without looking left or right the old lady **slowly** crossed the street.
A sports car approached the zebra crossing **at high speed** and had to brake **sharply.**
Quickly the policeman rushed into the road, picked up the child and carried him back to his mother.

Kurze Adverbien dieser Gruppe (*slowly, quickly,* etc.) erscheinen eher in Binnenstellung, längere eher in Endstellung.
Die Anfangsstellung ist seltener und hebt das Adverb besonders hervor.
(Bei *adverbial phrases* wie *at high speed* ist die Binnenstellung nicht möglich.)

Adverbien des Standpunkts und Kommentars: Anfangs- und Binnenstellung bevorzugt

Frankly, I wouldn't like to live in a busy street because of the noise. Ehrlich gesagt, ...
Living conditions could **probably** be improved if more money were spent on sound-proof windows.
Cars cause a lot of problems. But **of course,** we can't do without them.
(But we can't do without them, **of course**.)

In Anfangsstellung werden diese Adverbien z. T. durch Komma vom Restsatz abgetrennt.
Die Endstellung ist nur bei *of course* gebräuchlich.

H

1. a) She has **repeatedly** been stopped for driving too fast.
   b) But on the whole she has been **well** treated by the police.

   Vor allem Passivsätze enthalten oft zwei oder mehr Hilfsverben. Bei Binnenstellung des Adverbs ergeben sich dann zwei Möglichkeiten:
   a) Adverbien der unbestimmten Zeit oder Häufigkeit und Adverbien des Standpunkts und Kommentars stehen hinter dem ersten Hilfsverb.
   b) Adverbien der Art und Weise stehen meist nach dem letzten Hilfsverb, also vor dem Partizip des Vollverbs.

2. She is **undoubtedly** a dangerous driver.

   Wenn der Satz nur eine Form von *be* enthält, so tritt das Adverb bei Binnenstellung hinter diese *be*-Form.

⚠ Die im Deutschen sehr häufige Stellung des Adverbs zwischen Verb und direktem Objekt ist im Englischen nicht möglich.

Vgl.: Er nahm schnell das Geld an sich und lief weg.
He quickly took the money and ran away.

§ 5 Die Reihenfolge verschiedener Umstandsangaben am Satzende

The Sequence of Adverbials at the End of a Sentence

V Am Satzende folgen häufig mehrere Adverbien und andere Umstandsangaben aufeinander.

Normale Reihenfolge der Umstandsangaben: Art und Weise / Ort / Zeit

My father works **hard in the garden most weekends.**
My mother has to do her housework at night because she works **in an office during the day.**
She has to do her shopping **very quickly in the lunch-break.**

Häufig sind vor allem Zweierkombinationen, z. B. Ort + Zeit oder Art und Weise + Zeit.

Bestimmte Zeitangabe vor allgemeiner Zeitangabe

I have to leave for school **at eight on weekdays,** but I stay in bed **until ten o'clock on Sundays.**

H I often go to school **on Monday morning very unwillingly**.

Soll eine Umstandsangabe besonders hervorgehoben werden, so rückt sie ans Satzende, gleichgültig welchem Bedeutungstyp sie angehört.

§ 6 Die Wortstellung bei negativen und einschränkenden Umstandsangaben

Word Order with Negative and Restrictive Adverbials

V Während im Deutschen jede Umstandsangabe am Satzanfang die Umstellung des Subjekts (Inversion) bedingt, ist dies im Englischen nicht der Fall. (Vgl.: Heute **essen wir** auswärts./Today **we are** eating out.)
Im Englischen wird das Subjekt nur dann umgestellt, wenn eine negative oder einschränkende Umstandsangabe an den Satzanfang tritt.

Negative oder einschränkende Umstandsangabe in Anfangsstellung: Umstellung des Subjekts (Inversion)

***Hardly* had he** started his new job when the boss invited him to dinner.	Kaum hatte er ...
After the meal we all told Sandra how much we had enjoyed it.	
***Only then* did she tell** us that she had collected the mushrooms herself.	Erst dann ...
***Not until the waiter brought the bill* did he realize** that he had no money on him.	Erst als ...

Diese Wortstellung wird nur im gehobenen Stil gebraucht. Zu beachten ist, daß in *Present* und *Past Tense Simple* mit *do*-Formen umschrieben wird. Weitere negative und einschränkende Umstandsangaben sind: *never, not only, no sooner, scarcely* (kaum), *seldom* (selten), *sometimes only.*
Auch nach Adverbialsätzen mit *Not until* ... und *Not unless* ... erfolgt im Hauptsatz Inversion.
In der Umgangssprache wird die Binnen- oder Endstellung dieser Umstandsangaben oder Adverbialsätze bevorzugt, wobei die normale Wortstellung erhalten bleibt:
He had *hardly* started his new job when the boss invited him to dinner,
Sandra told us that she had collected the mushrooms herself ***only when we had eaten the meal.***

H There goes our bus. When's the next one?

Down came the rain and up went the umbrellas.

Auch Richtungsadverbien können in *Present-Tense-* und *Past-Tense-*Sätzen zur besonderen Hervorhebung an den Satzanfang treten und bedingen dabei die Umstellung des Subjekts, falls dieses ein Nomen ist. (Allerdings ohne *do*-Umschreibung.)

§ 7 Die Verneinung im Aussagesatz
Negation in Statements

F

	Hilfsverb + *not*	Vollverb	restlicher Satz
I	**can't**	**tell**	you anything new about Peter.
I	**haven't**	**seen**	him for a long time.
I	**don't**	**meet**	him very often anyway.
He	**doesn't**	**live**	round here any more and
he	**didn't**	**answer**	my last letter.

Die Verneinung wird im englischen Aussagesatz auf folgende Weise ausgedrückt:

1. Wenn der bejahte Satz bereits ein Hilfsverb enthält: durch die verneinte Form dieses Hilfsverbs.
2. Wenn der bejahte Satz nur ein Vollverb aufweist: durch *don't / doesn't / didn't* + Infinitiv des Vollverbs.

V

Verneinung mit *do*-Formen und anderen Hilfsverben

do-Form bei Vollverben in *Present* und *Past Tense Simple*

My sister **doesn't think** horoscopes come true.
Many people **don't walk** under ladders because it brings bad luck.
When I was a child I **didn't like** to be alone in a dark room.

Bei den zusammengesetzten Zeitformen, die mit Hilfsverben gebildet werden, ist die Verneinung einfach, ebenso bei Kombinationen mit modalen Hilfsverben wie *can*: *not* wird direkt an das Hilfsverb angehängt.
Bei den einfachen Zeitformen der Vollverben muß jedoch eine Form des Hilfsverbs *do* eintreten: *do / does* im *Present Tense Simple, did* im *Past Tense Simple.*

Have und *be* als Vollverben

Most English housewives **don't have to** cook lunch because their children have lunch at school.
This morning we **didn't have** breakfast together because Father left early.
The Bentleys have (got) five daughters, but they **haven't (got)** any sons.
This house **isn't** big enough for a large family.

Have und *be* können nicht nur als Hilfsverben zur Bildung der Zeitformen auftreten, sondern auch als Vollverben.
Have als Vollverb muß in den meisten Fällen mit Hilfe einer *do*-Form verneint werden. Nur in der Bedeutung ‚besitzen' kann die *do*-Umschreibung entfallen. Allerdings sind die Formen *haven't got / hasn't got* gebräuchlicher als *haven't / hasn't.* Vgl. § 84.
Be wird grundsätzlich ohne *do*-Umschreibung verneint, auch als Vollverb. Vgl. § 35.

Kurz- und Vollformen von Hilfsverben

I still **can't** find my pen. Have you seen it?
Dear Jane, I'm sorry I **didn't** write in time for your birthday.
Dear Sir, In reply to your letter we must inform you that we **cannot** deliver the articles you ordered. We **do not** expect to receive a new supply until November.

In der Umgangssprache (normales Gespräch, Briefe an Freunde, etc.) werden die Kurzformen der verneinten Hilfsverben bevorzugt, im gehobenen Stil (Aufsatz, Geschäftsbrief, öffentliche Rede, etc.) die Vollformen. (Diese Regel gilt auch für die bejahten Kurz- und Vollformen von *have, be, will, would.*)

H

1. He **never** goes out in the evening. **Nobody** ever visits him. He has **no** relatives to look after him.

   Die Verneinung kann auch durch *never, nobody, no* und andere verneinte Wörter ausgedrückt werden.

2. a) I promised **not to be** late. (Ich habe etwas versprochen.)
   b) I **didn't promise** to be here by ten. (Ich habe nichts versprochen.)

   Bei Sätzen, die eine Infinitivkonstruktion enthalten, ist folgendes zu beachten:
   a) Soll nur die Infinitivkonstruktion verneint werden, so wird ihr ein betontes **not** vorangestellt.
   b) Soll der ganze Satz verneint werden, so wird ein verneintes Hilfsverb benutzt.

§ 8 Bejahte und verneinte Aufforderungssätze
Positive and Negative Imperative Sentences

F

To get to the station

	go	straight on.	(Geh/Geht/Gehen Sie ...)
Don't	**turn**	left at the traffic lights.	

Look out! There's a car coming.
Don't cross until the lights change.

Aufforderungssätze, auch Befehlssätze genannt, werden mit dem Imperativ des Verbs gebildet. Er hat im Englischen im Singular und Plural die gleiche Form wie der Infinitiv.
Verneinte Aufforderungssätze werden immer mit *don't (do not)* gebildet.

Zeichensetzung: Das Ausrufezeichen wird nur bei wirklichen Ausrufen verwendet, z. B. zum Ausdruck der Überraschung. Sonst steht im Gegensatz zum deutschen Aufforderungssatz der Punkt.

V Aufforderungssätze können eine Reihe verschiedener Sprechabsichten wiedergeben:

Aufforderungssätze zum Ausdruck von Befehl/Verbot, Aufforderung/Bitte, Rat/Ermahnung

Come in.
Take a seat, please.
Have a cup of tea.
Help yourself to sugar and milk.

Don't worry about the test next week.
Don't forget to learn the new words.
Don't copy from your neighbour during the test.

Höfliche Aufforderungen und Bitten werden häufig durch *please* ergänzt.

Aufforderungssätze mit *be*

Be careful. He's an ex-boxer.
Be a man. Tell him what you think of him.

Don't be stupid.
Don't be a trouble-maker.

Aufforderungssätze kommen normalerweise nur bei Tätigkeitsverben (vgl. § 62) vor, da man jemanden nur zu einer Tätigkeit auffordern kann und nicht zu einem Zustand, einer Eigenschaft, etc.
Wenn *be* in einem Aufforderungssatz vorkommt, so drückt es deshalb nicht wie üblich eine Beziehung oder einen Zustand aus, sondern hat die Bedeutung „sich benehmen", „sich verhalten".

H

1. **Do sit** down. — Setzen Sie sich doch (bitte).
   Do take another piece of cake. — Nehmen Sie sich doch noch ein Stück Kuchen.

   Bejahte Aufforderungssätze können durch *do* verstärkt werden. Sie klingen dann besonders eindringlich oder übertrieben höflich.

2. Would you pass the sugar, please?
   Will you stay to supper?

   Höfliche Aufforderungen können auch durch Fragesätze ausgedrückt werden, die mit *will, would, can* oder *could* beginnen. (Vgl. § 76 V, 77, 80.)

§ 9 Entscheidungsfragen
Yes/No Questions

F

Hilfsverb im Fragesatz	Subjekt	Hilfsverb im Aussagesatz	Vollverb	restlicher Satz
	I	'll	**go and get**	something for lunch.
Shall	I		**go and get**	something for lunch?
Have	you		**tried**	the new shop yet?
	I		**go**	shopping twice a week.
Do	you		**go**	shopping every day?
Does	Jack		**do**	the shopping for you?
Did	you		**buy**	some bread?

Entscheidungsfragen werden immer durch ein Hilfsverb eingeleitet.

1. Ist bereits (im entsprechenden Aussagesatz) ein Hilfsverb vorhanden, so tritt dieses an den Anfang des Fragesatzes.
2. Ist (im entsprechenden Aussagesatz) nur ein Vollverb vorhanden, so tritt *do / does / did* an den Anfang des Fragesatzes.

V

Fragebildung mit *do*-Formen und anderen Hilfsverben

do-Form bei Vollverben in *Present* und *Past Tense Simple*

Do you sometimes **cook** for yourself?
Does it **cost** much to bake your own bread?

Did your friends **like** the cake I made for the party?

Bei den zusammengesetzten Zeitformen, die Hilfsverben enthalten, wird die Frage wie im Deutschen gebildet, ebenso bei Kombinationen mit modalen Hilfsverben wie *can:* Das Hilfsverb rückt an den Anfang des Fragesatzes. In den einfachen Zeitformen der Vollverben muß jedoch eine Form des Hilfsverbs *do* eintreten: *do / does* im *Present Tense Simple, did* im *Past Tense Simple.*

Have und *be* als Vollverben

Did you **have** a good time at the seaside?
Have you **(got)** enough money for the trip?

Is all the luggage in the car?

Have als Vollverb wird fast immer umschrieben. Nur in der Bedeutung ‚besitzen' kann die *do*-Umschreibung entfallen. Gebräuchlicher ist allerdings hier die Form *have got* (immer ohne Umschreibung, vgl. § 84).
Be wird in der Entscheidungsfrage grundsätzlich nicht umschrieben.

Verneinte Fragesätze

Can't you read? The sign says 'No smoking'.
Don't you know you mustn't smoke in the library?

People should know how dangerous smoking can be.
Or **do** they **not** want to see the facts?

Verneinte Fragesätze können auf zweierlei Art gebildet werden:
1. In der Umgangssprache tritt die verneinte Kurzform eines Hilfsverbs an den Anfang des Fragesatzes.
2. Im gehobenen Stil wird die Vollform *not* nach dem Subjekt eingeschoben.
Die *do*-Umschreibung tritt in denselben Fällen ein wie im bejahten Fragesatz.

H

You've finished that book already? You must be a fast reader.
Will der Sprecher Überraschung oder Skepsis ausdrücken, so kann auch ein Aussagesatz als Frage verwendet werden. Er wird dann mit steigender Satzmelodie gesprochen und durch ein Fragezeichen gekennzeichnet.

Nach den *do*-Formen steht der **Infinitiv.** Beachte deshalb:
Keine *s*-Endung beim Vollverb nach *does*! — Keine *Past-Tense*-Form nach *did*!

§ 10 Fragen mit Fragewörtern
Questions with Question Words

F

Fragewort	Hilfsverb	Subjekt	Hilfsverb	Vollverb	restlicher Satz
	Do	you		**live**	in London?
Where	**do**	you		**live?**	
How	**can**	I		**find**	a cheap hotel in London?
		Mr Clark		**works**	for London Transport.
		Who		**works**	for London Transport?
		Who	**can**	**show**	me to Mr Clark's office?

Zu unterscheiden sind zwei Arten von Fragen mit Fragewörtern:

1. Das Fragewort ist nicht Subjekt (oder Teil des Subjekts) des Fragesatzes.
   Die Wortstellung entspricht der einer Entscheidungsfrage. *Do*-Umschreibung tritt ein, wenn kein anderes Hilfsverb vorhanden ist.
2. Das Fragewort ist Subjekt des Fragesatzes (bzw. Teil des Subjekts).
   Die Wortstellung entspricht der eines Aussagesatzes. *Do*-Umschreibung tritt nicht ein.

Fragewort	restlicher Satz			Präposition zum Fragewort
Where	do	you	come	**from?**

Wird das Fragewort durch eine Präposition näher bestimmt, so tritt diese Präposition normalerweise ans Ende des Fragesatzes.

Zur Aussprache: Typisch für alle Fragewortfragen ist im Englischen die fallende Satzmelodie.

V

Fragesätze mit *where, when, why, how* werden (falls kein anderes Hilfsverb vorhanden ist) immer umschrieben, da diese Fragewörter nie Subjekt des Fragesatzes sein können.
Bei *who, what* und *which* ist auf die Funktion im Satz zu achten.

Fragewort ist (Präpositional-) Objekt: *Do*-Umschreibung	**Fragewort ist Subjekt: Keine Umschreibung**
***Who(m)* als Objekt**	***Who* als Subjekt**
Who (Whom) did you **take** to the pop concert? **Who (Whom) did** you **give** the spare ticket to?	**Who taught** you to play the guitar? **Who** first **introduced** you to country music?
Fragen mit *whom* (wen?/wem?) + Vollverb werden grundsätzlich umschrieben. In der Umgangssprache tritt meist *who* für *whom* ein.	Wenn *who?* im Sinn von *wer?* gebraucht wird, tritt keine Umschreibung ein.
***What / Which / Whose* als Objekt (oder Teil des Objekts)**	***What / Which / Whose* als Subjekt (oder Teil dessen)**
What do you **do** to keep fit? **Which** team **does** he **play** for? **Whose** football boots **did** you **borrow?**	**What keeps** going up until it runs out? (Oil, of course.) **Which** television personality **tells** the best jokes? **Whose** jokes **make** you laugh most?
Fragen mit *what* im Objektfall *(wen oder was?)* werden, falls kein anderes Hilfsverb vorhanden ist, mit *do*-Formen gebildet. Das gleiche gilt für Fragen mit *which* im Objektfall *(welchen?/welchem?)* und *whose* als Teil des Objekts.	Fragen mit *what* im Subjektsfall *(wer oder was?)* werden ohne *do*-Formen gebildet. Das gleiche gilt für Fragen mit *which* im Subjektfall *(welcher?)* und *whose* als Teil des Subjekts.

H **Which car** did you buy, the Ford or the Renault?
Which of the two cars has the lowest fuel consumption?

What kind of car have you bought?
What colour is your new car?
What extras has your new car got?

Für Auswahlfragen stehen im Englischen die Fragewörter *what* oder *which* zur Verfügung:

Which wählt aus einer begrenzten Anzahl von Gegenständen oder Personen aus. Es steht deshalb immer, wenn eine *of-phrase* unmittelbar folgt. (*Which of them,* etc.)

What wählt aus einer unbestimmten Anzahl von Gegenständen oder Personen aus. Es kann deshalb nie unmittelbar vor einer *of-phrase* stehen.

⚠ **Beachte:** *which* = *welcher* (aus einer begrenzten Anzahl)
what = *was für ein/welcher* (aus einer unbestimmten Anzahl)

§ 11 Bestätigungsfragen
Question Tags

F

Subjekt	Hilfs-verb	Voll-verb		Hilfs-verb	Subjekt
This	is		**a beautiful house,**	**isn't**	it?
You		**like**	your new room,	**don't**	you?

Bestätigungsfragen (auch *question tags* genannt) greifen Hilfsverb und Subjekt des vorangehenden Aussagesatzes wieder auf.
Enthält der Aussagesatz kein Hilfsverb, so treten *do / does* oder *did* ein.
Das Subjekt erscheint in Form eines Personalpronomens.

V Bestätigungsfragen gehören vor allem dem mündlichen Sprachgebrauch an. Sie stellen keine echten Fragen dar, sondern fordern den Gesprächspartner auf, der Aussage zuzustimmen. (Vgl. deutsch ‚nicht wahr?') Die **Satzmelodie** ist deshalb **fallend.** Für die Form der Bestätigungsfrage ist entscheidend, ob der Aussagesatz bejaht oder verneint ist.

Bejahter Aussagesatz: Verneinte Bestätigungsfrage	**Verneinter Aussagesatz: Bejahte Bestätigungsfrage**
You **moved** into the house last month, **didn't you?** Your old house **was** much too small, **wasn't it?** You**'ll be** much happier here, **won't you?**	The area **isn't** too noisy, **is it?** The house **hasn't** got a garage though, **has it?** And you **don't** want to park your car in the street, **do you?**
Im Deutschen wird in diesen Fällen ‚nicht?' oder ‚nicht wahr?' verwendet.	Im Deutschen wird in diesen Fällen ‚oder?' verwendet.

H

1. The Millers bought a new house last year, **didn't they?** — Yes, they did./No, they didn't./I don't know.
   Tom hasn't bought a new car recently, **has he?** — No, he hasn't./Yes, he has./I don't know.
   Mit **steigender Satzmelodie** gesprochen, läßt das *Question Tag* die Antwort des Gesprächspartners offen.
   Auch hier gilt: Bejahter Satz — verneintes *Question Tag;* verneinter Satz — bejahtes *Question Tag.*
2. What! That motor-bike is yours, **is it?** I can't believe it.
   Gelegentlich kann ein bejahter Aussagesatz ein bejahtes *Question Tag* bei sich haben. Die Satzmelodie ist dabei steigend. Solche Kombinationen drücken Zweifel oder Ironie aus.
3. **There** are lots of Japanese motor-bikes around these days, aren't **there**?
   Enthält der Aussagesatz das Vorsubjekt *there* (vgl. § 1), so wird dieses im *Question Tag* wiederaufgenommen.

§ 12 Kurzantworten
Short Answers

F

Hilfsv.	Subj.	Vollv.	restl. Satz	Subj.	Hilfsv.
Can	Peter	swim?		Yes, he	**can.** ['kæn]
				No, he	**can't.** ['ka:nt]
Does	Peggy	like	swimming?	Yes, she	**does.** ['dʌz]
				No, she	**doesn't.**

Die Kurzantwort greift Subjekt und Hilfsverb der vorangehenden Frage wieder auf. Das Subjekt erscheint in Form eines Personalpronomens. Bei den bejahten Hilfsverben wird die betonte Vollform gesprochen.

V

Während im Deutschen die Antwort auf Entscheidungsfragen gewöhnlich einfach *ja* oder *nein* lautet, werden im Englischen *yes* oder *no* meist durch einen Kurzsatz ergänzt. Auch Ausdrücke wie *of course, sorry, I'm afraid* können eine Kurzantwort einleiten.

Kurzantworten sind eine Reaktion auf Entscheidungsfragen

Can you ride a motor-bike? — Yes, I **can**.
Have you got a motor-bike yourself? — No, I **haven't**.
Would you like to have one? — Of course I **would**.

Do you have to wash your father's car? — Yes, I **do**.
Does your brother help you? — No, he **doesn't**.
Do you get paid for doing it? — I'm afraid I **don't**.

Entscheidungsfragen werden immer durch ein Hilfsverb eingeleitet (vgl. § 9). Dieses Hilfsverb wird auch in der Kurzantwort verwendet. Dies gilt für *do*-Formen ebenso wie für andere Hilfsverben.

H

1. Must I take off my shoes? — No, you needn't.

   Da *must* durch *needn't* verneint wird, muß *needn't* auch in der verneinten Kurzantwort auftreten. (Vgl. § 79)

2. Is **there** a swimming-pool in your town? — Yes, **there** is./No, **there** isn't.

   Enthält der Fragesatz das Vorsubjekt *there* (vgl. § 1), so wird dieses in der Kurzantwort wiederaufgegriffen.

3. Does the shop across the road sell picture postcards?
   — **I don't think so.** Ich glaube nicht.

   Bei Kurzantworten, die durch *I (don't) think* eingeleitet werden, kann der vorangehende Fragesatz durch einfaches *so* wiederaufgegriffen werden.

   Ebenso bei:
   I believe so. Ich glaube schon./Ich glaube ja.
   I hope so. Ich hoffe es. (Aber: I hope not. Ich hoffe nicht.)
   I suppose so. Ich nehme es an.

   Is the stationer's shop open?
   — **I don't know.** Ich weiß (es) nicht.

   Nach *I (don't) know* wird der vorangehende Satz nicht wiederaufgegriffen.

   Vergleiche auch:
   I forget. *(Present Tense!)* Ich habe es vergessen.
   I promise. Ich verspreche es.
   I (don't) remember. Ich erinnere mich (nicht) daran.

§ 13 Kurzsätze mit *so/nor/neither*
Short Responses with *so / nor / neither*

F

Subj.	Hilfsv.	Vollverb + restl. Satz		Hilfsv.	Subj.
I		**like** chips very much. —	So	**do**	I.
But I	**'m** not	very fond of fish. —	Nor	**am**	I.
			Neither	**am**	I.

Kurzsätze mit *so/nor/neither* greifen das Hilfsverb (bzw. die *be*-Form) des vorangehenden Aussagesatzes wieder auf. Enthält dieser nur ein Vollverb, so tritt im Kurzsatz eine *do*-Form ein. Das Subjekt wird ans Ende des Kurzsatzes gestellt und stark betont.

V Kurzsätze mit *so/nor/neither* entsprechen deutschen Kurzsätzen mit *auch/auch nicht:*

***so* nach bejahten Aussagesätzen: „auch“**	***nor/neither* nach verneinten Aussagesätzen: „auch nicht“**
I would like to have more pocket-money. — **So would I.** Ich hätte gern mehr Taschengeld. — Ich auch. My father and mother always ask a lot of questions when I need some extra money. — **So do *my* parents.** ... — *Meine* Eltern auch.	I didn't expect to get such a bad mark in English. — **Nor did I.** — Ich auch nicht. I wasn't very pleased with my last school report, **and neither were my parents.** ..., und meine Eltern auch nicht.

H My teacher doesn't want me to work all through the holidays, and my parents **don't either.** (... **nor do** my parents.)

Statt *nor/neither* wird in der Umgangssprache auch häufig *not... either* verwendet (ohne Umstellung des Subjekts).

§ 14 Hervorhebung von Sätzen durch *do*-Formen
Do-Forms Used to Emphasize Whole Sentences

F

I	don't	like folk music very much, but I	do	like modern jazz.
	Verneinung		bejahte Hervorhebung	

V Während im Deutschen ein Satz im Rahmen eines Texts meist durch verstärkende Adverbien wie *wirklich, tatsächlich, durchaus* hervorgehoben wird, können im Englischen dafür in bestimmten Fällen die *do*-Formen eintreten.

Betonte *do*-Form vor dem Vollverb	
Hervorhebung zum Zweck der Gegenüberstellung	
He himself had **no** idea that he smelt of onions, but plenty of other people **did** notice it.	... bemerkten es **durchaus/schon.**
Voraussetzung für diese kontrastierende Verwendung der *do*-Hervorhebung ist, daß der vorhergehende Satz eine verneinte Aussage enthält.	
Hervorhebung zum Ausdruck einer besonderen gefühlsmäßigen Reaktion	
I **did** enjoy that hamburger. It was really meaty and there was lots of ketchup on it.	Dieser Hamburger hat mir **wirklich** geschmeckt.
You **do** seem to be hungry. Haven't you had anything to eat today?	Du scheinst **wirklich** hungrig zu sein.

H

1. You **are** ['ɑ:] taking your time. You should have finished breakfast and left for school long ago.

   Sätze mit Hilfsverben können hervorgehoben werden, indem das Hilfsverb in der Vollform ausgesprochen und betont wird.

2. Zum Gebrauch von *do* in bejahten Aufforderungssätzen vgl. § 8.

§ 15 Hervorhebung von Satzteilen durch *it is/it was*
It is/it was Used to Emphasize Parts of a Sentence

F

		Subjekt	Verb	Objekt	Umstandsangabe
		Peter	broke	his leg	on his way home from school.
It was **Peter**	who		broke	his leg	on his way home from school.
It was **his leg**	(that)	Peter	broke		on his way home from school.
It was **on his way home from school**	that	Peter	broke	his leg.	

Durch die Konstruktion mit *it is/it was* können verschiedene Satzteile an den Satzanfang gestellt werden. Die restlichen Satzteile werden in Form eines Relativsatzes oder eines *that*-Satzes angeschlossen.

V Die Konstruktion mit *it is/it was* bietet die Möglichkeit, einen bestimmten Satzteil aus dem Satz „herauszunehmen" und auf diese Weise besonders hervorzuheben. Im Deutschen ist die entsprechende Konstruktion mit *es ist/es war* viel seltener.

it is/it was zur Hervorhebung einzelner Satzteile

It's yesterday's newspaper I'm looking for, not today's.	Ich suche **die gestrige Zeitung,** nicht die heutige.
I'm not going to pay the bill. **It was my brother** who ordered the magazine.	... **Mein Bruder** hat die Zeitschrift bestellt.
It's in the popular press that you find the most sensational stories.	Die sensationellsten Berichte findet man **in der Boulevardpresse.**

Diese Hervorhebung wird vor allem dann verwendet, wenn ein Gegensatz ausgedrückt werden soll.

it is/it was in Verbindung mit Pluralformen

It was the neighbours who told my father he'd left the lights of his car on.	**Es waren die Nachbarn,** die meinen Vater darauf aufmerksam machten, daß er seine Autoscheinwerfer nicht ausgeschaltet hatte.
It's friends you need when you are in trouble.	Was man braucht, wenn man in Schwierigkeiten ist, **sind Freunde.**

It is/it was stehen immer im Singular, auch wenn ein Nomen im Plural folgt. (Deutsch: „es sind/es waren ...")

It was not until/It was only after

It was not until three days after the gas explosion **that** the full extent of the damage became known.	**Erst drei Tage nach** der Gasexplosion wurde das volle Ausmaß des Schadens bekannt.
It was only after several fire engines had arrived **that** the fire was brought under control.	**Erst nachdem** mehrere Feuerwehrautos eingetroffen waren, konnte das Feuer unter Kontrolle gebracht werden.

Solche Sätze mögen aus deutscher Sicht umständlich erscheinen. Sie sind jedoch im Englischen durchaus gebräuchlich, vor allem im schriftlichen Ausdruck. Dabei wirken sie weniger förmlich und gewählt als Sätze mit Inversion.
(Not until three days after the gas explosion **did** the full extent of the damage **become known.** Vgl. § 6.)

H

1. **What** I need most urgently now **is money.** Was ich jetzt am dringendsten brauche, ist Geld.
Wie im Deutschen kann z. B. ein Objekt auch hervorgehoben werden, indem es ans Satzende gestellt wird, wobei die übrigen Satzteile in Form eines Relativsatzes vorausgehen.

2. After John had won the tennis championship
   several reporters interviewed him. (weniger betont)
   he was interviewed by **several reporters.** (hervorgehoben)

Eine weitere Möglichkeit, einen Satzteil durch Endstellung hervorzuheben, bieten Passivsätze (vgl. § 3).

§ 16 Satzverknüpfung durch Konjunktionen und Adverbien
Conjunctions and Adverbs Used to Link Sentences

V

1. Hauptsätze werden in englischen und deutschen Texten häufig durch satzverknüpfende Konjunktionen oder Adverbien verbunden.

Gebrauch häufig mißverstandener Konjunktionen oder Adverbien		
On the one hand Stratford is a beautiful little town, **on the other hand** it is overrun by tourists. **After all** it's the birthplace of one of the world's greatest playwrights. **Anyway,** I don't want to miss it. And **besides** the theatre alone would justify a visit to Stratford.	Einerseits ... andererseits ... Schließlich ist es ja ... / Immerhin ... Jedenfalls ... Und außerdem ...	Weitere satzverknüpfende Konjunktionen und Adverbien, die häufig falsch gebraucht werden, sind: *moreover* (überdies) *above all* (vor allem) *otherwise* (ansonsten) *however* (jedoch) *nevertheless* (trotzdem).

2. Satzverknüpfende Konjunktionen und Adverbien stehen normalerweise am Satzanfang, abgesehen von folgenden Ausnahmen:

Stellung von *too, as well, not either, also*	
If you ever pass through my home town don't just visit the cathedral, look at some of the smaller churches **as well.** The museum, **too,** is worth a visit. Unfortunately there is not much else to do in the town and there are **no** lakes or mountains nearby **either.** The only hotel in our town is quite expensive, but you can **also** get bed and breakfast at some of the pubs.	Das deutsche Adverb „auch" wird im Englischen häufig durch *too* oder *as well* wiedergegeben. Dem deutschen „auch nicht" entspricht *(not) either.* Diese Wörter treten ans Ende des Satzes oder hinter das Bezugswort; *also* erscheint meist in Binnenstellung. (Vgl. § 4.)

Im verneinten Satz erscheint nicht *too,* sondern *either.*

2 Nebensätze, Infinitiv-, *Gerund*- und Partizipialkonstruktionen

Subordinate Clauses; Infinitive, Gerund and Participle Structures

§ 17 Adverbialsätze und der Gebrauch von Konjunktionen

The Use of Conjunctions in Adverbial Clauses

F

Hauptsatz	**Umstandsangabe / Adverbialsatz**
He decided to go to the pictures	last night. when he left the office. because it was raining.
We'll go for a walk tomorrow	if it doesn't rain. unless it rains.

An die Stelle von Zeit- und anderen Umstandsangaben können adverbiale Nebensätze treten.
Sie werden durch Konjunktionen eingeleitet, z. B. Konjunktionen
der **Zeit** (wie *when:* wenn / als, *while, as soon as, after, before, until*),
des **Ortes** und der **Richtung** (wie *where:* wo / wohin / dort wo),
des **Grundes** (wie *because*),
des **Gegensatzes** (der **Einräumung**) (wie *though, although*),
der **Bedingung** (wie *if:* wenn / falls, *unless:* wenn nicht / falls nicht),
des **Vergleichs** (wie *as if:* als ob).

V

1. Beim Hören und Lesen ist zu beachten, daß bestimmte Konjunktionen mehrdeutig sind:

Nebensätze mit *since*	**Nebensätze mit *as***
Since the weather was so bad the concert could not be held in the open air. Da / weil ... **Since** the open air festival was founded they have always been unlucky with the weather. Seit ...	**As** the tickets for the opera are very expensive most people can't afford to go very often. Da / weil ... **As** we entered the theatre we met an old friend of ours. Als ... Before the show started my father bought a programme **as** he always does. ... wie immer. **As** I grow older I am getting more and more interested in classical ballet. Je älter ich werde ...
Since gibt — je nach Zusammenhang — einen Grund („da" / „weil") oder eine zeitliche Beziehung an („seit").	*As* kann Adverbialsätze des Grundes, der Zeit und verschiedene Arten von Vergleichssätzen einleiten.

2. Beim Sprechen und Schreiben sind bestimmte Konjunktionen von gleichbedeutenden Präpositionen zu unterscheiden:

Konjunktion + Nebensatz	**Präposition + Nomen**
***while:* „während" (= Konjunktion)**	***during:* „während" (= Präposition)**
While he was learning his lines the actor marched up and down the stage. Während er seinen Text auswendig lernte ...	**During** the first rehearsals [rɪˈhɜːslz] the actors wore their ordinary clothes. Während der ersten Proben ...
***though/although:* „obwohl"**	***in spite of:* „trotz"**
Though (Although) she tried very hard, the actress didn't impress the director. Obwohl sie sich sehr bemühte ...	**In spite of** his careful preparation the actor kept forgetting his lines. Trotz seiner sorgfältigen Vorbereitung ....

H 1. Viele Konjunktionen können auch mit Partizipialkonstruktionen, viele Präpositionen auch mit *Gerund*-Konstruktionen verbunden werden (vgl. § 18).

2. The young actor was short of money **because** he was out of work. — ..., weil ...
As/Since he was out of work the young actor was short of money. — Da ..., ...

Because leitet hauptsächlich **nachgestellte** Adverbialsätze des Grundes ein, bei **vorangestellten** werden die einsilbigen Konjunktionen *as* und *since* bevorzugt.

⚠ I wasn't terribly impressed **when** my parents took me to the theatre for the first time. — ... als ...
We must go to the theatre **when** you come and stay with us. — ... wenn („in der Zeit, da") ...
I would have become an actor **if** my father had let me. — ... wenn („falls") ...
When leitet Adverbialsätze der Zeit ein, *if* Bedingungssätze.

§ 18 Adverbialsätze und vergleichbare Konstruktionen
Adverbial Clauses and Corresponding Structures

F

Adverbialsatz/*Gerund*/Partizip	restlicher Satz
When he arrived	he looked very tired.
When arriving late at night	guests are requested to use the back entrance.
Arriving half an hour early	he went for a walk to pass the time.
On arriving at the station	he found that the train had already left.

An die Stelle eines Adverbialsatzes können folgende Konstruktionen treten:

— Konjunktion + Partizip
— Partizip (ohne Konjunktion)
— Präposition + *Gerund*

V 1. *Gerund*- und Partizipialkonstruktionen sind für den deutschen Hörer oder Leser manchmal schwer verständlich, da es im Deutschen meist keine direkte Entsprechung gibt.

Auslegung von Partizipalkonstruktionen als Nebensätze

When forced to travel in the holiday season always book your hotel in advance. — **(When you are forced** to travel ...)
Feeling hot and dusty after the long journey he decided to take a bath. — **(Since he felt** hot and dusty ...)
Living in a small village where nothing much happened I was fascinated by books about far-away countries. — **(Since I lived ... /When I lived** ...)

Partizipialkonstruktionen (mit *Present* und *Past Participle*) lassen sich als verkürzte Nebensätze auffassen.
Sie werden zum Teil durch die gleichen Konjunktionen eingeleitet wie die entsprechenden Adverbialsätze.
Wenn die Konjunktion fehlt, kommen oft mehrere Auslegungen in Frage (vor allem Angabe des Grundes und der Zeit).
Welche Auslegung vorzuziehen ist, wird meist aus dem Textzusammenhang klar.

Auslegung von *Gerund*-Konstruktionen

After looking through all the travel brochures we decided to go to Spain. — **(After we had looked** through ...)
On leaving the plane we were told that the hotel we had booked was full up. — **(When we left** ...)

Auch *Gerund*-Konstruktionen, die durch Präpositionen eingeleitet werden, lassen sich als Nebensätze verstehen
Allerdings gibt es im Englischen nur in einigen Fällen bedeutungsgleiche Adverbialsätze.
Im Deutschen entsprechen diesen *Gerund*-Konstruktionen teils Adverbialsätze, teils Infinitivkonstruktionen:

vgl.: **By working** during his holiday ... — **Indem er** während der Ferien **arbeitete** ...
In spite of saving money for his holiday ... — **Obwohl er** Geld für die Ferien **sparte** ...
Instead of/Without taking a holiday ... — **Anstatt/Ohne** Ferien **zu machen** ...

2. Die Wahl zwischen Adverbialsätzen und *ing*-Konstruktionen ist hauptsächlich eine Stilfrage:

Nebensätze wirken neutral — *ing*-Konstruktionen wirken meist gewählt

Although he talked a lot about his travels he didn't give us any useful hints.
Though taking an active part in the discussion on mass tourism he did not contribute anything valuable.
In spite of attacking mass tourism he was not able to present a real alternative.
} Obwohl ...

Partizipial- und *Gerund*-Konstruktionen klingen meist förmlicher als Nebensätze. Deshalb werden im Gespräch und im persönlichen Brief Nebensätze bevorzugt. Im sonstigen schriftlichen Gebrauch, z. B. in *comment, summary* und *essay,* sind *ing*-Konstruktionen aber durchaus am Platz.

***instead of / by / without* + *Gerund:* auf allen Stilebenen**

Instead of going to the local swimming-pool she always went swimming in the nearby lake.	Statt ... zu gehen ...
Without hesitating she jumped into the water and saved the child.	Ohne zu zögern ...
He earned some pocket money **by working** as a lifeguard.	... indem er ... arbeitete.

Diese Konstruktionen sind in mündlicher wie schriftlicher Verwendung üblich, da sie im Englischen nicht durch gebräuchliche Nebensätze ersetzt werden können.

Angabe des Zwecks: *Gerund* und Infinitiv auf allen Stilebenen

In most caravans gas is used **for cooking.**	... zum Kochen ...
Modern tents are designed **to offer** maximum space and comfort.	... so konstruiert, daß sie ... bieten.
They drove as fast as they could **to reach** the camping site before dark.	... um ... zu erreichen.

Zur Angabe von Zweck oder Absicht werden praktisch nur *Gerund*- und Infinitiv-Konstruktionen verwendet, da entsprechende Nebensätze (z. B. ... *so that they would reach the camping site before dark*) zu schwerfällig wirken bzw. gar nicht möglich sind.

§ 19 *That*-Sätze und vergleichbare Konstruktionen
That-Clauses and Corresponding Structures

F

Subj.	Verb	Objekt des Hauptsatzes		
I	know	**that**	Jim **(he)**	**has got** a sailing boat.
I	'd like		**him**	**to take** me sailing.
We	saw		a car ferry	**enter** the harbour.
We	watched		an oil tanker	**entering** the harbour.
Jill	can't stand		Jim and **me**	**talking** about boats all the time.
			eigenes logisches Subjekt	

Objekt eines Satzes kann nicht nur ein Nomen sein, sondern z. B. auch ein *that*-Satz, eine Infinitivkonstruktion (mit und ohne *to*) oder eine *ing*-Konstruktion.
Die Infinitiv- oder *ing*-Konstruktion kann, ebenso wie der *that*-Satz, ein eigenes logisches Subjekt haben.
Im Gegensatz zum *that*-Satz steht das logische Subjekt der Infinitiv- oder *ing*-Konstruktion im Objektsfall, d. h. es werden die Objektsformen der Personalpronomen verwendet (*him, me,* etc. Vgl. § 32).

H

I wish	**I** could go	sailing with Jim.
I should like	to go	sailing with Jim.

Ist das Subjekt das gleiche wie im Hauptsatz, so wird es in der Infinitiv- oder *ing*-Konstruktion nicht genannt.

V 1. Zum Verständnis von Konstruktionen mit eigenem logischem Subjekt ist zu beachten:

Auslegung von Infinitiv- und *Gerund*-Konstruktionen als Objektsätze

The Wilsons want their eldest son to take over the farm later. (The Wilsons want something = direktes Objekt)	Wilsons möchten, daß ihr ältester Sohn später den Hof übernimmt.
Farmers always complain about tourists walking across their fields. (Farmers always complain about something = Präpositionalobjekt)	Die Bauern beklagen sich immer darüber, daß die Touristen über ihre Felder gehen.

Infinitiv- und *Gerund*-Konstruktionen mit eigenem logischem Subjekt lassen sich als Objektsätze auffassen. Dabei spielt es keine Rolle, ob die Konstruktion direkt ans Verb angeschlossen wird (vgl. *want*) oder mit Hilfe einer Präposition (vgl. *complain about*). Wichtig ist, daß das Nomen nach dem Verb als **Teil des Objekts** verstanden wird.

2. Beim eigenen Gebrauch von *that*-Sätzen und vergleichbaren Konstruktionen ist zu beachten:

that-Sätze sind nicht nach allen Verben möglich

Nach Verben des Sagens: *that*-Sätze

The old man **told** us **that** he had been a farmer all his life.
I wouldn't like to live in the country. I **know** I would miss things like the theatre and the cinema.

That-Sätze sind vor allem in der indirekten Rede verbreitet (vgl. § 25), also nach Verben wie *say, remark, answer,* aber auch nach Verben des Wissens und Vermutens, wie *know, believe, think.*
Die Konjunktion *that* kann entfallen. Im Gegensatz zum Deutschen steht kein Komma.

Nach Verben der Willensäußerung: Infinitiv

Do you **want us to help** you in the garden?	Willst du, daß wir dir im Garten helfen?
Father **expects the work to be done** by the weekend.	Vater erwartet („will" oder „nimmt an"), daß die Arbeit ...

Nach *want* kann nur der Infinitiv stehen; nach *wish* und *expect* ist oft auch ein *that*-Satz möglich. Allerdings kommt bei *expect* + *that*-Satz nur die Auslegung „annehmen", „vermuten" in Frage. (Zu *wish* + *that*-Satz vgl. § 27 V 2.)

Nach Verb + Präposition und nach *don't mind, can't stand: Gerund*

I **don't mind Peter believing** in a simple life, but I sometimes **worry about him living** alone on that farm.

Nach einer Reihe von Verben ist nur die *ing*-Form zulässig. Dazu gehören alle Verben mit Präposition sowie *don't mind* und *can't stand.* (Vgl. § 90.)

H 1. Few people mind **the farmers' (the farmers)** being so rich, but many object to **their (them)** paying such low taxes.
Im förmlichen Stil kann das logische Subjekt einer *Gerund*-Konstruktion auch durch einen *s*-Genitiv bzw. einen Possessivbegleiter wiedergegeben werden.

2. The farmers are waiting **for the rain to stop** before they start making hay. (... warten darauf, daß ...)
Auch die Konstruktion *for* + Nomen / Pronomen + Infinitiv läßt sich oft als Objektsatz auffassen.

§ 20 Relativsätze
Relative Clauses

F

	Relativsatz				
		Subjekt			
The lady		**who**	answered the phone		wasn't very helpful.
The information	**(which)**	she	gave me		was incorrect.
The office		she	sent me	**to**	didn't exist.
	Objekt			Präp.	

Relativsätze können mit und ohne Relativpronomen gebildet werden.
Man unterscheidet:

- Relativsätze, in denen das Pronomen Subjekt ist (stets mit Relativpronomen);
- Relativsätze, in denen das Pronomen Objekt ist (Pronomen entfällt häufig).

Präpositionen werden im Relativsatz häufig nachgestellt.

V

Entscheidend für Form und Gebrauch der Relativsätze im Englischen ist, ob der Relativsatz notwendig für das Verständnis des Gesamtsatzes ist oder ob er nur eine zusätzliche, nicht unbedingt nötige Information bietet. Im Deutschen ist diese Unterscheidung für die Form des Relativsatzes ohne Bedeutung.

Notwendiger Relativsatz

Kein Komma, keine Sprechpausen

People **who live in Europe** often have no idea of living conditions in other parts of the world.
The countries **which have the lowest standard of living** normally have a high birth-rate too.

Der notwendige Relativsatz ist im schriftlichen wie im mündlichen Gebrauch sehr verbreitet. Da er die Bedeutung des Nomens einschränkt, ist er ein wesentlicher Bestandteil des Gesamtsatzes. Deshalb wird er nicht durch Komma oder Sprechpausen vom Hauptsatz getrennt.

Nachstellung der Präposition üblich

The problems **which the third world is faced *with*** are difficult to solve.
The girl **I was talking *to* the other day** was a Kenyan student.
A fact **that she was particularly proud *of*** was that her country was now doing well without much help from outside.

Die Präposition wird im notwendigen Relativsatz normalerweise nachgestellt. Beim Relativsatz mit *that* und beim Wegfall des Relativpronomens **muß** sie sogar nachgestellt werden.

Nicht-notwendiger Relativsatz

Abtrennung durch Komma und Sprechpausen

My friend Jim, // **who is an engineer,** // is at present working for Oxfam in India.
India, // **which has long been a major tea-producing nation,** // is now developing her industry.

Der nicht-notwendige Relativsatz erscheint vorwiegend in der geschriebenen Sprache. Er ist ein zusätzlicher Einschub, der durch Komma und Sprechpausen vom Hauptsatz abgehoben wird.

Präposition meist vor dem Relativpronomen

Uncle Henry, ***with* whom I spent the weekend,** has seen a good deal of the world.
Australia, ***to* which he first travelled as a young man,** has become his second home.

Die Präposition bleibt im nicht-notwendigen Relativsatz wie im Deutschen meist vor dem Relativpronomen.

Relativpronomen im notwendigen Relativsatz

who (whom), which

The people ***who* are worst off today** are the neglected minorities such as the American Indians.
There is hardly a country in the world ***which* doesn't have a minority problem.**
A large number of the young black men ***whom (who)* you see in the streets of Harlem** are out of work.
Many of the jobs ***which* coloured people do in Britain** are the ones ***which* white people don't want to do.**

Für Personen tritt im Subjektsfall *who* ein. Im Objektsfall verwendet man im förmlichen Stil *whom*, in der Umgangssprache gewöhnlich *who* (falls das Relativpronomen nicht ganz entfällt).
Für Sachen tritt im Subjekts- und Objektsfall *which* ein.

that als Alternative zu *who (whom), which*

The immigrants ***that (who)* have come from the West Indies** usually have no language problems.
More than other immigrants the Pakistanis keep up the customs ***that (which)* they have brought from their home country.**
If you would like to eat something ***that (which)* is cheap and tasty,** go to an Indian restaurant.

That kann sowohl im Subjektsfall als auch im Objektsfall verwendet werden, und zwar vorwiegend mit Bezug auf Dinge, gelegentlich aber auch auf Personen.
That wird bevorzugt nach *only, all, everything, something, anything, first, last* und nach Superlativen.

Wegfall des Relativpronomens *(contact clause)*

Most of the cassette-recorders **you find in the shops these days** have been made in the Far East.
What do you think of the Chinese lamp-shade **I bought this morning?**

Diese Konstruktion ist möglich, wenn das Relativpronomen das Objekt (bzw. Präpositionalobjekt) des Relativsatzes wäre. In der Umgangssprache entfällt das Relativpronomen hier fast immer.

Relativpronomen im nicht-notwendigen Relativsatz

who, whom, which als einzig mögliche Pronomen

The Indians, ***who* once owned the whole area of the present USA,** are now trying to get back some of their former land.
The Sioux, ***whom* the white Americans only defeated after a long struggle,** are among the most famous Indian tribes.
One of the best-known Indian place names in the USA is Massachusetts, ***which* is quite difficult to pronounce.**
The Navaho Reservation in Arizona, ***which* I visited last year,** is the largest Indian reservation in the USA. It is about the size of Austria.

Das Relativpronomen kann im nicht-notwendigen Relativsatz nie weggelassen oder durch *that* ersetzt werden.
Für Personen treten *who* oder *whom* ein, und zwar *who* im Subjektsfall, *whom* im Objektsfall.
Für Sachen tritt immer *which* ein.

H

1. India is one of those countries **whose birth-rate is still rising.**
   My brother John, **whose wife comes from New Delhi,** has just begun to learn Hindi.

   Auch *whose* (Relativbegleiter) kann sowohl notwendige als auch nicht-notwendige Relativsätze einleiten.

   In der Schriftsprache wird bei Sachen statt *whose* gelegentlich auch *of which* verwendet *(... one of those countries the birth-rate of which ...).*

2. In many of the new African states several different languages are spoken, **which causes great problems.**
   ... was große Probleme verursacht.

   Das Relativpronomen *which* kann sich nicht nur auf ein Nomen beziehen, sondern auch auf einen ganzen Satz. Es entspricht dann dem deutschen Relativpronomen „was". Auch diese Form des Relativsatzes enthält eine zusätzliche, nicht-notwendige Information und wird deshalb durch Komma und Sprechpause vom Hauptsatz abgetrennt.

3. **Whoever** told you that India was a Muslim country was mistaken.
   My friend Peter is prepared to work in **whichever** Third World country needs qualified engineers.

   Durch den Zusatz *-ever* werden *who, what* und *which* zu verallgemeinernden Relativpronomen in der Bedeutung von „wer / was / welcher auch immer" bzw. „jeder der", „alles was". Sätze mit *whoever, whichever, whatever* können verschiedene Satzteile ersetzen.

§ 21 Relativsätze und vergleichbare Konstruktionen
Relative Clauses and Corresponding Structures

F

	Relativsatz / Partizipial- oder Infinitivkonstruktion		
The man	who	lives next door	sells picture postcards in front of the cathedral.
The man		**living** next door	sells picture postcards in front of the cathedral.
The postcards	which	are sold outside the castle	are of poor quality.
The postcards		**sold** outside the castle	are of poor quality.
The first country	which	used postage stamps	was Britain.
The first country		**to use** postage stamps	was Britain
	Subjekt des Relativsatzes		

Relativsätze, in denen das Relativpronomen Subjekt ist, können durch folgende Strukturen ersetzt werden:
- durch Partizipialkonstruktionen.
  Dabei tritt das *Present Participle* für aktive Verbformen im Relativsatz ein, das *Past Participle* für passive Verbformen.
- durch Infinitivkonstruktionen.
  Dies ist jedoch nur in bestimmten Fällen möglich.

V

Partizipialkonstruktionen: nach allen Nomen möglich	**Infinitivkonstruktionen: nach *the first, the last, the only one,* etc.**
The ships sailing to America in the sixteenth and seventeenth centuries took several weeks to get there. **The food supplied** to the passengers on early sailing ships was unhealthy and tasted terrible.	Armstrong was **the first (man) to set** foot on the moon. Australia was **the last continent to be discovered.** The two Italians were **the only members** of the expedition **to return.** All the others had been killed in a blizzard.
Diese Struktur ist sowohl im geschriebenen als auch im gesprochenen Englisch sehr verbreitet. Auch im Deutschen gibt es ähnliche Partizipialkonstruktionen („ein auf dem Meer treibendes Boot“, „ein vom Sturm aufgepeitschter Ozean“), doch werden sie weitaus seltener benutzt als im Englischen. Im Gegensatz zum Deutschen wird die Partizipialkonstruktion im Englischen dem Nomen nachgestellt.	Die Infinitivkonstruktion ist nur nach Superlativen und Zahlenangaben wie *the first, the last, the few* möglich. *The first* und *the last* können allein stehen. *The only* muß mit einem Nomen oder dem Stützwort *one/ones* verbunden werden.

H

The film **to see** this week is 'Crazy Planets'. It's extremely funny.
(The film **which you should see** this week ...)
The man **to talk to** is my uncle. He knows all about space research.
(The man **you should talk to** ...)

Die Infinitivkonstruktion kann auch anstelle eines Relativsatzes eintreten, in dem das Relativpronomen Objekt ist bzw. entfällt *(contact clause)*, aber nur dann, wenn dieser Relativsatz ein modales Hilfsverb *(should, must,* etc.) enthält.

§ 22 Infinitivkonstruktionen mit Fragewort
Infinitive Structures Starting with Question Words

F

	Fragewort	**S**	**Hv**	**V**	**Ergänzung**
Tourists often don't know	where	they	can	get	a cheap meal.
	where		**to get**		
	Fragewort + Infinitiv				

Manche indirekte Fragesätze können durch Infinitivkonstruktionen verkürzt werden.

V

Fragewort + Infinitiv statt indirekter Fragesätze mit modalen Hilfsverben

People who travel by plane for the first time often have no idea ...	**where to** put their hand luggage.	(where they can put ...)	Indirekte Fragesätze, die ein modales Hilfsverb (*can, should,* etc.) enthalten, werden im Englischen vermieden. Statt dessen benutzt man Infinitivkonstruktionen.
	when to fasten their seat belts.	(when they must fasten ...)	
	what to do if they feel sick.	(what they should do ...)	
	how to use their life jackets.	(how they should use ...)	

§ 23 Kommentierende und satzverknüpfende Infinitivkonstruktionen
Infinitive Structures Used as Comments and Links

F

Adverb / Infinitivkonstr.	**zugehöriger Satz**
Frankly, To be frank,	I always feel lost in big cities.

An Stelle von kommentierenden Adverbien (*frankly, certainly,* etc.) und satzverknüpfenden Adverbien (*firstly, then, besides,* etc.) können auch Infinitivkonstruktionen verwendet werden. Sie werden meist durch Komma vom zugehörigen Satz abgetrennt. (Vgl. § 16)

V Beim Hören und Lesen ist zu beachten:

Infinitivkonstruktion als Einschub im Text

Kommentierende Infinitivkonstruktionen

To be sure, London is one of the most exciting cities in the world.	Gewiß ist ...
I was very impressed by London, but, **to tell the truth,** I wouldn't like to live there.	... aber ehrlich gesagt ...

Weitere kommentierende Infinitivkonstruktionen sind *to be honest, to be frank.*

Satzverknüpfende Infinitivkonstruktionen

To start with the guide took us on a quick tour of the main sights of London ...	Als erstes/Zunächst ...
... **To be brief,** for the tourist London is a must.	... Kurz gesagt, ..

Satzverknüpfende Infinitivkonstruktionen können zur Einleitung einer Aufzählung *(to start with, to begin with)* verwendet werden oder zur Zusammenfassung eines Gedankengangs *(to sum up, to be brief).*

§ 24 Satzreihen und Partizipialkonstruktionen
Linking Sentences with Participle Structures

F

Erster Satz			Folgesatz/Partizipialkonstruktion	
	Gleiches Subjekt			
The interpreter	spoke very slowly.		He	pronounced every word carefully and clearly.
The interpreter	spoke very slowly,			**pronouncing** every word carefully and clearly.
	Verschiedene Subjekte			
The foreign visitors	listened attentively.		Some of them	were making notes.
The foreign visitors	listened attentively,	**(with)**	**some of them**	**making** notes.

An die Stelle von Satzfolgen können folgende Partizipalkonstruktionen treten:

1. Partizipialkonstruktionen **ohne** eigenes logisches Subjekt, wenn das Subjekt der beiden Sätze übereinstimmt.
2. Partizipialkonstruktionen **mit** eigenem logischem Subjekt, wenn beide Sätze verschiedene Subjekte haben (absolute Partizipialkonstruktion). Dabei kann die Partizipialkonstruktion direkt oder durch *with* angeschlossen werden.

V

Die hier besprochenen Partizipialkonstruktionen gehören im allgemeinen der gehobenen Schriftsprache an.
Die *with* + *Participle*-Konstruktion wird jedoch auch in der Umgangssprache verwendet.

Auslegung der *with* + *Participle*-Konstruktion als Hauptsatz oder Nebensatz

Most of the London newspapers showed understanding for the postmen's strike, **with only the Daily Telegraph disapproving.**	... Nur der Daily Telegraph äußerte Kritik.
With the Olympic Games approaching, the newspapers were full of interviews, forecasts and news about the national team.	Die Olympischen Spiele kamen näher, und ... Als/Da die Olympischen Spiele näherkamen, ...

Man muß sich unbedingt klarmachen, daß *with* hier nicht als Präposition verwendet wird, wie etwa in:
He did it **with** *his own hands* (= mit ...). Vielmehr deutet *with* hier nur eine lose Verbindung mit dem Hauptsatz an.
Die *with* + *Participle*-Konstruktion läßt sich deshalb als eine Folge von Hauptsätzen auslegen.
Je nach Zusammenhang können ihr im Deutschen auch Nebensätze mit *als, wobei, indem, weil, wenn* entsprechen.

Diese Auslegungsmöglichkeiten gelten auch für die absoluten Partizipialkonstruktionen ohne *with.* Vgl.:

Television has had a serious effect on the profits of the entertainment industry, **the cinema being hit the hardest.**	... Dabei wurde das Kino am stärksten betroffen. ... wobei das Kino am stärksten betroffen wurde.

3 Gebrauch von Zeitformen und Zeitangaben im Text

The Use of Tenses and Time Adverbials in Texts

§ 25 Zeitenfolge in der Erzählung und in der Indirekten Rede

Sequence of Tenses in Narration and Indirect Speech

Bei der Wahl der Zeitform des Verbs muß man stets die Zeitformen in den vorangehenden Sätzen mit berücksichtigen, d. h. man muß die Zeitenfolge einhalten. Man unterscheidet dabei zwischen gegenwartsbezogener und vergangenheitsbezogener Zeitenfolge.
Zu den einzelnen Zeitformen vgl. § 62–75.

F

Gegenwarts-bezogene Zeitenfolge		Vergangenheit *Past Tense* oder *Present Perfect*	Gegenwart *Present Tense*	Zukunft *will-Future*
Vergangenheits-bezogene Zeitenfolge	Vor-Vergangenheit *Past Perfect*	Vergangenheit (Erzählzeit) *Past Tense*	Zukunft in der Vergangenheit *Conditional*	
Bei allgemein gültigen Aussagen ist das *Present Tense Simple* immer möglich.				

V

1. Die vergangenheitsbezogene Zeitenfolge gilt nicht nur für die Erzählung, sondern auch für die indirekte Rede.

Vergangenheitsbezogene Zeitenfolge in Erzählung und indirekter Rede

Last summer my sister and I **spent** three weeks travelling around the West of the USA by bus. It **was** great fun, and very exciting for me, as I **had** never **been** there before. First we **visited** San Francisco, which **is** a 'must' for all tourists. Then we **went** on to Los Angeles to visit some friends who **had invited** us to stay. We **didn't know** if we **would get** as far as the Grand Canyon, but in fact we **did.**

Vor-Vergangenheit — Normale Erzählzeit — ‚Zukunft in der Vergangenheit' — Allgemeine Gültigkeit

Last week at the club Mark **told** me that he and his elder brother **had found** an old gypsy caravan somewhere in the woods, and that they **had** already **started** repairing it. He **seemed** to be very proud of the fact that they **were using** all sorts of things other people just **throw** in the dustbin. He **said** they **planned** to paint it blue and yellow in gypsy style, and that they **were hoping** their uncle **would lend** them a horse for a trip round the Lake District next summer.

In allen Formen der Erzählung (z. B. Erlebnisberichte, Geschichten) steht ein Zeitraum der Vergangenheit im Mittelpunkt.
Dies führt dazu, daß die *Past Tense*-Formen überwiegen. Handlungen vor dieser Zeit werden durch das *Past Perfect* wiedergegeben. Was damals als Zukunft gesehen wurde, wird zu *Future in the Past (Conditional)*. Nur allgemein gültige Aussagen können im *Present Tense* stehen.

Die Indirekte Rede ist im Englischen eine Form des Erzählens. Wenn das Einführungsverb im *Past Tense* steht (z. B. *He said . . .*), dann gilt deshalb auch hier die vergangenheitsbezogene Zeitenfolge. (Im Deutschen wird dagegen der Konjunktiv benutzt: She said she **was** tired. – Sie sagte, sie **sei** müde.)

H

1. There we **were,** sitting by the river, peacefully fishing, when without any reason Jack suddenly **stands** up, **loses** his balance and **falls** in. I nearly **died** laughing.

Besonders spannende Phasen einer Erzählung werden, wie im Deutschen, manchmal im *Present Tense* wiedergegeben.

2. I've just heard from Mark. He **says** that he**'s spending** all his free time repairing an old gypsy caravan that he **found** somewhere in the woods.
   He **hopes** that it **will be** finished soon.

Bei der indirekten Rede mit Einführungsverb im *Present Tense* (z. B. *He says*) gilt die gegenwartsbezogene Zeitenfolge, d. h. die Zeitformen der direkten Rede bleiben erhalten.

V 2. Bei der Umsetzung von direkter Rede in indirekte Rede mit Einführungsverb im *Past Tense* wird die gegenwartsbezogene durch die vergangenheitsbezogene Zeitenfolge ersetzt.

Direkte Rede → Indirekte Rede

Verschiebung der Zeitformen bei Vollverben

Direkte Rede			Indirekte Rede
From an interview with a stuntman:			
"... Sure, **I'm** a stuntman in the movie industry.	*Present Tense* (Gegenwart)	*Past Tense*	Jim told me that he **was** a stuntman in the movie industry, and
... **I've worked** in the job for ten years without a serious accident.	*Pres. Perfect*	*Past Perfect*	that he **had worked** in the job for ten years without a serious accident.
... As a boy I **was** good at athletics and I **did** some judo.	*Past Tense*	*Past Perfect*	He said he **had been** good at athletics as a boy and **had done** some judo.
... Yes, I hope **I'll be** able to continue for a few more years.	*will-Future*	*Conditional*	He said he hoped he **would be** able to continue a few more years, and explained
... Of course, most stuntmen **retire** very early, perhaps at 35 or 40."	*Present Tense* (allg. Gültigkeit)	*Present Tense/ Past Tense*	that most stuntmen **retire (retired)** very early, perhaps at 35 or 40.

Verschiebung bei modalen Hilfsverben

Direkte Rede			Indirekte Rede
"... A stuntman **may** be asked to jump from the top of a house —	*may*	*might*	Jim went on to say that a stuntman **might** be asked to jump from the top of a house,
... I **can** show you several ways to do it!	*can*	*could*	and added that he **could** show me several ways to do it.
... Of course, something **might** go wrong, but a stuntman **needn't** do a job if he thinks it's too dangerous.	*might/could* *need*	*might/could* *need*	He admitted that something **might** go wrong, but said a stuntman **needn't** do a job if he thought it was too dangerous.
... I know it **must** sound crazy to drive a car off a bridge, and you	*must* (Annahme)	*must*	He said he knew it **must** sound crazy to drive a car off a bridge and that you
certainly **must** have good nerves, but it's no problem for an expert."	*must* (Notwendigkeit)	*had to*	certainly **had to** have good nerves, but that it was no problem for an expert.

Umwandlung von Frage- und Aufforderungssätzen

Direkte Rede			Indirekte Rede
From an interview with a movie director: **"Do you often use** stuntmen in your movies?"	Entscheidungsfrage	*if-/whether-* Nebensatz	The reporter asked the director **if (whether) he often used** stuntmen in his movies, and also wanted to know
"**What** kind of advice **do you give** them?"	Fragewortfrage	Fragewort-Nebensatz	**what** kind of advice he **gave** them.
Some advice given to a stuntman: "**Don't take** your eyes off the actor, **study** his movements closely and **imitate** them exactly."	Aufforderungssatz (Imperativ)	Infinitivkonstruktion	The director told the stuntman **not to take** his eyes off the actor, **to study** his movements closely and **to imitate** them exactly.

Frage- und Aufforderungssätze werden in der indirekten Rede **stets** in Nebensätze bzw. Infinitivkonstruktionen umgewandelt (z. B. auch nach *He asks ...*). Steht das Einführungsverb im *Past Tense (He asked ...)*, so tritt bei Fragen außerdem die vergangenheitsbezogene Zeitenfolge ein. Bei Infinitivkonstruktionen spielt die Zeitenfolge natürlich keine Rolle.

H "I arrived on Monday." She told me that she arrived on Monday. (= ... that she had arrived ...)

In Originaltexten trifft man gelegentlich auf Abweichungen von den Regeln der Zeitenfolge. Um Mißverständnisse zu vermeiden, sollte man aber beim eigenen Sprechen und Schreiben die Regeln einhalten.

§ 26 Gegenwartsbezogene und vergangenheitsbezogene Zeitangaben im Text
Time Adverbials Referring to Present and Past Time

F

gegenwartsbezogen	vergangenheitsbezogen
three months **ago**	three months **before**
last Monday	(on) the Monday **before**
yesterday	(on) the day **before**
this week	(in) **that** week
today	(on) **that** day
tomorrow	(on) **the following** day
next year	(in) **the following** year

Eine Zeitangabe kann entweder eine Zeit absolut festlegen (z. B. *in the 19th century; on the fourth of July, 1980)* oder die Zeit nur relativ zu einem Zeitpunkt oder Zeitraum angeben. Bei dieser Gruppe von 'relativen' Zeitangaben unterscheidet man zwischen gegenwartsbezogenen Zeitangaben und solchen, die sich auf einen Zeitpunkt oder Zeitraum der Vergangenheit beziehen.
Zu weiteren Einzelheiten über die Zeitangaben vgl. § 59.

V

1. Die Verwendung der Zeitangaben in Texten entspricht im Englischen im allgemeinen dem deutschen Sprachgebrauch. Zu beachten ist vor allem der unterschiedliche Gebrauch von *ago* und *before*, die beide nachgestellt werden.

Gegenwartsbezogene Zeitangaben	Vergangenheitsbezogene Zeitangaben
I'm so tired I can hardly keep my eyes open today. We only got back from Mallorca late **last night.**	On the first day of term I was terribly tired. We had returned from Mallorca only **the night before.**
How time flies! The school term started exactly **six weeks ago** today, and some people are already counting the days to Christmas. ... **vor** sechs Wochen ...	By November we were able to carry on a simple conversation in Spanish. **Six weeks before** none of us had been able to speak a word of the language. ... Sechs Wochen **vorher** ...

2. Bei der Umsetzung von direkter in indirekte Rede mit Einführungsverb im *Past Tense* müssen in bestimmten Fällen vergangenheitsbezogene Zeitangaben eintreten.

Direkte Rede	Indirekte Rede	
	mit gleicher Zeitangabe	**mit veränderter Zeitangabe**
(It is Tuesday morning.) Jack: I made a really stupid mistake in our maths test **yesterday!**	(It is Tuesday evening.) Dave: Jack told me that he had made a stupid mistake in their maths test **yesterday.**	(It is Friday.) Dave: When I met Jack on Tuesday he said that he had made a stupid mistake in their maths test **the day before.**
Die Zeitangabe *yesterday* bedeutet für den Sprecher (Jack): „am Montag" (gegenwartsbezogene Zeitangabe).	Da für Dave *yesterday* immer noch „am Montag" bedeutet, benutzt er ebenfalls die gegenwartsbezogene Zeitangabe.	Ein paar Tage später jedoch muß Dave eine vergangenheitsbezogene Zeitangabe benutzen.

H Jane (in a letter to her American pen-friend): We have a big comprehensive school **here.**

Jane's pen-friend (in America): Jane wrote they had a big comprehensive school **in her home town.**

Auch Ortsangaben müssen bei der Umwandlung von direkter in indirekte Rede manchmal verändert werden, wenn sich der berichtende Sprecher nicht (mehr) an dem Ort befindet, über den berichtet wird.

§ 27 Konjunktivischer Zeitengebrauch bei Bedingungen und Wünschen
The Modal Use of Tenses to Express Conditions and Wishes

F

Normaler Zeitengebrauch	Konjunktivischer Zeitengebrauch
When he left . . . Als er wegging . . .	If he **left** . . . Wenn er weggingе . . .
After he **had left** . . . Nachdem er weggegangen war . . .	If he **had left** . . . Wenn er weggegangen wäre . . .
As he **couldn't** drive . . . Da er nicht fahren konnte . . .	If he **could** drive . . . Wenn er fahren könnte . . .

Die *Past Tense-* und *Past Perfect*-Formen der Vollverben drücken manchmal ein nur vorgestelltes Geschehen aus. Sie entsprechen dann deutschen Konjunktivformen.

Auch modale Hilfsverben können konjunktivische Bedeutung haben (vgl. § 76–82).

V

1. Besonders häufig ist der konjunktivische Zeitengebrauch in bestimmten Arten von Bedingungssätzen. Wesentlich für die Wahl der Zeitformen ist, ob der Sprecher die Bedingung für erfüllbar hält oder nicht. Folgende Typen der Zeitenfolge sind besonders häufig (wobei die Reihenfolge von Nebensatz und Hauptsatz auch umgekehrt sein kann):

Durchaus erfüllbare Bedingung **if-Satz: *Present Tense***	**– Folge für die Zukunft** **Hauptsatz: *will*-Futur / Imperativ / *can, may, must, needn't***
If you **are** hungry	you**'ll find** something to eat in the fridge.
If Peter **comes** home before I'm back	**tell** him to get lunch ready.
If you **are** in a hurry	you **needn't do** the washing up. (I'll do it for you.)
Im *if*-Satz erscheint nie das *will*-Futur, auch wenn sich die Bedingung oft auf die Zukunft bezieht. (Vgl. § 69.)	
Nicht oder nur theoretisch erfüllbare Bedingung ***if*-Satz: *Past Tense***	**– nur gedachte Folge für Gegenwart oder Zukunft** **Hauptsatz: *Conditional / could, might***
If we **bought** a dishwasher	we **could save** a lot of time.
If Susan **were (was)** more careful	she **wouldn't break** so many cups and plates.
Das Verb *be* hat spezielle Konjunktivformen, die im *if*-Satz verwendet werden: *If I/he/she/it were . . .* In der Umgangssprache werden sie aber zunehmend durch die normalen *Past Tense*-Formen ersetzt: *If I/he/she/it* ***was . . .*** (Im Hauptsatz steht dagegen in jedem Fall das *Conditional: I/he/she/it* ***would be*** . . .)	
Nicht mehr erfüllbare Bedingung ***if*-Satz: *Past Perfect***	**– nur gedachte Folge für die Vergangenheit** **Hauptsatz: *Conditional Perfect / could have, might have***
If John **had locked** his bike	it **wouldn't have been** stolen.
If the police **had arrived** a little sooner	they **might have caught** the thieves
Das hier Ausgemalte steht im Widerspruch zu dem, was tatsächlich in der Vergangenheit geschah. (Im Hauptsatz kann auch das einfache *Conditional* stehen, wenn eine Folge für die Gegenwart dargestellt werden soll: *If my brother* ***hadn't lost*** *the keys to the house, we* **would** *all* **feel** *much safer now.*)	

H

1. If one of us **should lose** his keys, we**'ll** (we**'d**) **have to** change the lock of our front door.
Wenn einer von uns seinen Schlüssel verlieren sollte, müssen (müßten) wir . . .

Should im *if*-Satz kann auf eine reelle oder nur theoretische Möglichkeit hinweisen.
Im Hauptsatz kann deshalb *will*-Futur oder *Conditional* eintreten.

2. **Provided** we pay our rent regularly the house owner will have no reason to throw us out.
Unless something extraordinary happens we'll never move to another part of the country.
Suppose your father were offered a better job somewhere else. Would he accept, do you think?

Bedingungssätze können auch durch *provided (that)* (= *if*) oder *unless* (= *if not*) eingeleitet werden.
Suppose (Angenommen ...) leitet häufig einen Hauptsatz ein, der einem *if*-Nebensatz entspricht.

Im *if*-Nebensatz darf kein *will* oder *would* erscheinen, wenn er eine echte Bedingung ausdrückt. (Soll jedoch ein Wollen, ein Wunsch oder eine Bitte ausgedrückt werden, so ist *will* oder *would* auch im *if*-Satz möglich, vgl. V 2, unten.)

2. Auch außerhalb von Bedingungssätzen gilt der konjunktivische Zeitengebrauch, wenn man von etwas spricht, das man sich nur vorstellt (wünscht, für ratsam hält, erbittet, usw.).

Konjunktivischer Zeitengebrauch zum Ausdruck von Wünschen und Bitten:
I wish, I'd rather, if (only), it's time

mit konjunktivischem *Past Tense*	**mit *would***
I wish I **were** a millionaire. — Ich wünschte, ich wäre ... If only I **had** enough money for a trip to America! — Wenn ich nur ... hätte. It's high time father **gave up** betting on horses. — Es ist höchste Zeit, daß Vater ... aufgibt. I'd rather you **stopped** spending so much money on records. — Es wäre mir lieber, wenn du aufhörtest ...	I wish you **would stop** talking about your girl-friends all the time. If only Betty **would leave** me alone! I'd like to have a chance to dance with other girls as well this evening. We'd be very grateful if you **would lend** us a hand in preparing the party.
Diese Sätze drücken häufig Wünsche aus, die für unerfüllbar gehalten werden. Im Deutschen verwendet man zum Teil den Konjunktiv (vgl. *wäre, hätte*), zum Teil den Indikativ (vgl. *aufgibt*).	Auch *would* kann zur Wiedergabe von Wünschen verwendet werden. Solche Sätze sind stets auf die Zukunft bezogen und drücken Wünsche aus, die von jemandem erfüllt werden können. Auch in einem *if*-Nebensatz kann ein *would* auftreten, wenn es sich hier um einen solchen Wunsch oder eine Bitte handelt und nicht um eine echte Bedingung.

1. Long **live** the Queen! — Es **lebe** die Königin.
God **bless** you! — Gott **segne** dich.

In einigen formelhaften Wünschen und Ausrufen wird noch der Konjunktiv Präsens verwendet.
Diese Form ist daran erkennbar, daß die 3. Person Singular keine *s*-Endung hat.

2. The President suggested that many more alternative forms of energy **be** developed. (... **should be** developed.)

Der Konjunktiv Präsens erscheint auch in *that*-Sätzen nach Verben des Forderns und Vorschlagens, vor allem im amerikanischen Englisch. Er kann in dieser Verwendung durch *should* + Infinitiv ersetzt werden.

Zweiter Teil: Wortarten und Satzteile

Part Two: Parts of Speech and their Functions

4 Nomen, Pronomen und Begleiter

Nouns, Pronouns and Determiners

§ 28 Singular- und Pluralformen des Nomens

The Singular and Plural Forms of Nouns

F

Singular	Plural auf *-s*	
one cat one basket	two cats two baskets	[s]
one dog one chicken	three dogs five chickens	[z]
one box a sandwich	two boxes some sandwiches	[ɪz]
one potato a hero	lots of potatoes [z] the heroes [z] of ancient Greece	
one thief one wolf	a gang of thieves [vz] a pack of wolves [vz]	
one dead body one boy	two dead bodies [ɪz] two boys [z]	

1. Plural auf *-s*

Die Pluralform wird im Englischen bei der überwiegenden Zahl der Nomen auf *-s* gebildet.
Aussprache: [-s] nach stimmlosem Laut [p, t, k, etc.], sonst [-z].

Nach Zischlauten [s, z, ʃ, tʃ, dʒ] kann die *s*-Endung nicht direkt angefügt werden. Es tritt *-es* ein. **Aussprache:** [-ɪz].

Bei einigen Nomen auf *-o* [-əʊ] wird ebenfalls *-es* angehängt.
Aber: *photos, radios, studios*

Nomen, die auf *-f* oder *-fe* enden, bilden den Plural zumeist auf *-ves.*
Aber: *roofs, proofs, chiefs, handkerchiefs*

Bei Nomen, die auf Konsonant + *-y* enden, tritt im Plural *-ies* ein.
Nach Vokal bleibt jedoch das *-y* erhalten.

Singular	Umlaut-Plural / Plural auf *-en* Endungsloser Plural
one man/woman one foot/tooth one ox a child	two men/women two feet/teeth two oxen many children
one fish one sheep	hundreds of fish a flock of sheep

2. Sonstige Pluralformen

Bei einigen Nomen wird die Pluralform durch Umlaut gebildet (vgl. Deutsch: *Fuß/Füße).*
Weitere Beispiele: *goose/geese, mouse/mice*
Bei *ox* und *child* wird der Plural auf *-(r)en* gebildet.

Einige wenige Nomen weisen für Singular und Plural die gleiche Form auf („endungsloser Plural").

H

bacillus — bacilli [aɪ]
crisis — crises [i:z]

Einige Wörter, die aus dem Lateinischen oder Griechischen übernommen wurden, haben im Englischen ihre ursprüngliche Pluralform beibehalten.

§ 29 Nomen, die nur im Singular oder nur im Plural auftreten
Nouns Used Only in the Singular or Only in the Plural

V

1. Wie im Deutschen kommen im Englischen viele Stoffbezeichnungen *(milk)* und Abstrakta *(music)* nur im Singular vor, andere Nomen nur im Plural (z. B. *parents*/ Eltern). In manchen Fällen weicht der englische Sprachgebrauch jedoch vom deutschen ab:

Im Englischen nur Singular

Sammelbegriffe wie *furniture*

The furniture in the living-room is getting very shabby.
Die Möbel ... werden ...
Father's **hair** is getting thin on top.
Vaters Haare werden ...

Ebenso: *machinery* (Maschinen), *garbage* (Abfälle)

Abstrakte Nomen wie *knowledge*

Our knowledge of outer space is still very limited.
Unsere Kenntnisse ... sind ...
Great **progress** in space research has been made with the help of satellites and spacelabs.
Große Fortschritte ... sind ...

Ebenso: *information* (Information/Informationen), *advice* (Rat/Ratschläge)

Im Englischen nur Plural

Sammelbegriffe wie *clothes*

Ladies' **clothes** are on the first floor.
Damenkleidung befindet sich ...
The stairs are over there in the corner.
Die Treppe ist ...

Ebenso: *goods* (Ware), *wages* (Lohn), *earnings* (Verdienst), *surroundings* (Umgebung)

"Doubles" wie *trousers*

He always wears **trousers,** never **shorts** even on the hottest day. ... eine lange Hose, nie eine kurze Hose ...

I have never seen him without his dark **glasses.**
... ohne seine dunkle Brille ...

Kennzeichen von "doubles" ist, daß sie jeweils aus zwei Teilen bestehen. Weitere Beispiele: *jeans, pyjamas* (Schlafanzug), *scissors* (Schere), *scales* (Waage)

2. Im Deutschen richten sich die Personalform des Verbs, die Pronomen und die Begleiter grundsätzlich nach der äußeren Form (Singular oder Plural) des Nomens. Im Englischen dagegen ist ausschlaggebend, ob das Nomen als **Einheit** aufgefaßt wird (*physics:* **ein** Fach) oder als **„Vielheit"** (*the police:* **viele** Polizisten):

Nomen mit Pluralendung aber: Verbform, Pronomen, Begleiter im Singular

Physics is my favourite subject. **It** is difficult, but never boring.
The USA leads the world in space research.

Diese Nomen werden trotz Pluralendung als Einheit aufgefaßt und wie die Singularformen anderer Nomen verwendet. Ebenso: *mathematics, electronics, economics, politics, statistics* (als Lehrfach); Spiele wie *billards, darts,* etc.; *news (Here is the news.); the UN, the Netherlands.*

Nomen mit Singular-Form aber: Verbform, Pronomen, Begleiter im Plural

The police patrol the streets day and night. **They carry** walkie-talkies to call headquarters in an emergency.
Die Polizei patroulliert ...
Most people work a five-day week. **They** can't imagine working on Saturdays as **their** parents often had to.

Diese Gruppenbezeichnungen werden stets als Summe ihrer Mitglieder, als „Vielheit" aufgefaßt und wie die Pluralformen anderer Nomen verwendet. Ebenso: *cattle* (Vieh, Rinder), *clergy* (Klerus, Geistliche)

3. Nomen, die nur im Singular oder Plural auftreten, können nicht mit Zahlwörtern oder mit dem unbestimmten Artikel verbunden werden (Ausnahme: *four people*). Soweit Mengenangaben sinnvoll und nötig sind, verwendet man daher eine Umschreibung:

Mengenangaben mit *pair of* bei "doubles"

A pair of pyjamas	ein Schlafanzug
Five pairs of shorts	fünf kurze Hosen

H The Eskimoes are **a** peaceful **people.**
The **peoples** of the world hope for lasting peace.

In der Bedeutung „Volk" kommt *people* sowohl im Singular als auch im Plural vor.

Beachte auch folgende Bedeutungsunterschiede:

to look at **the pictures** in a book (... **Bilder** ...)
to go to **the pictures** (ins **Kino** gehen)

the customs of a people (... **Sitten** ...)
to smuggle s.th. through **the customs** (... durch den **Zoll** ...)

a table **cloth** [klɒθ], two table **cloths** [klɒθs] (Tisch**tuch**/-**tücher**)
ladies' **clothes** [kləʊðz] (Damen**kleidung**/-**kleider**)

Mengenangaben mit *some/piece of*

bei Stoffbezeichnungen

Would you like **some tea** and **a piece of cake?**

Je nach Art des Stoffes werden auch andere Mengenangaben verwendet (vgl. § 61).
Zum Gebrauch von *some/any* als Mengenangaben vgl. § 44.

bei Abstrakta

Here is **some information** for visitors from abroad.
... eine Information ...

bei Sammelbegriffen

There were several beautiful **pieces of furniture** in the shop window. ... einige schöne Möbel(stücke) ...

§ 30 Gruppenbezeichnungen wie *family/team*
Collective Nouns such as *family/team*

V *Family* und einige andere Gruppenbezeichnungen können — im Gegensatz zu *police* (§ 29 V 2) — ganz normal Singular und Plural bilden *(two families)*. Im Singular gibt es dabei zwei Möglichkeiten:

Gruppe als Summe der Mitglieder: Verbform, Pronomen, Begleiter im Plural

The family **have** all come together to celebrate grandmother's 90th birthday. **They are** sitting around the table and enjoying the birthday cake.
Our team always **lose their heads** in important matches.

Hier wird betont, was die einzelnen Mitglieder tun, nicht die Gruppe als Ganzes. Diese Betrachtungsweise ist im Englischen sehr häufig, vor allem auch bei *audience, class, club, crew, crowd, government.*

Gruppe als Einheit: Verbform, Pronomen, Begleiter im Singular

My family **has** lived in Brighton since the early 18th century. **It has** always been one of the leading families in the town.

Our local football team **is** not at **its** best this season.

Hier werden — wie stets im Deutschen — *family* und *team* als Einheit aufgefaßt, da es auf die Gesamtheit der Familie bzw. der Mannschaft ankommt, nicht auf die einzelnen Mitglieder.

H **A large number** of cars **were** involved in the accident.
Half of the cars **were** seriously damaged.
The majority of road accidents **are** caused by carelessness.

Bei diesen Mengenangaben stehen die Verbformen im Plural, d. h. es herrscht die Vorstellung von der Summe der Bestandteile vor.

§ 31 Nationalitätenbezeichnungen
Nationality Words

F

Country	Adjective	Individuals	The People
Germany	a **German** firm	a German/ several Germans	the Germans
Japan	a **Japanese** camera	a Japanese	the Japanese
England	an **English** pub	an Englishman/ an Englishwoman	the English
France	a **French** bistro	a Frenchman/-woman	the French
Spain	a **Spanish** dance	a Spaniard/ some Spaniards	the Spanish/ the Spaniards

Zur Verwendung ist zu beachten:

1. *German, American, Canadian,* etc. werden wie normale Nomen mit Plural-*s* gebraucht.
2. Nationalitätenbezeichnungen auf *-ese* erscheinen nie mit Plural-*s*.
3. *English, French* und andere Nationalitätenbezeichnungen auf *-sh* und *-ch* können nur die Gesamtheit eines Volkes, nicht einzelne Einwohner bezeichnen (vgl. § 48).

§ 32 Subjekts- und Objektsformen des Personalpronomens
The Subject and Object Forms of Personal Pronouns

F

Subjektsformen	I	you	he	she	it	we	you	they
Objektsformen	me	you	him	her	it	us	you	them

Für die meisten Personen weist das Personalpronomen neben der Subjektsform eine besondere Objektsform auf.

V

Die Objektsform des Personalpronomens übernimmt grundsätzlich die Funktionen der deutschen Akkusativ- und Dativform.
Vergleiche: *Yesterday we saw* ***them*** (sie) *at the bus stop and offered* ***them*** (ihnen) *a lift.*
Darüber hinaus wird die Objektsform in folgenden Fällen an Stelle der deutschen Nominativform gebraucht:

Objektsform nach dem Verb *be*

"It's **me,** Linda."	**Ich** bin's, Linda.
"That must be **him.**"	Das muß **er** sein.
"You needn't worry. It's only **us.**"	... **Wir** sind's nur.

Nach den Formen von *be* wird vorwiegend die Objektsform verwendet, vor allem in der Umgangssprache.

Objektsform in Vergleichen

"I scarcely recognized you. You're as tall as **me** now and much bigger than **him.**"
"Young people today are much more adventurous than **us.**"
(Aber: They are much more adventurous than **we** are.)

In Vergleichen tritt die Objektsform ein, wenn das Pronomen nicht einen Nebensatz einleitet.

H

They say that schooldays are the happiest days of one's life. But I think that's rubbish.
You never know what can happen in an oral exam. The examiners pass **you** or fail **you,** just as they like.

Oft beziehen sich *they* und *you* nicht auf bestimmte Personen, sondern entsprechen den unpersönlichen Pronomen *man* bzw. *einem/einen.*

V

§ 33 Die Personalpronomen *he/she/it* und das Genus der Nomen
The Personal Pronouns *he/she/it* and the Gender of Nouns

Welches Genus (grammatisches Geschlecht) ein Nomen im Englischen besitzt, geht aus dem Artikel nicht hervor. Das Genus zeigt sich jedoch, wenn das Nomen durch *he/she/it* vertreten wird. Nach dem Prinzip des natürlichen Geschlechts unterscheidet man grundsätzlich zwischen **Personen** und **Dingen.**

Verwendung von *he* und *she*

generell für Personen

he: boy, Mr Scott, husband, uncle, actor, etc.
she: girl, Mrs Scott, wife, aunt, actress, etc.

teacher, cook, etc.

Do you like our English **teacher? — She**'s very friendly, isn't **she? —** And what about the Maths **teacher? — He** looks rather strict, but **he** isn't really.

Nomen wie *teacher, doctor, nurse, cook, driver, reader* können je nach Sinnzusammenhang eine männliche oder eine weibliche Person bezeichnen.

child, baby

"Look at the **baby!** Isn't **she** funny?"

Je nach Geschlecht tritt *he* oder *she* ein.

Tiere

This is **Leo. He** is the oldest **lion** in our zoo.
Look at **Pussy** drinking that saucer of milk. **She** is always thirsty.

Für Tiere, zu denen der Sprecher eine besondere Beziehung hat (z. B. Haustiere), können *he* oder *she* eintreten. Meist haben solche Tiere Namen.

Verwendung von *it*

generell für Dinge

"Where's Aunt Margaret's **letter**?" ... Brief?
"**It**'s on the bookshelf." **Er** ist ...

"Where's the **newspaper**?" ... die Zeitung?
"**It**'s on the floor." **Sie** ist ...

"Where's the **book** I'm reading?" ... das Buch ...?
"**It**'s in the bedroom where you left **it**." **Es** ist ...

child, baby

A small **child** needs a lot of sleep. **It** must go to bed early.

In allgemeinen Aussagen erscheint gelegentlich *it.*

Tiere

A **cat** isn't much trouble. **It** looks after itself most of the time.
That **wasp** is getting on my nerves. **It** keeps flying round my head.

Für Tiere, zu denen keine persönliche Beziehung besteht, verwendet man *it.*

H

"What do you think of my new **car?** Isn't **she (it)** a beauty?"
The **Queen Elizabeth** was a wonderful **ship. She (It)** was something the whole nation was proud of.

She kann auch für **Dinge** stehen, zu denen der Sprecher ein besonderes, persönliches Verhältnis hat, besonders für Autos und Schiffe.

North Sea oil has changed many things in **Scotland. She (It)** is no longer one of the poorer nations in Europe.

Auch Länder und Nationen können mit *she* bezeichnet werden, vor allem wenn sie nicht als geographische Begriffe, sondern als wirtschaftliche oder politische Mächte aufgefaßt werden.

§ 34 Das Pronomen auf *-self / -selves*
The Pronouns Ending in *-self/-selves*

F

myself, yourself, himself, herself, itself, oneself
ourselves, yourselves, themselves

Die Singularformen enden auf *-self,* die Pluralformen auf *-selves.*

V

Das Pronomen auf *-self/-selves* tritt in zwei verschiedenen Funktionen auf:

Verstärkender Gebrauch

We like **the house itself,** but it's at a very busy crossing.
... das Haus selbst ...
The **house owners themselves** helped us with the repairs.
... die Hauseigentümer selbst ...
Henry has redecorated his room **himself.**
Henry ... selbst ...
When we moved into our new flat **we** installed the central heating **ourselves.** ... wir ... selbst ...

Das Pronomen auf *-self/-selves* kann zur Hervorhebung eines Nomens oder Pronomens dienen. Es tritt direkt hinter das hervorzuhebende Wort. Wenn das Subjekt hervorgehoben wird, steht es jedoch häufig auch am Satzende.

⚠

1. Zu beachten ist, daß die Pluralform der 2. Person mit *-selves* gebildet wird. (**euch** = *yourselves*)
2. *Remember* wird nie reflexiv konstruiert.

Reflexiver Gebrauch (im Englischen eingeschränkt!)

"May I **introduce myself?** My name is Smith."
Darf ich mich vorstellen?
"Help yourselves. The drinks are on the table."
Bedient Euch!

Das Pronomen auf *-self/-selves* wird reflexiv (rückbezüglich) verwendet, wenn Subjekt und Objekt dieselbe Person bezeichnen.

englisch: nicht reflexiv/deutsch: reflexiv

He suddenly **remembered** his promise to prepare breakfast for the family. ... erinnerte sich ...
He jumped out of bed and **dressed** (himself) quickly.
... zog sich ... an

Das Reflexivpronomen ist im Englischen weit seltener als im Deutschen. Vielen reflexiven deutschen Verben entspricht im Englischen ein nicht reflexiver Ausdruck, z. B. *sich erinnern: to remember.* Weitere häufige Fälle sind:

sich fürchten	*be afraid*	sich freuen auf	*look forward to*
sich entschuldigen	*apologise*	sich bewegen	*move*
sich ändern	*change*	sich öffnen	*open*
sich ereignen	*happen*	sich erinnern	*remember*
sich beeilen	*hurry*	sich setzen	*sit down*
sich vorstellen	*imagine*	sich fragen	*wonder*

Bei *wash, shave, dress* und *hide* ist das Reflexivpronomen möglich, aber nicht nötig.

§ 35 Reflexivpronomen und reziproke Pronomen
Reflexive and Reciprocal Pronouns

V

Das Reflexivpronomen der 3. Person Plural *(themselves)* ist zu unterscheiden von den reziproken Pronomen *(each other/ one another).* Im Deutschen steht für beide Fälle *sich.*

Reflexivpronomen: sich selbst

The travellers defended **themselves** against the bandits.

Reziproke Pronomen: sich gegenseitig/einander

The two bandits helped **each other** to escape from prison.
Criminals often don't trust **one another.**

Each other wird vornehmlich bei zwei, *one another* bei mehreren Personen gebraucht.

§ 36 Der Possessivbegleiter und seine Verstärkung durch *own*
Possessive Determiners and the Effect of Adding *own*

F

my jacket	**our** shoes
your scarf	**your** boots
his jeans, **her** blouse, **its** buttons	**their** clothes

Die Formen des Possessivbegleiters sind mit denen des Personalpronomens verwandt: *me/my, you/your,* etc.; *her* kann sowohl Possessivbegleiter als auch Personalpronomen sein. Zu den Formen des Possessivpronomens vgl. § 38

V

1. Der Possessivbegleiter tritt im Englischen häufiger auf als im Deutschen, vor allem bei Körperteilen und Kleidungsstücken, sowie bei einigen abstrakten Begriffen wie *life* und *mind.*

Possessivbegleiter bei Körperteilen, Kleidungsstücken und einigen abstrakten Begriffen	
The other day **one of my friends** fell off his motorbike and broke **his leg.** ... sich **das** Bein. **He** also hit **his head** and injured **his left arm.** ... **den** Kopf ... **He** never takes off **his crash helmet** even if he stops for a cup of coffee. ... **den** Sturzhelm ...	Der Possessivbegleiter muß bei Körperteilen oder Kleidungsstücken einer Person verwendet werden, wenn diese Subjekt des Satzes ist.
Possessivbegleiter bei *life* und *mind* My friend nearly lost **her** life on holiday. She has now changed **her** mind about the joys of swimming in the sea.	Auch *life* und *mind* werden mit dem Possessivbegleiter verbunden.

H Thousands of people lose **their lives** in road accidents every year. ... kommen ... ums Leben.

Steht das Subjekt des Satzes im Plural, so müssen auch die Pluralformen *lives* und *minds* verwendet werden.

⚠ Der Possessivbegleiter *its* darf nicht mit der Kurzform *it's (it is)* verwechselt werden.

V

2. Der Possessivbegleiter kann durch *own* verstärkt werden.

Possessivbegleiter + *own* vor dem Nomen	***of* + Possessivbegleiter + *own* nach dem Nomen**
Margaret's got **her own** TV set now. In our new house the children will all have **their own** rooms.	Peter doesn't spend much time with the family because he's got **a** TV set **of his own.** ... einen eigenen Fernsehapparat. In the new house the children will have **a** bathroom **of their own.** ... ein eigenes Bad ...
Possessivbegleiter + *own* können vor dem Nomen stehen, wenn kein unbestimmter Artikel oder Zahlwort vorausgeht.	Soll ein unbestimmter Artikel oder ein Zahlwort verwendet werden, so wird *own* in der Form *of my own, of her own,* etc. dem Nomen nachgestellt.

⚠ Im Gegensatz zum deutschen *eigen* muß dem englischen *own* immer ein Possessivbegleiter vorangehen.

§ 37 *S*-Genitiv und *of-phrase*

The *s*-Genitive and the *of*-Phrase

F

Father's pipe ['fɑːðəz] My **parents'** records ['peərənts]	Regelmäßige Bildung des s-Genitivs: Im Singular treten Apostroph + *s* an das Nomen; im Plural wird an das Plural-*s* ein Apostroph angefügt.
The **children's** books ['tʃɪldrənz] **James's** tapes ['dʒeɪmzɪz] **Dickens'** books; ['dɪkɪnz]/['dɪkɪnzɪz] Mrs **Jones's** hat ['dʒəʊnzɪz]	Bei unregelmäßigen Pluralformen, die nicht auf -*s* enden: Apostroph + *s* Bei Vornamen auf -*s*: Apostroph + *s* (Aussprache [-ɪz]) Bei Familiennamen auf -*s*: Apostroph + *s* oder nur ein Apostroph Zur Aussprache [s]/[z]/[ɪz] vgl. die Bemerkungen zum Plural-*s* in § 28.
The headlights **of the car**	*Of* wird immer als Schwachform ausgesprochen: [əv].

V Wichtig für die Wahl von *s*-Genitiv oder *of-phrase* ist die Unterscheidung von Personen und Dingen.

S-Genitiv

generell bei Personen

I've brought **your son's guitar.**
He left it behind at **the Browns' party** last night.

bei Tieren

I've put **Tibby's basket** near the radiator to keep her warm.
A bird's cage should be kept well away from cats.

Der *s*-Genitiv ist bei Tieren selbst dann möglich, wenn man das Personalpronomen *it* verwenden würde (vgl. § 33).

bei Ländern, Ortsnamen, Institutionen

What do you think of **England's chances** of winning the World Cup?
WOLVERHAMPTON'S STADIUM TO BE MODERNIZED

Auch bei Ländern, Ortsnamen und Institutionen (wie *government*) ist der *s*-Genitiv verbreitet.

bei Zeitangaben

There is a travel section in **today's newspaper.**
A three weeks' holiday is more than I can afford.
(Möglich auch: A three-week holiday ...)

Auch bei Zeitangaben wie *day, minute, evening, today, yesterday* wird häufig der *s*-Genitiv verwendet.

of-phrase

generell bei Dingen

He's got safety belts on **the back seats of his car.**
The lights of that lorry don't work properly.

bei Personen

a) Where is **the luggage of the lady from New York?**
b) **The portrait of Churchill** was destroyed by his wife.

Die *of-phrase* bei Personen ist nur in Sonderfällen möglich, z. B.
a) wenn sonst ein besonders langer Ausdruck im Genitiv erscheinen würde, oder
b) um klarzustellen, daß kein Besitz- oder Urheberverhältnis vorliegt. *The portrait of Churchill* bedeutet: Churchill ist auf dem Bild dargestellt. *Churchill's portrait* dagegen könnte auch bedeuten: Das Portrait gehört Churchill, oder: Churchill hat es gemalt.

bei Entfernungs- und Mengenangaben

On the school outing the class walked **a distance of 20 miles.**
A group of students was waiting for the teacher.

Die *of-phrase* wird bei Entfernungsangaben, vor allem aber bei Mengenangaben benutzt (vgl. § 61).

§ 38 Der *s*-Genitiv ohne nachfolgendes Nomen und das Possessivpronomen
The *s*-Genitive without a Noun and the Possessive Pronouns

F

Whose house is this?	It's **Bob's.**	It's **the Bartons'.**
	It's **mine/yours.**	It's **ours/yours.**
	It's **his/hers.**	It's **theirs.**

Zu den Formen des *s*-Genitivs vgl. § 37.

Das Possessivpronomen besteht, außer bei *mine* und *his,* aus Possessivbegleiter und *s*-Endung (vgl. § 36).

V

Der *s*-Genitiv kann gelegentlich ohne Bezugswort (= nachfolgendes Nomen) stehen, nämlich dann, wenn dieses aus dem Sinnzusammenhang erschlossen werden kann. Entsprechend kann für Possessivbegleiter *(my)* + Bezugswort ein Possessivpronomen *(mine)* eintreten.

s-Genitiv ohne Bezugswort / Possessivpronomen statt Possessivbegleiter + Bezugswort	
Bezugswort vorher genannt	**Ausdrücke wie *at the newsagent's***
That's a really nice **camera.** Is it **yours?** — No, it's **my father's.** **Whose bike** is that outside? — It must be **Peter's.** **Whose books** are those on the dining-room table? — They are **mine.** I'll put them away in a minute.	If you want to buy picture postcards you can get them at **Smith's** in the High Street or at any **newsagent's.** We can buy some stamps on the way to **Aunt Mary's.** I think I'll send my family this postcard of **St Paul's.**
Wurde das Bezugswort schon vorher genannt, so braucht es nicht wiederholt zu werden. Dies ist z. B. meistens der Fall bei Fragen mit *whose.*	Bei Geschäften, Privatwohnungen und bekannten Gebäuden wird das Bezugswort (*shop, house, cathedral,* etc.) als bekannt vorausgesetzt, auch wenn es nicht vorher erwähnt wurde.

H

The new headmaster is **a friend of my father's.**	... ein Freund (aus dem Freundeskreis) meines Vaters.
Last term **two essays of mine** were printed in the school magazine.	... zwei Aufsätze von mir ...

Wenn vor dem Bezugswort *(friend, essay)* der unbestimmte Artikel oder ein Zahlwort steht, wird der „doppelte Genitiv" verwendet. Er besteht aus *of-phrase* und *s*-Genitiv bzw. Possessivpronomen.

§ 39 Der bestimmte Artikel
The Definite Article

F

the [ðə]	**the** [ðɪ]
the plane the flight the new airport the European airlines the USA	the English plane the early flight the airport the hour of departure the SAS plane
'Freeway' is **the** ['ði:] travel agency for charter flights.	

Der bestimmte Artikel wird immer *the* geschrieben.
Die Aussprache ist vor Konsonanten [ðə], vor Vokalen [ðɪ].

Ausschlaggebend ist dabei, wie der Anlaut des folgenden Wortes ausgesprochen wird, nicht wie er geschrieben wird (vgl.: *the USA* [ðəju:es'eɪ], *the hour* [ðɪ 'aʊə]).

Wird der bestimmte Artikel besonders betont, so wird er auch vor Konsonanten [ði:] ausgesprochen.

V Der bestimmte Artikel dient im Englischen nicht zur Klärung des Genus und ist seltener als im Deutschen. Er tritt nur dann auf, wenn Personen und Dinge tatsächlich näher bestimmt werden. (*The hospital* bedeutet z. B. fast immer *this* oder *that hospital.*)

Nomen nicht näher bestimmt: OHNE Artikel	Nomen näher bestimmt: MIT Artikel
Stoffbezeichnungen und Abstrakta	**Stoffbezeichnungen und Abstrakta**
Water is scarce in many parts of the world. **Rice** is mainly grown in the Far East. **Life** is often hard. **History/Modern history** is full of disasters.	**The water in our rivers** is often polluted. **The rice I like best** comes from Bali. **The life of an Indian coolie** is very hard. He is an expert on **the history of India.**
Beachte: Auch wenn ein Adjektiv vorausgeht, können Abstrakta als allgemeine Begriffe aufgefaßt werden und stehen dann ohne Artikel.	Werden Stoffbezeichnungen oder Abstrakta auf besondere Fälle eingeschränkt, z. B. durch einen Relativsatz oder eine *of-phrase,* so steht der bestimmte Artikel.
Institutionen und Verkehrsmittel	**Institutionen und Verkehrsmittel**
School usually begins at nine in England. Not many people go to **church** every Sunday. My sister had to spend Christmas in **hospital.** Few people know what life in **prison** is like. Today more people travel **by car** than **by train.**	**The school** I go to is very modern. **The church** in the market place was built in 1425. **The hospital** is right next to **the prison.** **The bus** to London leaves from the town hall.
Der bestimmte Artikel steht nicht, wenn an den Zweck der Institution (Unterricht, Gottesdienst, etc.) gedacht wird. Bei *by* + Verkehrsmittel ist die Verkehrsverbindung gemeint.	Der bestimmte Artikel wird verwendet, wenn an eine ganz bestimmte Schule, Kirche, etc., ein bestimmtes Gebäude oder Fahrzeug gedacht wird.
Jahreszeiten, Monate, Wochentage, Mahlzeiten	**Jahreszeiten, Monate, Wochentage, Mahlzeiten**
Spring seems to be late this year. **July** and **August** are the most popular holiday months. The working week starts on **Monday.** On weekdays **breakfast** is often eaten in a hurry and **lunch** is rarely more than a snack.	**The summer (The July) of 1976** was unusually hot and dry. I'll never forget **the Monday I started my new job.** **The English breakfast** is quite a large meal. **The lunch we had at the hotel** cost over £ 10.
Diese Nomen stehen ohne den bestimmten Artikel, wenn sie im allgemeinen Sinne verwendet werden.	Der bestimmte Artikel tritt ein, wenn diese Nomen durch eine nähere Bestimmung auf einen konkreten Fall begrenzt werden.

H Zum Gebrauch von Präpositionen bei Zeitangaben s. § 59. Zum Datum s. § 56.

§ 40 Der bestimmte Artikel bei Namen
The Definite Article with Names

V Namen (darunter fallen auch geographische Namen) bezeichnen im Singular etwas Einzigartiges und müssen deshalb nicht näher bestimmt werden. Sie treten im Englischen meist ohne den bestimmten Artikel auf.

OHNE bestimmten Artikel	MIT bestimmtem Artikel
Personennamen im Singular	**Personennamen im Plural**
Peter often goes to the cinema with **Margaret.** **Father** and **Mother** watch TV most evenings. **Poor old Tom** hasn't even got a radio.	**The Scotts** and **the Whites** are neighbours. **The Bartons** are the only family I know who haven't got a television set.
Personennamen im Singular und wie Namen gebrauchte Verwandtschaftsbezeichnungen stehen ohne den bestimmten Artikel, auch dann, wenn ihnen ein Adjektiv vorausgeht.	Familiennamen im Plural stehen mit dem bestimmten Artikel.
Ländernamen im Singular, Berggipfel	**Ländernamen im Plural, Gebirge**
Some people believe that **Mont Blanc** is situated in **Switzerland,** but in fact it is in France. (... **der** Mont Blanc ... in **der** Schweiz ...) **Snowdon** is the highest mountain in Wales.	**The United States** and **the Netherlands** are both members of NATO. **The Alps** and **the Rocky Mountains** contain some of the most dramatic scenery in the world.
Die meisten Ländernamen im Singular und Namen von Berggipfeln stehen ohne den bestimmten Artikel. (Ausnahmen: The USSR, the Sudan)	Außer Familiennamen stehen auch alle anderen im Plural gebrauchten Eigennamen mit dem bestimmten Artikel.
Seen	**Flüsse und Meere (oder Meeresteile)**
Lake Constance lies between Switzerland, Austria and Germany. **Der** Bodensee ...	**The Rhine** flows into **the North Sea.** **The English Channel** connects **the North Sea** and **the Atlantic.**
Gebäude und Straßen	
Buckingham Palace is surrounded by parks and gardens. **Oxford Street** is London's most popular shopping street.	

H Namen, die eine *of-phrase* enthalten, haben stets den bestimmten Artikel bei sich, z. B. *the Isle of Man, the Cape of Good Hope, the Gulf of Mexico.* Bei bekannten Sehenswürdigkeiten kann die *of-phrase* entfallen, z. B. *the Tower (of London), the House (of Commons).*

§ 41 Der unbestimmte Artikel
The Indefinite Article

F

a [ə]	**an** [ən]
a plane	an English plane
a large airport	an airport
a UFO	an SAS plane
a European airline	an hour's wait

Der unbestimmte Artikel lautet vor Konsonanten *a* [ə], vor Vokalen *an* [ən].

Ausschlaggebend ist dabei, wie der Anlaut des folgenden Worts gesprochen wird, nicht wie er geschrieben wird. (Vgl. § 39 F)

V

1. Bei der Angabe von Beruf, Nationalität und Religion unterscheidet sich die Verwendung des unbestimmten Artikels vom Deutschen:

MIT unbestimmtem Artikel	**OHNE unbestimmten Artikel**
Berufsbezeichnungen	**Titel**
Jennifer Brown is **a stewardess** with British Airways. ... ist Stewardess ... Jim is employed as **a bus driver.** ... als Busfahrer.	Elizabeth II became **Queen** at the age of 28. Not many people would like to be **President** of the USA.
Nationalität, Religion	Der unbestimmte Artikel entfällt vor Titeln, die als einmalig empfunden werden. Dabei ist es unerheblich, daß es auf der Welt z. B. mehrere Präsidenten oder Königinnen gibt.
Carmen is **a Spaniard,** ... ist Spanierin, but her husband **an Englishman.** ... ist Engländer. Jack is **a Catholic,** ... ist Katholik, but his wife is **a Baptist.** ... ist Baptistin.	

H

Carmen is **Spanish.** Zur Angabe der Nationalität kann statt des Nomens auch ein Adjektiv verwendet werden.

V

2. Beachte zur Stellung des unbestimmten Artikels:

Normalstellung des unbestimmten Artikels	**Nachstellung des unbestimmten Artikels**
It was **a very** hot day. "**A quarter** pound of tea, please."	**What a** lovely day! It was **such a** hot day that he decided to take a shower. He often spends **half an** hour under the shower. Cold water can be **quite a** shock.
Normalerweise hat der unbestimmte Artikel die gleiche Stellung wie im Deutschen.	Bei *what!* (was für!), *quite, such, half* wird der unbestimmte Artikel nachgestellt.

H

Bob was in **a** hurry, as he always is. He looked very tired and said he had **a** headache.

Abweichend vom Deutschen steht der unbestimmte Artikel auch bei Ausdrücken wie *in a hurry, to have a headache.*

§ 42 Der unbestimmte Artikel bei Maß- und Zeiteinheiten
The Indefinite Article with Units of Quantity and Time

V

Der unbestimmte Artikel in der Bedeutung von *pro/je*	
bei Maßeinheiten	**bei Zeiteinheiten**
In winter tomatoes are 50p **a** pound. ... 50p **pro/je** Pfund. Good French wine can cost as much as £15 **a** bottle. ... £15 **pro/je** Flasche.	Mrs Black goes shopping once **a** week. ... **in der** Woche ... She spends about £150 **a** month on food. ... **im** Monat ...

§ 43 *Much/many* und ihre Ersatzformen
Much/many and Related Expressions

V Ob *much* oder *many* gebraucht wird, hängt davon ab, ob das zugehörige Nomen im Singular oder Plural steht. *Much* und *many* sind in keinem Fall austauschbar.

***Much* bei Stoffnamen und Abstrakta (Singular)**	***Many* bei Pluralformen**
***Much* in verneinten Sätzen und Fragen**	***Many* in allen Satztypen**
How **much** money do you spend on books? — Not **much.** I wouldn't like to study medicine, it's too **much** work.	The average student can't afford **many** books these days. Do you read **many** short stories at school? There are **many (lots of)** school programmes on radio and television these days. **Many (A large number of)** film and television programmes are used in schools today.
Much erscheint außer in verneinten Sätzen und Fragen auch in den Verbindungen *very much, too much, so much, as much.*	
Ersatzformen in bejahten Sätzen	
People say that doctors earn **a great deal of** money. Doctors in hospitals certainly have **a lot of** work to do.	*Many* kommt in allen Satztypen vor. Im bejahten Satz können aber auch Ausdrücke wie *a lot of, lots of* usw. stehen.
Im bejahten Satz treten Ersatzformen wie *a lot of, a good deal of,* etc. ein.	

H I wish I were a doctor. There are **few** jobs that are more satisfying.
I get **little** satisfaction from my present job.

Parallel zu *much* und *many* wird *little* (wenig) bei Singularformen (Stoffnamen und Abstrakta) verwendet, *few* (wenige) bei Pluralformen.

⚠ Zu beachten ist, daß *much* und *little* (= wenig) nie mit Pluralformen verwendet werden.

§ 44 *Some/any* als Mengenangaben
Some/any Used as Quantifiers

F

We need **some** milk and **some** potatoes.

We haven't got **any** tea in the house.
We haven't got **any** biscuits either.

There's **no** sugar left.
There is**n't any** sugar left.

Als Mengenangaben werden *some* und *any* unbetont ausgesprochen:
some [səm/sm], *any* [ˌenɪ].

In anderen Bedeutungen werden *some/any* betont (vgl. § 45).

Statt *not any* kann *no* verwendet werden, doch ist *not any* häufiger.

V

Soll eine nicht näher bestimmte Menge bezeichnet werden, so kann im Englischen das Nomen nicht allein stehen. Deshalb werden vor Stoffbezeichnungen und Abstrakta sowie vor Pluralformen entweder *some* oder *any* verwendet: *Some* steht, wenn der Sprecher davon ausgeht, daß etwas tatsächlich vorhanden oder möglich ist, sonst tritt *any* ein.

Positive Sicht: *some*	**Negative Sicht oder Ungewißheit: *any***
Bejahte Aussagesätze	**Verneinte Aussagesätze**
Look, they've got **some** fresh farm eggs in that shop. ... frische Landeier ... Let's buy **some** of those eggs and **some** bacon for breakfast tomorrow. ... ein paar von diesen Eiern ... etwas Speck ... It takes **some** time to find where things are in a modern supermarket. Man braucht (schon etwas) Zeit ...	Sorry, we have**n't** got **any** peaches. We're sold out. We wo**n't** have **any** fresh fruit until Monday morning. **Einschränkende Adverbien** There are **hardly any** grocers these days, only supermarkets. Nach einschränkenden Adverbien wie *scarcely, hardly* steht *any.*
Fragesätze	**Fragesätze**
Would you like **some** cake with your tea? No, thank you. Could I have **some** biscuits instead?	Is there **any** tea left in the pot? Have you got **any** chocolate biscuits?
Some wird auch in Fragesätzen verwendet, wenn eine positive Antwort erwartet wird. Die Fragen sind dabei im Grunde Bitten, Aufforderungen oder Vorschläge, **also nur der Form nach Fragen.**	*Any* wird verwendet, wenn der Sprecher nicht weiß, ob die Antwort ja oder nein lautet. Es handelt sich hier also um **echte Fragen.**

H

Could I have **something** to eat? I haven't had **anything** since breakfast.
Somebody (someone) came to see me just after one o'clock and by the time he left I couldn't go out for lunch because there wasn't **anywhere** open.

Die Erläuterungen zu *some/any* gelten entsprechend auch für Zusammensetzungen mit *some/any (-body, -one, -where, -thing).*

§ 45 *Some/any/each/every/all*

V 1. In folgenden Bedeutungen wird *some* betont und mit vollem Vokal ausgesprochen (vgl. § 44):

Some **[sʌm]: irgendein**	***Some*** **[sʌm] . . . *others:* manche . . . andere**
The Blacks have moved to **some place in the North,** but I can't remember its name. **Some man** was asking for the Blacks yesterday.	**Some (people)** enjoy living in big cities, **others** prefer the peace of the countryside.
Some bezeichnet hier eine nicht näher bekannte Person oder Sache.	*Some* in der Bedeutung „manche" wird häufig mit *others* kontrastiert.

2. Dem deutschen *jeder* entsprechen im Englischen *any* (betont), *each* und *every.*
Sie haben verschiedene Bedeutungen und sind deshalb nicht beliebig austauschbar.
Bei *all* sind zwei Verwendungen zu unterscheiden.

Every: jeder, **ohne Ausnahme**	***Each: jeder*** **aus einer Gruppe**
Every house in the street has a small front garden and a larger back garden. **Every weekend in summer** our next-door neighbour cuts the grass in his garden.	**Each of the houses in our street** has a garden. **Each / every garden in our street** is well kept.
Every bezeichnet jeden, ohne Ausnahme. Der Bedeutungsunterschied gegenüber *each* ist gering. Man könnte auch sagen: *Each house in the street . . .,* *Each weekend in summer . . .* (Vgl. rechte Spalte).	*Each* muß verwendet werden, wenn die Gruppe durch eine *of-phrase* näher bezeichnet wird. Außerdem kann es im gleichen Zusammenhang wie *every* auftreten und bedeutet dann „jeder einzelne für sich gesehen".
Any: jeder **beliebige**	***All: alle***
Any time you are in our part of the town come and see us. You can take **any of the buses** going to Stockwell.	***All*** **ohne Artikel** **All English families** would like to have a garden.
Das betonte *any* wird gebraucht, wenn man keine bestimmte Person oder Sache im Auge hat: gleichgültig welcher, jeder beliebige, irgendeiner. In dieser Bedeutung kann *any* auch im bejahten Satz auftreten, vor allem, wenn er ein Hilfsverb enthält (*can, will may,* etc.).	*All* ohne Artikel bezeichnet alle, ohne Ausnahme. (Vgl. *every*) ***All*** **mit Artikel** **All the families in our street** have got cars. *All the* bezeichnet alle aus einer begrenzten Anzahl. (Vgl. *each*).

H 1. **Everybody** in the village knows him. **Anybody** will tell you where he lives.

Die gleichen Bedeutungsunterschiede wie zwischen *every* und *any* (betont) bestehen auch zwischen ihren Zusammensetzungen *(-body, -one, -thing, -where).*

2. **Nobody** wanted to look after our dog when we were on holiday. **None of** our neighbours have got pets.

Von den negativen Formen haben *nobody* und *no one* die Bedeutung „keiner ohne Ausnahme".
None [nʌn] dagegen bezieht sich auf eine begrenzte Gruppe und tritt oft in Verbindung mit einer *of-phrase* auf.

§ 46 *Both/either/neither*

V Während *both* sich auf die Gesamtheit einer Zweiergruppe bezieht, betonen *either* und *neither* deren Bestandteile.

both: **(alle) beide**	***either/neither:*** **irgendeiner/keiner von beiden**
Both of these TV sets have got big screens. There are cowboy films on at **both** local cinemas. **Both** films were made in the 1950s.	**Either** TV set will do. Which one shall we buy? I **don't** want to see **either** of the films. **Neither** of these films was very successful.
Both bedeutet: beide = der eine **und** der andere. Im Gegensatz zum Deutschen *beide* ist es immer betont und hat nie den bestimmten Artikel vor sich.	*Either* bedeutet: der eine **oder** der andere. *Not ... either* und *neither* bedeuten: **weder** der eine **noch** der andere.

H

1. Are there no other newspapers on sale apart from **the two** local ones?
   Both our local newspapers have got detailed TV programmes.
   The two (die beiden/die zwei) betont, daß es sich um zwei und nicht um eine andere Anzahl handelt.
   Bei *both* (beide) ist es von vornherein klar, daß es sich um zwei handelt; betont wird, daß beide betroffen sind.
2. Our school has **neither** a tennis court **nor** a swimming-pool.
   If you want to play tennis you can **either** join a club **or** play on the public tennis courts.
   As our town has an indoor swimming-pool you can go swimming **both** in summer **and** in winter.

Beachte folgende Kombinationen:

neither ... nor	weder ... noch
either ... or	entweder ... oder
both ... and	sowohl ... als auch

§ 47 Demonstrativbegleiter und Demonstrativpronomen
Demonstrative Determiners and Pronouns

F

Singular:	**this** boy	**that** girl
Plural:	**these** boys	**those** girls

Beachte die unterschiedliche Aussprache von *this* [ðɪs] und *these* [ði:z].

V *This/these* und *that/those* werden oft zur Gegenüberstellung benutzt.

this/these **weisen auf Näherliegendes hin**	***that/those*** **weisen auf Entferntes hin**
örtlich näherliegend	**örtlich entfernt**
This department sells shirts and ties, ... How much are **these** cardigans here on the counter, ...	and **that** one over there sells suits and overcoats. and how much are **those** pullovers on the shelf?
zeitlich näherliegend	**zeitlich entfernt**
Earlier **this** week I went shopping in Oxford Street with my grandmother. The old lady was surprised to see that so many girls wear jeans **these** days.	The last time my grandmother went shopping in Oxford Street was in the fifties. **That** was a long time ago. In **those** days women rarely wore trousers.

H **This/That** is my book. Falls keine Gegenüberstellung beabsichtigt ist, können in der Umgangssprache *this* oder *that* verwendet werden.

5 Adjektiv und Adverb
Adjectives and Adverbs

§ 48 Das Adjektiv als Nomen
Adjectives Used as Nouns

F

Adjektiv — Nomen
a **poor** man — help for **the poor**

Adjektive haben, wenn sie wie Nomen benutzt werden, den bestimmten Artikel bei sich, jedoch kein Plural-*s*, auch wenn sie sich auf viele Menschen beziehen.

V

Im Gegensatz zum Deutschen können Adjektive im Englischen nur in sehr begrenztem Umfang als Nomen benutzt werden; häufig sind Umschreibungen nötig.

Bezeichnung einer *Gesamtgruppe* von Personen	**Bezeichnung *einzelner* Personen**
The blind are educated in special schools where, among other things, they are taught Braille. [breɪl]	**A blind person** usually has a guide dog these days. Ein Blinder ...
Als Nomen gebrauchte Adjektive beziehen sich auf die Gesamtheit einer Gruppe von Menschen: *the blind* = die Blinden allgemein / alle Blinden.	Sind einzelne Personen gemeint, so muß das Adjektiv durch ein Nomen wie *person, woman, people* ergänzt werden.
Bezeichnung einer Nation als *Gesamtheit*	**Bezeichnung *einzelner* Mitglieder einer Nation**
The English and **the Irish** have never got on very well. **The French** are among the world's leading wine producers.	You can tell an **Englishman** from an **Irishman** or a **Scotsman** as soon as he opens his mouth. There are few **Frenchmen** who never drink a glass of wine.
Auch Nationalitätenadjektive auf *-sh* und *-ch* werden ohne Plural-*s* und mit Artikel zur Bezeichnung des ganzen Volkes verwendet. (Vgl. § 31)	Sind einzelne Einwohner gemeint, so werden Zusammensetzungen mit *-man, -woman* oder sonstige Sonderformen verwendet. (Vgl. § 31)

H

1. Doctors often seem to achieve **the impossible.** (... das Unmögliche ...)
   The **good thing** about living near a hospital is that help is always close at hand. (Das Gute ...)
   Auch zum Ausdruck eines allgemeinen abstrakten Begriffs kann das Adjektiv als Nomen verwendet werden. Bezieht es sich jedoch auf einen speziellen Fall, so muß es durch ein Stützwort wie *thing* ergänzt werden.
2. The **blacks** feel that they have been badly treated by the **whites** for centuries.
   Einige wenige Adjektive können als echte Nomen mit Plural-*s* verwendet werden.

§ 49 Das Stützwort *one / ones* beim Adjektiv
The Use of the Prop Word *one/ones* with an Adjective

F

the new carpet and the old **one**
the new curtains and the old **ones**

Im Singular wird als Stützwort *one,* im Plural *ones* verwendet. Da die Betonung immer auf dem vorangehenden Adjektiv liegt, werden *one/ones* unbetont ausgesprochen.

V

Vorher genanntes Nomen ersetzt durch *one/ones*

Which of these **cameras** is yours? — The small **one** with the flash. ... Die kleine ... I don't like coloured **photos** very much, I prefer black-and-white **ones**. ... schwarz-weiße ...	Soll ein zählbares Nomen nicht wiederholt werden, so wird es durch *one/ones* ersetzt. Das Adjektiv kann nicht, wie im Deutschen, allein stehen.

H

Here are two **pictures** of me. **Which (one)** do you like best, **this one** or **that one**?
Don't worry, I'm not going to show you all my **photos** — but you must see **the ones** I took in Greece.

Das Stützwort *one/ones* vertritt ein Nomen auch nach *the, which, this* und *that.*

§ 50 Die Steigerung des Adjektivs
The Comparison of Adjectives

F

What you can say about things or persons:

a room:	**small**	— **smaller**	— **smallest**
a poster:	**nice**	— **nicer**	— **nicest**
a meal:	**big**	— **bigger**	— **biggest**
coffee:	**strong**	— **stronger**	— **strongest**
	[strɒŋ]	[ˈstrɒŋgə]	[ˈstrɒŋgɪst]
a road:	**narrow**	— **narrower**	— **narrowest**
a boy or girl:	**clever**	— **cleverer**	— **cleverest**
a trick:	**simple**	— **simpler**	— **simplest**
a joke:	**funny**	— **funnier**	— **funniest**

1. Auf *-er/-est* werden gesteigert:
a) alle einsilbigen Adjektive.
Beachte beim Schreiben:
Der Endkonsonant wird nach kurzem betontem Vokal verdoppelt.
Beachte beim Sprechen:
Nach *-ng* [-ŋ] wird bei den Steigerungsformen zusätzlich ein [g] gesprochen.
b) zweisilbige Adjektive auf *-ow, -er, -le* und *-y.*

Beachte beim Schreiben: Nach Konsonant wird *-y* zu *-i-*.

a dress:
beautiful — more beautiful — most beautiful
a student in an exam:
nervous — more nervous — most nervous

2. Mit *more/most* werden gesteigert:
a) Adjektive mit mehr als zwei Silben.
b) zweisilbige Adjektive, die nicht auf *-ow, -er, -le* oder *-y* enden. (Vgl. 1 b)

an idea:	**good**	— **better**	— **best**
a plan:	**bad**	— **worse**	— **worst**
people:	**many**	— **more**	— **most**
money:	**much**	— **more**	— **most**
work:	**little**	— **less**	— **least**

3. Unregelmäßige Steigerung haben:
good, bad, many, much, little.

Beachte: *little* = *klein* hat keine Vergleichsformen.
Statt dessen kann *smaller/smallest* benutzt werden

H

1. Uncle George is my mother's **eldest** brother.
Bei Verwandtschaftsnamen werden statt der Normalformen *older/oldest* auch die Sonderformen *elder/eldest* verwendet.

2. Now that we've moved it's much **farther** to the shops. Where's the **nearest** bus stop, please?
A **further** disadvantage is that it's too **far** to walk to the station. We must get off at the **next** stop.
Farther (Komparativ zu *far*) wird nur im räumlichen Sinn verwendet, *further* auch zur Bezeichnung der Reihenfolge.
Ähnliches gilt für *nearest* (räumlich) und *next* (nur Reihenfolge).

§ 51 Der Vergleich
Ways of Expressing Comparison

V Bei Vergleichssätzen lassen sich zwei Grundmuster unterscheiden:

Gleichheit

□ = □ **as** big **as** / **as** exciting **as**

New York is about **as big as** London.
Sightseeing in Edinburgh can be **as exciting as** it is in London.
Few big cities have got **as many** parks **as** London.

Ungleichheit

□ > □ bigg**er than** / **more** dangerous **than**

London buses are **bigger than** buses in New York.
Living in a large modern city can be **more dangerous than** living in the country.
Americans are said to drink **more** coffee **than** English people.

□ < □ **not as** / **not so** } big **as** / interesting **as**

Cologne is **not as (not so)** big **as** London.
For many people Birmingham is **not as (not so)** interesting **as** London.
It doesn't rain **as** much (**so** much) in Italy **as** it does in London.

H

1. For many people

Birmingham is	**less**	interesting **than**	London.
	not as	interesting **as**	

Vergleiche mit *less . . . than* (weniger . . . als) haben etwa die gleiche Bedeutung wie Vergleiche mit *not as . . . as.*

2. **The bigger** a city is, **the easier** it is to get lost.
Je größer . . ., desto leichter . . .

⚠ *Than* darf nicht mit *then* (dann) verwechselt werden.

§ 52 Das Adverb
The Adverb

F

Adjektiv	**Adverb**
a **bad** accident	to be **badly** injured
a **careful** driver	to drive **carefully**
an **angry** policeman	to shout **angrily**
a **terrible** mistake	I'm **terribly** sorry
an **automatic** reaction	to react **automatically**
a **true** hero	a **truly** brave action
a **fast** car	to drive **fast**
a **daily** journey	to travel **daily**
a friendly chap	to welcome s. o. **in a friendly way**
a **good** interpreter	to speak English **well**

1. Von den meisten Adjektiven lassen sich Adverbien ableiten.

Adverbien auf *-ly* bilden die Mehrzahl der abgeleiteten Adverbien. Beachte:
— *-y* wird zu *-ily*
— Die Adjektivendung *-le* nach Konsonant entfällt
— *-ic* wird zu *-ically* (Ausnahme: *publicly*)
— Das stumme End-*e* entfällt bei *true/truly, whole/wholly*

Gleiche Form wie das Adjektiv haben
— einige einsilbige Adverbien wie *fast, long, low.*
— Zeitadverbien auf *-ly,* wie *daily, weekly,* etc.

Eine Umschreibung ist nötig, wenn das Adjektiv auf *-ly* endet (außer bei *daily,* etc.)
Zu *good* lautet das Adverb *well.* (Daneben gibt es *well* auch als Adjektiv: *to be well* = gesund sein.)

We have a small house at the seaside with a kitchen **downstairs** and two bedrooms **upstairs.** We **often** drive **there** for the weekend, but **never** on a bank holiday.

2. Wie im Deutschen gibt es auch im Englischen Adverbien, zu denen es keine entsprechenden Adjektive gibt, vor allem Zeit- und Ortsadverbien wie *today, soon, always, often, sometimes, seldom, never; downstairs, there,* etc.

H Einige Adverbien haben Doppelformen mit unterschiedlicher Bedeutung:

In football, as in other sports, you are supposed to play **fair** (fair).
But fouls are **fairly** (ziemlich) common in professional football.

Our local football team have been training **hard** (schwer) to improve their fitness.
But they will **hardly** (kaum) manage to get into the first division.

I've **just** (gerade) been watching some horse racing on television.
In my opinion it is **justly** (zu Recht) called the sport of kings.

Some of the young ice skaters danced very **prettily** (hübsch).
Ice hockey is a **pretty** (ziemlich) rough game.

V Adverbien können ihrer Funktion im Satz entsprechend in zwei Hauptgruppen unterteilt werden:

1. Ein Adverb kann ein Adjektiv oder ein anderes Adverb in seiner Bedeutung **verstärken** oder **einschränken.** Solche Adverbien werden *Adverbien des Grades* genannt.

Nähere Bestimmung eines Adjektivs oder Adverbs

There are some **very** good sports programmes on TV.
Some people get **extremely** excited while watching sports programmes on TV.
Yesterday's programme about the Davis Cup was **rather** disappointing.
Our team simply wasn't good **enough.**

Das Adverb des Grades tritt wie im Deutschen vor das zugehörige Wort. Nur *enough* wird nachgestellt.

2. Ein Adverb kann sich auch auf das Verb oder den ganzen Satz beziehen. Es kann angeben:
   - **wann, wie oft** und **wo** eine Handlung stattfindet *(Angabe der Zeit, der Häufigkeit, des Orts und der Richtung),*
   - **wie** eine Tätigkeit ausgeführt wird *(Angabe der Art und Weise),*
   - unter welchem **Gesichtspunkt** der Sprecher das Geschehen sieht *(Angabe des Standpunktes, kommentierendes Adverb).*

   Statt durch *Adverbien* können diese Angaben auch durch zusammengesetzte Ausdrücke *(adverbial phrases)* wiedergegeben werden.

Nähere Bestimmung des Verbs oder des ganzen Satzes

Every morning my father turns on the radio as soon as he gets up. *(Zeit)*
He **always** listens to the eight o'clock news. *(Häufigkeit)*
He has got a stereo radio **in his car.** *(Ort)*
Whenever he drives **to town** he listens to the traffic information. *(Richtung)*
He studies the Radio Times **carefully,** looking for interesting programmes. *(Art und Weise)*
Obviously, he would be lost without the radio. *(Standpunkt, Kommentar)*

Die einzelnen Arten von Angaben erscheinen an unterschiedlichen Stellen im Satz. Vgl. § 4.

§ 53 Adjektiv und Adverb nach Verben
Adjectives and Adverbs after Verbs

V

1. Die meisten Verben beschreiben eine Tätigkeit und werden durch ein Adverb der Art und Weise näher bestimmt (vgl. § 52 V2). Daneben gibt es aber eine Reihe von Verben, die auf eine Eigenschaft oder einen Zustand des Subjekts verweisen. Sie werden mit einem Adjektiv verbunden.

Zustands-/Vorgangsverb + Adjektiv

be, seem, remain, stay

The band **was wonderful** last night.
The audience **seemed** rather **enthusiastic**.

Diese Verben werden immer mit dem Adjektiv verbunden.

become, get, grow, turn

Every time I ask my Dad for some money he **becomes (gets) angry**.
I always **grow nervous** when I see a police car following me.
As soon as the girl spoke to him he **turned red**.

Vorgangsverben mit der Bedeutung ‚werden' verweisen auf einen zukünftigen Zustand (das Resultat des Vorgangs) und haben daher ebenfalls das Adjektiv nach sich.

Tätigkeitsverb + Adverb

The band always **plays wonderfully** when the audience is enthusiastic.
They **clapped enthusiastically.**

When his father refused to let him go to the disco, John rushed out of the room and **slammed** the door **angrily**.
Whenever he is worried about something he **bites** his fingernails **nervously**.

Das Adverb beschreibt hier die Art und Weise, in der etwas getan wird. Es bezieht sich auf das Verb (und seine Ergänzungen).

2. Eine kleine Gruppe von Verben können entweder als Zustandsverben (mit Adjektiv) oder als Tätigkeitsverben (mit Adverb) verwendet werden.

look, taste, smell, sound als Zustandsverben

What do you think of those cakes in the shop window? Don't they **look nice**?
The food they serve in the cafeteria **smells unpleasant** and **tastes awful**.
My brother has told me a lot about Mexican food. It **sounds interesting.**

Wenn diese Verben Aussehen, Geruch, Geschmack, Klang als Zustand bzw. Eigenschaft beschreiben, haben sie das Adjektiv bei sich.

look, taste, smell, sound als Tätigkeitsverben

The little boy **looked sadly** at the cakes in the shop window.
The cook **tasted** the soup **carefully** because it was very hot.
He **smelt** the meal **suspiciously** because he had never had Mexican food before.
When I saw smoke coming from the kitchen I **immediately sounded** the alarm.

look, taste, smell und *sound* können auch Handlungen (schauen, probieren, beriechen, betätigen) ausdrücken. In diesem Fall wird das Adverb verwendet.

What was the band **like**? What **did** they look **like**?
How did the band play?

Nach einer Eigenschaft oder einem Zustand fragt man mit *what... like?*, nach der Art und Weise einer Tätigkeit mit *how?*.

§ 54 Die Steigerung des Adverbs
The Comparison of Adverbs

F

to pronounce: **clearly — more clearly — most clearly** to handle school books: **carefully — more carefully — most carefully** to look up words in the dictionary: **often — more often — most often**	1. **Auf *more/most* werden gesteigert:** a) Adverbien auf *-ly* (außer *early*). b) andere mehrsilbigen Adverbien
to study: **hard — harder — hardest** to read: **fast — faster — fastest** to arrive at school: **early — earlier — earliest**	2. **Auf *-er/-est* werden gesteigert:** einsilbige Adverbien und *early.*
to sing: **well — better — best** to draw: **badly — worse — worst** to work: **little — less — least** to enjoy art lessons: very **much — more — most**	3. **Unregelmäßige Steigerung haben:** *well, badly, little, much*

H

1. Though Peter lives a long way from the school he usually arrives **earlier than** his friends.
He is the youngest boy in the class, but he can run **as fast as** some of the older boys.
Although he was born in the USA he does**n't** speak English **as well as** you might expect.

   In Vergleichssätzen ergeben sich die gleichen Strukturen wie beim Adjektiv (vgl. § 51).

2. Briggs won the motor racing championship last year and he will **most probably** win it again this year.

   Most kann auch die Bedeutung „sehr, äußerst, höchst“ haben.

6 Zahlen, Zeit-, Orts- und Mengenangaben

Numbers, Expressions of Time, Place and Quantity

§ 55 Grund- und Ordnungszahlen

Cardinal and Ordinal Numbers

F

1	one [wʌn]	1st	the first [fɜ:st]
2	two [tu:]	2nd	the second ['sekənd]
3	three [θri:]	3rd	the third [θɜ:d]
4	four [fɔ:]	4th	the fourth [fɔ:θ]
5	five [faɪv]	5th	the fifth [fɪfθ]
6	six [sɪks]	6th	the sixth [sɪksθ]
7	seven ['sevn]	7th	the seventh ['sevnθ]
8	eight [eɪt]	8th	the eighth [eɪtθ]
9	nine [naɪn]	9th	the ninth [naɪnθ]
10	ten [ten]	10th	the tenth [tenθ]
11	eleven [ɪ'levn]	11th	the eleventh [ɪ'levnθ]
12	twelve [twelv]	12th	the twelfth [twelfθ]
13	thirteen ['θɜ:'ti:n]	13th	the thirteenth ['θɜ:'ti:nθ]
14	fourteen ['-'-]	14th	the fourteenth
15	fifteen ['fɪf'ti:n]	15th	the fifteenth
16	sixteen ['-'-]	16th	the sixteenth
17	seventeen ['--'-]	17th	the seventeenth
18	eighteen ['-'-]	18th	the eighteenth
19	nineteen ['-'-]	19th	the nineteenth
20	twenty ['twentɪ]	20th	the twentieth ['twentɪɪθ]
21	twenty-one [ˌ--'-]	21st	the twenty-first
22	twenty-two [ˌ--'-]	22nd	the twenty-second
30	thirty ['θɜ:tɪ]	30th	the thirtieth ['θɜ:tɪɪθ]
40	forty ['fɔ:tɪ]	40th	the fortieth
50	fifty ['fɪftɪ]	50th	the fiftieth
60	sixty ['sɪkstɪ]	60th	the sixtieth
70	seventy ['sevntɪ]	70th	the seventieth
80	eighty ['eɪtɪ]	80th	the eightieth
90	ninety ['naɪntɪ]	90th	the ninetieth
100	a (one) hundred ['hʌndrəd]	100th	the hundredth
1,000	a (one) thousand ['θaʊzənd]	1,000th	the thousandth
3,853	three thousand eight hundred and fifty-three	3,853rd	the three thousand eight hundred and fifty-third
1,000,000	a (one) million ['mɪljən]	1,000,000th	the millionth
2,000,000	two million	2,000,000th	the two millionth

Grundzahlen

1. Einer- und Zehnerzahlen werden durch *and* an Hunderter- und Tausenderzahlen angeschlossen: *a hundred and two.*
2. Vor *hundred* und *thousand* (als Zahlwörtern) steht immer ein anderes Zahlwort oder *a.*
3. *Hundred, thousand* und *million* erhalten nur dann ein *s,* wenn sie als Substantive gebraucht werden: *five hundred years — hundreds of years.*
4. Zehner und Einer werden durch Bindestrich miteinander verbunden: *thirty-two, seventy-three.*
5. Von 1000 ab werden je drei Stellen von rechts durch ein Komma abgeteilt: *4,635,826.*
   Im Gegensatz zum Deutschen bezeichnet das Komma im Englischen also nicht eine Dezimalstelle, sondern eine Tausenderzahl.
   Dezimalzahlen werden im Englischen durch einen Punkt gekennzeichnet: *3.5 (three point five).*

Ordnungszahlen

1. *First, second, third* sind unregelmäßige Formen. Beachte: Auch bei zusammengesetzten Grundzahlen, die auf *one, two, three* enden, tritt *first, second, third* ein: *the twenty-second, the hundred and third.*
   Alle anderen Ordnungszahlen werden auf *-th* gebildet. Beachte jedoch die Zehnerzahlen auf *-tieth* (zwei Silben) und die farbig unterstrichenen Formen.
2. Nach einer Ordnungszahl steht nicht wie im Deutschen ein Punkt, sondern die beiden letzten Buchstaben des Wortes: *first = 1st; second = 2nd; third = 3rd; fourth = 4th;* etc.
3. Auch die römischen Ziffern nach Herrschernamen stehen ohne Punkt: *Henry VIII (Henry the Eighth); Elizabeth II*

H

Für die Ziffer 0 gibt es im Englischen verschiedene Bezeichnungen. Man sagt z. B.:

nought [nɔ:t]	für den Zahlenwert 0. *Three minus three leaves nought.*
zero ['zɪərəʊ]	für den Nullpunkt einer Skala: *The temperature is ten below zero.*
o [əʊ]	in Fernsprechnummern: 55040 *(double five-o-four-o).*
nil [nɪl]	für Sportergebnisse: *The match ended 5:0 (five nil).*

§ 56 Das Datum
The Date

F

Schreibung	Aussprache
June 2nd, 1985 June 2, 1985 2nd June (,) 1985 2 June (,) 1985 2/6/1985	"June the second, nineteen eighty-five." "The second of June, nineteen eighty-five."

H

Zu beachten ist der Unterschied in der Schreibung:
Englisch 24 / 12 / 1985 (Tag / Monat / Jahr); amerikanisch 12 / 24 / 1985 (Monat / Tag / Jahr).

§ 57 Wiederholungszahlen und Zahlen der Reihenfolge
Expressions of Frequency and Sequence

F

Mrs Black only goes shopping	**once** a week.
She does the washing-up	**twice** a day,
rings her husband at the office	**three times** a day,
and makes herself a cup of tea at least	**ten times** every day.

1. Den Grundzahlen *one* und *two* entsprechen die Wiederholungszahlen *once* und *twice*.
Die übrigen Wiederholungszahlen werden aus der Grundzahl und *times* gebildet.

If you want to redecorate your room

first	decide what colour you want,
second,	buy the paint,
third,	wash the walls thoroughly, and
fourth,	paint the walls with a large brush.

2. Zur Angabe der Reihenfolge können die Ordnungszahlen (vgl. § 55) verwendet werden. Gelegentlich finden sich auch Ausdrücke wie *firstly, secondly,* etc. und *in the first place, in the second place,* etc.

§ 58 Die Uhrzeit
Telling the Time

F

five **to** one
ten **to** one
a quarter to one
twenty-nine **minutes to** one
twelve **o'clock**

half past twelve
five **past** twelve
eight **minutes past** twelve
a quarter past twelve
twenty-one **minutes past** twelve

1. Die Zeitangaben der ersten halben Stunde bezieht man auf die vorhergehende Stunde, die Zeitangaben der zweiten halben Stunde auf die folgende Stunde.
2. Bei Fünferzahlen fehlt gewöhnlich das Wort *minutes*. Bei allen anderen Minutenangaben muß *minutes* stehen.

H

1. The shop opens at **8 a.m.** and closes at **6 p.m.**
Die Stunden von 0—12 Uhr werden durch *a.m.* [ˌeɪˈem] (lat. **ante** meridiem = **vor** Mittag), die von 12—24 Uhr mit *p.m.* [ˌpiːˈem] (lat. **post** meridiem = **nach** Mittag) bezeichnet, um Verwechslungen zu vermeiden.
2. Eine andere Möglichkeit, die Uhrzeit zu nennen, ist folgende: 9.15: *nine fifteen;* 9.32: *nine thirty-two;* 9.59 *nine fifty-nine.*
3. Im internationalen Reiseverkehr hat sich die 24-Stunden-Uhr durchgesetzt:
The plane will take off at 18.00 [ˈeɪtiːn ˈaʊəz]. It will land at 20.05 [ˈtwentɪ əʊ ˈfaɪv].
Im amerikanischen Englisch gibt es auch die Aussprachevariante „eighteen hundred hours" für 18.00.

§ 59 Präpositionen in Zeitangaben
Prepositions in Expressions of Time

V

1. *At, on, in:* Als allgemeine Richtlinie gilt: Mit *at* wird meist die Vorstellung eines Zeit**punkts** verbunden *(at this moment)*, mit *on* und *in* meist die Vorstellung eines Zeit**raums** *(on this day, in summer)*.

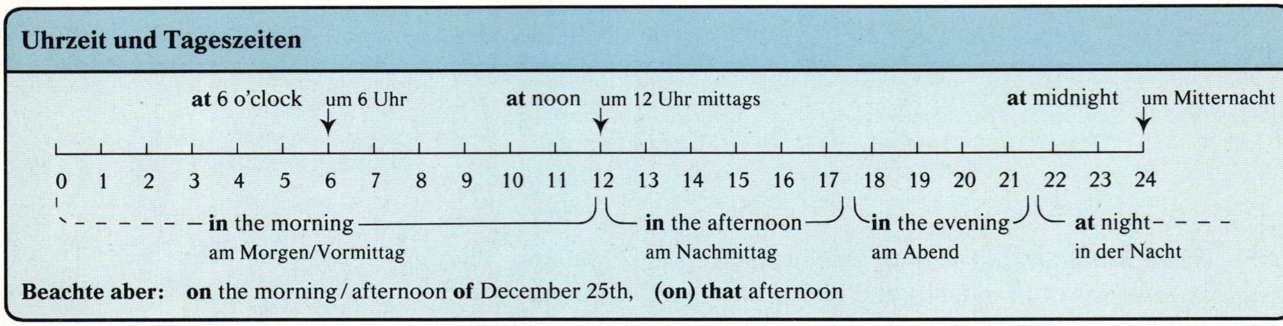

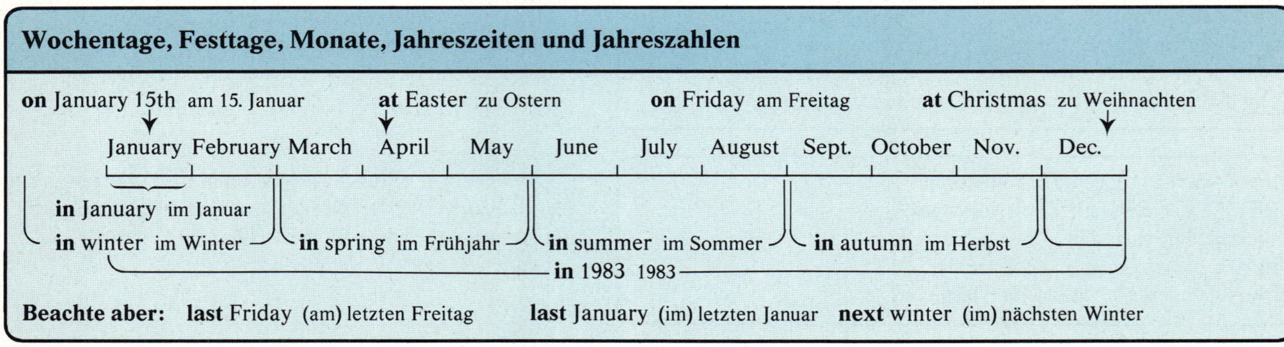

2. Weitere Präpositionen in Zeitangaben:

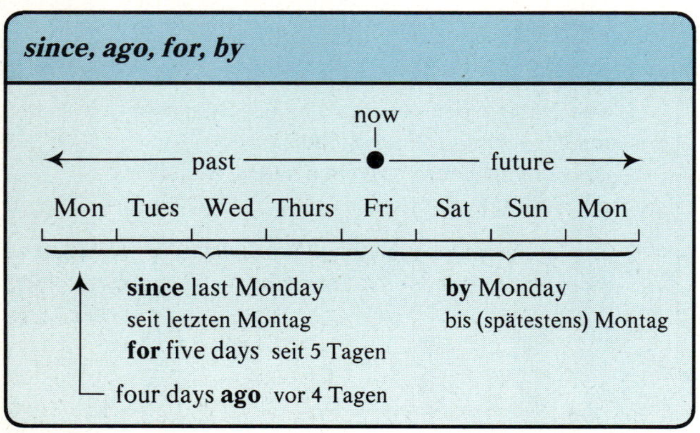

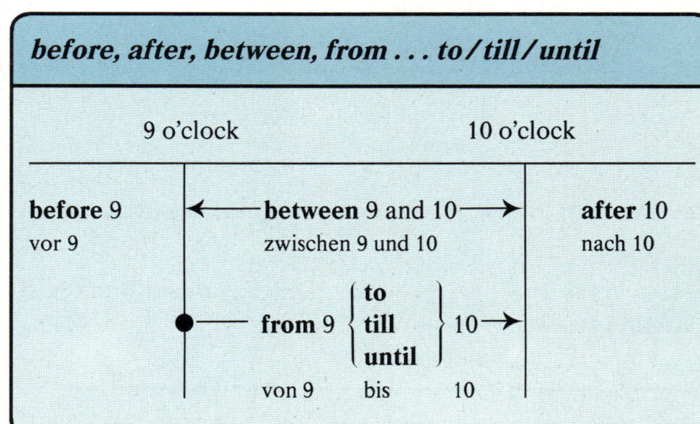

H

He has been playing the trumpet **for about five years** now. (. . . **seit** etwa 5 Jahren . . .)
He played in Mike's band **for more than two years** (. . . über 2 Jahre **lang** . . .), but now he has got a band of his own.
Next summer the band is going on tour **for two months** (. . . **für** 2 Monate . . .).
Zeitangaben mit *for* beziehen sich nicht immer auf das Jetzt. Sie können auch einen Zeitraum der Vergangenheit oder Zukunft bezeichnen.

§ 60 Präpositionen in Orts- und Richtungsangaben
Prepositions in Expressions of Place and Direction

V

Ortspräpositionen

by, near	the door
at **under** **on** **over**	the table
above **below**	the book-shelf
in front of, before **behind** **in** **outside**	the house
round	the fire
opposite	the lady
among	his friends
between	her parents
beside	his mother

Richtungspräpositionen

on, onto **from, off**	the roof
over	the fence
towards **to** **into** **out of** **past**	the house
along **across**	the road
against	the wall
after	the thieves
up **down**	the hill
through **round**	the trees

H

1. I live **in** London and my friend lives **in** Cardiff.
   On the way to Swansea the train stops **at** Cardiff.

   in: Die Stadt wird als (Wohn-, Lebens-)Raum betrachtet.
   at: Die Stadt wird als Punkt (auf der Reiseroute) betrachtet.

2. Since his parents died he has been living **with** his aunt.
   He always spends his summer holiday **at** his aunt**'s**.

   ... **bei** seiner Tante (ständig).
   ... **bei** seiner Tante (vorübergehend). Zum *s*-Genitiv vgl. § 38.

3. She went **into** the snackbar to buy a cup of coffee. — She put six lumps of sugar **in** her coffee.
   Bei Richtungsangaben erscheint normalerweise *into* bzw. *onto.* Nach *put* ist jedoch *in* bzw. *on* gebräuchlich.

§ 61 Mengenangaben mit der Präposition *of*
Expressions of Quantity with the Preposition *of*

V

Mengenangaben und Stoffbezeichnungen werden im Englischen nie direkt, sondern stets durch die Präposition *of* miteinander verbunden. Dasselbe gilt für Gruppenbezeichnungen bei Menschen und Tieren. Wie im Deutschen gibt es eine Reihe mehr oder weniger fester Verbindungen. Hier eine Auswahl:

Mengenbezeichnungen bei Nahrungsmitteln			Gruppenbezeichnungen bei Menschen und Tieren		
a **pound of** butter	a **box of** eggs		a **crowd of** people	a **herd of** cattle	
a **packet of** biscuits	a **bar of** chocolate		a **group of** young girls	a **flock of** sheep	
a **tin of** sardines	a **lump of** sugar	(ein Stück Zucker)	a **gang of** thieves	a **shoal of** fish	(ein Schwarm Fische)
a **cup (pot) of** tea	a **loaf of** bread	(ein Laib Brot)	a **team of** scientists	a **pack of** wolves	(ein Rudel Wölfe)

H

Wenn auch die Umstellung auf die internationalen Maße *Liter* und *Gramm* geplant ist, sind im Englischen noch *pint (0,57 litres), gallon (4,54 litres)* und *ounce (28,35 grams)* üblich. Das englische *pound (16 ounces)* hat 454 Gramm.

7 Die Zeitformen des Verbs

The Tenses of the Verb

§ 62 *Continuous* und *Simple Form:* Grundsätzliches zur Verwendung

The Use of Continuous and Simple Forms: Basic Principles

V Die *Continuous Form* (auch *Progressive Form* genannt) betont stets den Ablauf eines Geschehens. Deshalb kann sie nur bei solchen Verben verwendet werden, die in irgendeiner Form einen Ablauf beschreiben können. Die *Simple Form* dagegen ist bei allen Verben möglich.

Continuous Form	*Simple Form*
Mr Brown **is working** on an important article at the moment. As I **was walking** home from work, Jim passed me in his car. Let's take a rest, **I'm getting** tired.	Mr Brown **works** as a reporter for the *Daily Star.* I **walked** all the way to the office this morning. After a long day's work, everybody **gets** tired.
	Have you **noticed** that Jim is growing a beard? Most boys **like** girls with long hair. I **wish** I had fair hair like you. This bottle **contains** one pint, The milk **seems** to be sour.
I **'m thinking** of going camping this year. Ich überlege, ob ... Our neighbours **are seeing** to the cat while we're away. ... kümmern sich um ... The travel agency is making all the arrangements. They **are being** very helpful. ... sind/verhalten sich ...	I **think** June is the best month for a holiday. Ich glaube ... I **see** you are studying the travel brochures. Ich sehe ... Spain **is** still very cheap.

1. Die *Continuous Form* ist möglich bei Verben, die eine Tätigkeit oder einen Vorgang beschreiben. Tätigkeitsverben sind z. B. *work, walk, read.* (Sie bilden die größte Gruppe aller Verben.) Vorgangsverben sind z. B. *become, grow, get* (= werden).

2. Folgende Verben erscheinen normalerweise nicht in der *Continuous Form:*

a) Verben der Sinneswahrnehmung, z. B. *notice, see, hear, feel.*

b) Verben, die Wissen, Meinungen, Gefühle oder Wünsche ausdrücken, z. B. *know, believe, think, like, want, wish.*

c) Verben, die einen Zustand, eine Maßangabe, ein Besitzverhältnis oder eine sonstige Beziehung ausdrücken, z. B. *be, seem, contain, consist of, cost, have, possess, belong.*

3. Wenn Verben wie *think, see, be* und *have* in der *Continuous Form* erscheinen, so haben sie eine andere Bedeutung, nämlich die eines Tätigkeitsverbs.

Vgl. auch § 84 zu *have* und § 85 zu *be.*

H **I've been wanting** to meet her for ages. Seit ewigen Zeiten war es mein größter Wunsch, sie zu treffen.

Gelegentlich erscheint die *Continuous Form* auch bei *want* und *wish,* die normalerweise nur die *Simple Form* zulassen. Die *Continuous Form* betont hier die Stärke des Gefühls.

§ 63 *Present Tense Continuous* und *Present Tense Simple*

F

Present Tense Continuous

I	**am**	**walking** on the beach.
He / She	**is**	**swimming.**
The sun	**is**	**shining.**
We / You / They	**are**	**lying** in the sun.

Das *Present Tense Continuous* setzt sich zusammen aus *am / is / are* + *Present Participle* (*ing*-Form).
Beachte beim Anfügen der *ing*-Endung:
- Der Endkonsonant wird verdoppelt nach kurzem, betontem Vokal.
- Stummes End-*e* entfällt *(shine — shining, write — writing).*
- *-ie* wird zu *-y- (lie — lying, die — dying).*

Present Tense Simple

I / You / We / They	**speak**		English.
He / She	**speaks**	[-s]	English.
It often	**rains**	[-z]	in England.
The Thames seldom	**freezes**	[-ɪz].	

Die 3. Person Singular wird auf *-s* gebildet, alle anderen Formen entsprechen dem Infinitiv.
Beachte bei der *s*-Endung:
- Nach stimmlosem Laut wird [s] gesprochen, sonst [z].
- Nach Zischlaut tritt *-es* [ɪz] ein *(freezes, watches).*
- Schreibung *-ies* nach Konsonant: *fly — flies, hurry — hurries.*
- Sonderformen: *goes* [gəʊz], *does* [dʌz], *says* [sez].

V

Das *Present Tense Continuous* wird normalerweise nur bei Tätigkeits- und Vorgangsverben gebraucht. Es betont, daß ein Vorgang gerade abläuft und von vorübergehender Dauer ist. Das *Present Tense Simple* wird benützt, wenn die Dauer nicht eingeschränkt ist.

Present Tense Continuous:

gerade ablaufende Handlungen

At the moment Dad **is watching** the boat race on TV.
Look, one of the boats **is sinking!**
Our rowing team **is doing** very well this summer.

Das *Present Continuous* beschreibt Handlungen, die im Augenblick des Sprechens oder — im weiteren Sinn — während des gegenwärtigen Zeitraums ablaufen (z. B. *this summer*).

Present Tense Simple

allgemeingültige Tatsachen

Water **freezes** at 0 °C. — Still waters **run** deep.
The Rhine **flows** into the North Sea.

Es geht hier um Aussagen, die nicht nur im Augenblick des Sprechens gültig sind. (Naturgesetze, Sprichwörter, etc.)

Gewohnheiten

My sister **goes** for a swim every morning before work.
Jean always **beats** me at tennis.

Wenn etwas wiederholt wird oder immer geschieht (z. B. bei *always, often, sometimes*), steht grundsätzlich die *Simple Form.*

Handlungsfolgen

... McCabe **stops** the ball, **passes** it to Joe Brown ...
Brown **runs** down the wing, **beats** two opponents,
slips it to McTavish and — it's a goal!

Handlungsfolgen (z. B. in Sportberichten, Gebrauchsanweisungen und spannenden Erzählungen), bei denen die Dauer keine Rolle spielt, werden im *Present Tense Simple* wiedergegeben.

H

1. You'**re always pronouncing** that word wrong.
   She'**s continually criticizing** the way I speak.

   Always und *continually* werden gelegentlich auch mit der *Continuous Form* verbunden. Es handelt sich dann aber nicht um sachliche Angaben der Häufigkeit, sondern um Übertreibungen, mit denen der Sprecher z. B. seine Verärgerung ausdrückt.

2. Zum Gebrauch von *Present Tense Continuous* und *Simple* zur Wiedergabe der Zukunft vgl. §§ 70 und 72.

§ 64 *Past Tense* und *Present Perfect* (Zu den Formen vgl. § 65 und § 66.)

V Während im Deutschen zwischen Präteritum *(ich ging)* und Perfekt *(ich bin gegangen)* oft nur ein stilistischer Unterschied besteht, drücken *Past Tense* und *Present Perfect* zwei völlig verschiedene Betrachtungsweisen der Vergangenheit aus.

Past Tense: Geschehen in der Vergangenheit betont

bei Zeitangaben wie *yesterday, a week ago*

Jimmy **fell** down the stairs yesterday.
Sandra **broke** her leg while skiing last winter.

Benutzt der Sprecher eine Zeitangabe der Vergangenheit, so betont er gleichzeitig, daß das Geschehen vorbei ist. Es kommt nur das *Past Tense* in Frage.

bei temporalen Nebensätzen

I **visited** her twice while she was in hospital.
She **went** back to work as soon as she was able to walk.

Auch ein temporaler Nebensatz (mit *when, while,* etc.) kann einen Zeitpunkt oder Zeitraum der Vergangenheit angeben. Im Hauptsatz muß dann das *Past Tense* stehen.

Zeitliche Festlegung durch den Zusammenhang

Last year's flu epidemic **was** the worst for years. Dad **was** the only one in our family who **did not catch** it.
I **missed** the Spiders' concert because I **was** ill. **Did** you **go**?

Auch wenn der Satz keine Zeitangabe enthält, kann aus dem Sinn- oder Textzusammenhang hervorgehen, daß eine frühere Zeit gemeint ist. Auch hier steht das *Past Tense.*

Present Perfect: Bezug zur Gegenwart betont

bei Zeitangaben mit *since, for, up to now,* etc.

Betty **has been** blind since birth. (... since she was born.)
My uncle **has been taking** these pills for a long time.

Zeitangaben mit *since, for, up to now, so far* sowie Nebensätze mit *since* (= seit) bezeichnen meist einen Zeitraum, der von der Vergangenheit bis hin zur Gegenwart reicht. Hier muß das *Present Perfect* verwendet werden. (Zum Gebrauch von *since* und *for* vgl. § 66 H 2.)

bei *ever/never*

Have you ever **been** in hospital? ... schon einmal ...?
No, **I've** never **been** seriously ill. ... noch nie ...

Auch Sätze mit *ever* und *never* können sich auf einen Zeitraum beziehen, der von der Vergangenheit bis zur Gegenwart reicht, und stehen dann im *Present Perfect.*

gegenwärtiges Resultat im Vordergrund

Jenny **has eaten** all the cake. No wonder she's feeling sick.
Some more tea? — No thanks, **I've had** enough.

Soll das Ergebnis einer Handlung betont werden, so benutzt man das *Present Perfect:* Die Handlung an sich ist zwar vorbei, aber der Zustand der sich daraus ergeben hat, besteht immer noch. (Allerdings darf der Satz dann keine Zeitangabe wie *yesterday* enthalten.)

H

1. The match **has** just started.

   Bei *just* („gerade eben") steht das *Present Perfect*, da das Geschehen fast noch als Gegenwart empfunden wird.

2. Mr Barrett **hasn't had** a holiday yet *this year*, but he's hoping to spend a week in Austria over Christmas.
   We **didn't have** a holiday *this year.* We're saving the money for a trip to Australia next year.

   Bei *today, this week/month/year* wird je nach Betrachtungsweise *Present Perfect* oder *Past Tense* benutzt.

§ 65 *Past Tense Continuous* und *Past Tense Simple*

F

Past Tense Continuous			
You/We/They	**were**	**walking**	home.
I/He/She	**was**	**waiting**	for the bus.
It	**was**	**raining**.	

Das *Past Tense Continuous* wird gebildet aus *was / were* + *Present Participle* (*ing*-Form).

Zur Schreibung des *Present Participle* vgl. § 63 F.

Past Tense Simple			
I/You/He/	**listened**	[d]	to the radio.
She/We/They	**liked**	[t]	the concert.
It	**ended**	[ɪd]	at nine.
I	**saw**	the match on TV.	

Beim *Past Tense Simple* unterscheidet man regelmäßige und unregelmäßige Formen.
Die regelmäßigen Formen werden auf *-ed* gebildet.
Aussprache: [d] nach stimmhaftem Laut, [t] nach stimmlosem Laut, [ɪd] nach [t] und [d].
Schreibung: *-y* wird zu *-ied* nach Konsonanten *(cry — cried, hurry — hurried).* Konsonantenverdoppelung nach kurzem betontem Vokal *stop — stopped).*

Zu den unregelmäßigen Formen s. Anhang.

V

Beide *Past Tense*-Formen betonen, daß ein Geschehen vorbei ist (vgl. § 64). Die Betrachtungsweise ist jedoch verschieden:
Das *Past Tense Continuous* (nur bei Tätigkeits- und Vorgangsverben!) betont den Verlauf der Handlung.
Das *Past Tense Simple* stellt das Ereignis als Ganzes dar.

Past Tense Continuous

Hintergrundshandlungen

We **were watching** TV when the electricity went off.
While we **were sitting** in the dark my father started to tell a ghost story.

Unter Hintergrundshandlung verstehen wir einen Vorgang, der gerade in Gang und noch nicht zu Ende war, als sich etwas Neues ereignete. Die Hintergrundshandlung steht im *Past Tense Continuous*, die neu eintretende Handlung jedoch im *Past Tense Simple.*

Gleichzeitig ablaufende Handlungen

While Jimmy **was doing** his homework, his sister **was practising** the guitar.
It was chaos — the dogs **were barking**, the children **were screaming** and Peter **was shouting** at them all to keep quiet.

Soll betont werden, daß mehrere Handlungen gleichzeitig abliefen, so wird die *Continuous Form* bevorzugt.
Dies trifft vor allem auf Sätze mit *while* zu.

Past Tense Simple

Einzelhandlungen

The President of the USA **arrived** in London this morning for talks on energy problems.
Yesterday's heavy snowstorm **caused** a power failure in the Manchester area.

Für einzelne Ereignisse der Vergangenheit wird in der Regel das *Past Tense Simple* benutzt, da es meist um das Ereignis an sich geht und nicht um den momentanen Ablauf.

Handlungsfolgen

Colorado Bill **grabbed** the money, **jumped** on his horse and **rode** away at top speed.
The film was so silly that I **turned off** the TV set and **went** to bed.

Aufeinanderfolgende Handlungen werden grundsätzlich durch die *Simple Form* wiedergegeben. Das *Past Tense Simple* ist deshalb die typische Zeitform für Erzählung und Bericht.

§ 66 *Present Perfect Continuous* und *Present Perfect Simple*

F

Present Perfect Continuous	
I/You/We/They	**have been waiting.**
He/She	**has been walking.**
It	**has been raining.**

Das *Present Perfect Continuous* setzt sich zusammen aus *have/has* + *been* + *Present Participle* (*ing*-Form). Zur Schreibung des *Present Participle* vgl. § 63 F.

Present Perfect Simple	
I/You/We/They	**have phoned.**
He/She	**has arrived.**
It	**has grown** dark.

Das *Present Perfect Simple* wird gebildet aus *have/has* + *Past Participle*. Beim *Past Participle* unterscheidet man regelmäßige Formen auf *-ed* (zu Schreibung und Aussprache vgl. § 65 F) und unregelmäßige Formen (s. Anhang).

V

Beide *Present-Perfect*-Formen betonen im Gegensatz zu den *Past-Tense*-Formen, daß ein Geschehen in Beziehung zur Gegenwart steht (vgl. § 64). Vom *Present Tense* abgesehen, treten beim *Present Perfect* die Unterschiede zwischen *Continuous* und *Simple Form* am deutlichsten hervor.

Present Perfect Continuous:

Tätigkeit oder Vorgang dauert noch an

It's time you put out the light. You**'ve been reading** long enough. Du hast lange genug gelesen.
My cousin is very talented. She **has been writing** poems since she was very young. Sie schreibt schon seit ihrer frühen Kindheit Gedichte.

Das *Present Perfect Continuous* betont, daß eine Handlung von der Vergangenheit bis jetzt angedauert hat bzw. immer noch andauert. Es ist in der Regel nur bei Tätigkeits- und Vorgangsverben möglich (vgl. § 62) und tritt meistens in Verbindung mit Zeitangaben wie *since* ... und *for* ... auf. Im Deutschen erscheint häufig das Präsens in Verbindung mit ‚schon'.

Present Perfect Simple:

Resultat betont

Sue **has hurt** her hand – she can't write at the moment.
I've written six letters in the last two hours.
I've tried to ring him up several times, but he doesn't seem to be at home.

Soll das Ergebnis einer vergangenen Handlung betont werden, so kommt nur das *Present Perfect Simple* in Frage. Dabei kann es sich auch um ein mehrfach wiederholtes Geschehen mit Angabe der Häufigkeit handeln (vgl. *six letters, several times*).

Zustand dauert noch an

You needn't tell me how to spell 'address'. **I've known** that for ages! Ich weiß das schon ewig.
John is not very interested in reading. He **has** always **preferred** playing football. Er hat schon immer lieber Fußball gespielt.

Bei Verben, die keine *Continuous Form* zulassen, wird das *Present Perfect Simple* benutzt, um die Handlungsdauer bis zur Gegenwart auszudrücken. In dieser Verwendung tritt das *Present Perfect Simple* nur in Verbindung mit Zeitangaben wie *since* ..., *for* ..., *up to now*, etc. auf.

H

1. Someone**'s been sending** us anonymous letters.
   The phone **has been ringing** all day.

   Das *Present Perfect Continuous* kann auch eine mehrfach wiederholte Handlung ausdrücken. Oft schwingt dabei Verärgerung mit. Solche Sätze dürfen aber keine Angabe der Häufigkeit enthalten. (The phone **has rung** *ten times* today.)

2. Dem deutschen „seit" entspricht im Englischen entweder *since* oder *for:*

   It's been raining **since** Monday.

   It's been raining **for** four days.

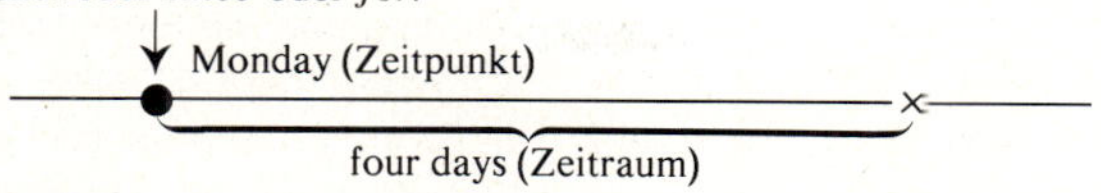

   Since bezieht sich auf den Zeitpunkt, zu dem die Handlung begonnen hat, *for* auf den Zeitraum, den sie bereits andauert.

§ 67 *Past Perfect Continuous* und *Past Perfect Simple*

F

Past Perfect Continuous	
I / You / He / She / We / They	**had been waiting.**
It	**had been raining.**

Das *Past Perfect Continuous* wird gebildet aus
had + *been* + *Present Participle* (*ing*-Form).
Zur Schreibung des *Present Participle* vgl. § 63 F.

Past Perfect Simple	
I / You / He / She / We / They	**had arrived.**
They	**had gone home.**

Das *Past Perfect Simple* wird gebildet aus
had + *Past Participle.*
Zum *Past Participle* vgl. § 66 F.

V

Das *Past Perfect* bezeichnet Handlungen, die vor einem bestimmten Zeitpunkt der Vergangenheit einsetzten.
Es drückt also Vorzeitigkeit gegenüber einem Bezugspunkt der Vergangenheit aus.

Das *Past Perfect* erscheint vor allem in der indirekten Rede vom Typ *He said* . . . sowie in Erzählungen und Berichten.
(Zum System der Zeitenfolge vgl. § 25.)

Das *Past Perfect Continuous* wird normalerweise nur bei Tätigkeits- und Vorgangsverben verwendet (vgl. § 62).
Außerdem sind folgende Unterschiede zwischen der *Continuous* und der *Simple Form* des *Past Perfect* zu beachten:

Past Perfect Continuous: **Dauer und Ablauf der vorzeitigen Handlung betont**	***Past Perfect Simple:*** **Vorzeitigkeit an sich betont**
After the soup **had been boiling** for ten minutes she turned the heat down. We **had been working** in the kitchen all day, so we were too tired to enjoy the party.	After he **had added** the eggs he beat the mixture with the electric mixer. Aunt Dorothy's apple pie tasted great, of course. She **had** always **been** a good cook.

§ 68 Die Wiedergabe der Zukunft: Formen und Sprechabsichten (Übersicht)

Ways of Expressing Future Time: Verb Forms and Speech Intentions (Table)

F Zukünftiges Geschehen kann im Englischen durch eine Reihe von Formen wiedergegeben werden, und zwar durch:

We'**ll travel** / We **are going to travel** / We **are travelling** / We'**ll be travelling**	to London next week.
Our plane **leaves** at 7.30.	
We'**ll have arrived** before lunchtime.	

1. *will*-Futur (vgl. § 69)
2. *going-to*-Futur (vgl. § 70)
3. *Present Tense Continuous* (vgl. § 70)
4. *Future Continuous* (vgl. § 71)
5. *Present Tense Simple* (eingeschränkter Gebrauch, vgl. § 72)
6. *Future Perfect* (§ 73)

V Über zukünftiges Geschehen lassen sich keine verbindlichen Aussagen machen wie über die Gegenwart oder die Vergangenheit. Deshalb drücken alle Futur-Formen bestimmte Einstellungen oder Sprechabsichten aus.

Zukünftiges Geschehen vom persönlichen Willen abhängig	Zukünftiges Geschehen von äußeren Umständen abhängig
***will*-Futur: Versprechen, Willenserklärung**	***will*-Futur, *Future Perfect:* Vorhersage**
I'**ll send** you a postcard from Ireland.	It **will take** us two hours to drive to Dover. By 10 o'clock at the latest we **will have** reached Paris.
***going-to*-Futur: Absicht**	***going-to*-Futur: Gewißheit, Schlußfolgerung**
Barbara and I **are going to hitchhike** from Munich to Athens.	We won't be able to sleep on the bus. It'**s going to be** a very tiring journey.
***Present Tense Continuous:* Plan, Vereinbarung**	***Present Tense Simple:* feststehender Termin**
My cousin **is travelling** with us. We'**re meeting** at Victoria Station.	Our train **leaves** at 10.15 a.m. When **does** the ferry **arrive** in Calais?

Erwartete Entwicklung: *Future Continuous*
I suppose your rich aunt **will be going** to Switzerland again this winter.

H Außer *will* können auch die anderen modalen Hilfsverben sowie Infinitivkonstruktionen auf zukünftiges Geschehen hinweisen. (Vgl. § 76, 87 und 91.)

§ 69 *Will*-Futur

Will-Future

F

I/You/He/She/It/We/They	**will**	**start** tomorrow.
(I/We	**shall**)	
I/You/He/She/It/We/They	**'ll**	
I/You/He/She/It/We/They	**won't**	

Das *will*-Futur wird aus *will* + Infinitiv gebildet.
In der ersten Person wird statt *will* gelegentlich auch *shall* gebraucht.
In der Umgangssprache werden statt *will / will not* die Kurzform *'ll / won't* verwendet.

V Beim *will*-Futur lassen sich zwei Anwendungsbereiche unterscheiden:

will-Futur bei Willenserklärungen / Versprechen

Of course we**'ll help** you to cut the hedge.
I **won't let** the grass grow so high again.

Will enthält hier neben dem Verweis auf zukünftiges Geschehen noch eine weitere Sprechabsicht: Versprechen, Bereitschaft.
Will kann außerdem eine Reihe anderer Sprechabsichten ausdrücken: vgl. § 80.

will-Futur zur Vorhersage

allgemeine Vorhersagen

The West **will have** cloudy skies with occasional showers.
The harvest **will be** very good this year.

Das *will*-Futur bezieht sich hier auf zukünftige Ereignisse, die nicht von einer persönlichen Entscheidung abhängen, sondern von äußeren Umständen.

Bedingungssätze

If there is any more frost, the roses **will be** ruined.
We**'ll pick** the apples if it stops raining.

Ob ein zukünftiges Geschehen eintritt, hängt oft von einer Bedingung ab. Deshalb erscheint das *will*-Futur sehr häufig in Hauptsätzen von Bedingungsgefügen.
Beachte: Im *if*-Satz steht das *Present Tense* (vgl. § 27).

H I hope the weather **will be** fine tomorrow.

Das *will*-Futur erscheint auch in Nebensätzen, die von Verben und Ausdrücken des Hoffens und Befürchtens abhängig sind.

§ 70 *Going-to*-Futur und *Present Tense Continuous*
Going-to-Future and Present Tense Continuous

F

I	**am going to**	**be** late.
You / We / They	**are going to**	
He / She / It	**is going to**	

Das *going-to*-Futur wird gebildet aus *am / are / is* + *going to* + Infinitiv.

Zu den Formen des *Present Tense Continuous* vgl. § 63 F.

V Sowohl das *going-to*-Futur als auch das *Present Tense Continuous* können zukünftiges Geschehen ausdrücken, das vom Willen des Handelnden abhängt. Folgende Bedeutungsunterschiede sind zu beachten:

going-to-Futur: Vorhaben, Absicht

We're **going to buy** Judy a violin for her birthday.
Bobby says he's **going to be** a famous musician when he grows up.

Das *going-to*-Futur drückt ein mehr oder weniger festes Vorhaben aus. Es bezieht sich häufig, aber nicht immer, auf die nahe Zukunft.

Present Tense Continuous: fester Plan, Vereinbarung

The London Philharmonic **is playing** at the City Theatre on the 17th.
We**'re meeting** Bill and Sue after the concert tonight.

Das *Present Tense Continuous* (nur bei Tätigkeits- und Vorgangsverben! Vgl. § 62) drückt fest arrangierte Pläne, Vereinbarungen oder Verabredungen des Handelnden aus.

Um Verwechslungen mit gegenwärtigen Handlungen auszuschließen, wird meist eine Zeitangabe wie *soon, next week*, etc. benutzt.

H Look at those clouds — it's **going to rain** soon.

Das *going-to*-Futur kann auch ein Ereignis vorhersagen, das von äußeren Umständen abhängt. (Vgl. § 68.)
Es drückt dann eine ziemlich große Gewißheit aus.

§ 71 *Future Continuous*

F

I/You/He/She/We/They	**will**	**be coming** later.
(I/We	**shall)**	
I/You/He/She/We/They	**'ll**	

Das *Future Continuous* setzt sich zusammen aus *will (shall)* + *be* + *Present Participle.*
Zu *will/shall* vgl. § 69 F, zum *Present Participle* vgl. § 63 F.

V Das *Future Continuous* ist nur bei Vorgangs- und Tätigkeitsverben üblich (vgl. § 62). Es hat zwei Anwendungsbereiche:

Verlauf der zukünftigen Handlung betont	Erwartete Handlung in der Zukunft
This time tomorrow **I'll be lying** on the beach on Capri! When Mrs Williams gets back from her holiday a lot of work **will be waiting** for her.	I suppose you**'ll be going** sailing again next week-end. You needn't phone Jim to make plans for the camping trip. **I'll be meeting** him at the Youth Club tonight.
Das *Future Continuous* kann einen Vorgang bezeichnen, der zu einem bestimmten zukünftigen Zeitpunkt gerade ablaufen wird. Häufig handelt es sich um eine ‚Hintergrundshandlung', vor allem in Verbindung mit einem *when*-Satz (vgl. § 65).	Durch das *Future Continuous* kann der Sprecher auch ausdrücken, daß er eine zukünftige Handlung für so gut wie sicher hält, ohne zu sagen, ob es sich um eine Absicht, eine Verabredung oder ein Versprechen handelt. (‚Es wird sich eben so ergeben.')

§ 72 *Present Tense Simple* zur Wiedergabe der Zukunft
Present Tense Simple to Express Future Time

F Zu den Formen vgl. § 63 F.

V Im Gegensatz zum deutschen Präsens kann das *Present Tense Simple* nur begrenzt zur Wiedergabe der Zukunft verwendet werden:

Present Tense Simple in Hauptsätzen: bei feststehenden Terminen	*Present Tense Simple* in temporalen Nebensätzen
The sightseeing tour **starts** at 10 a.m. The coach **leaves** from the station at eight.	When I **find** out what the ticket costs, I'll let you know. He'll ring us up as soon as he **lands** at Dublin Airport.
Das *Present Tense Simple* tritt nur ein, wenn der Termin nicht vom Sprecher oder vom Handelnden selbst festgelegt ist, sondern z. B. von einer Institution. Dies ist häufig der Fall bei Fahrplanangaben, so daß man auch vom ‚timetable future' spricht.	In temporalen Nebensätzen, die sich auf die Zukunft beziehen — z. B. mit *when, as soon as, before* — tritt das *Present Tense Simple* ein. Im zugehörigen Hauptsatz dagegen steht meist das *will*-Futur, nie das *Present Tense Simple.* (Zur Verwendung in *if*-Sätzen vgl. § 27 und § 69.)

§ 73 *Future Perfect*

F

I/You/He/She/We/They	**will**	
(I/We	**shall)**	**have finished** soon.
I/You/He/She/We/They	**'ll**	

Das *Future Perfect Simple* setzt sich zusammen aus *will (shall) + have + Past Participle.*
Zu *will/shall* vgl. § 69 F, zum *Past Participle* vgl. § 66 F.

V

Future Perfect: Handlung zu einem zukünftigen Zeitpunkt abgeschlossen

By the time Mum gets home, we**'ll have painted** all the doors.
I hope they**'ll have repaired** the central heating before it gets cold.

Das *Future Perfect* sagt vorher, daß eine Handlung zu einem bestimmten Zeitpunkt der Zukunft abgeschlossen sein wird. Dieser Zeitpunkt wird meist durch eine Zeitangabe wie *soon, by Saturday* (= bis spätestens Samstag) oder einen temporalen Nebensatz (*when, as soon as,* etc.) bestimmt.

§ 74 *Conditional* und *Conditional Perfect*

F

I/You/He/She/We/They	**would**	**do** it differently.
(I/We	**should)**	
I/You/He/She/We/They	**would**	**have done** it differently.
(I/We	**should)**	
I/You/He/She/We/They	**'d**	**do** it differently.
I/You/He/She/We/They	**wouldn't**	**have done** it differently.

1. Das *Conditional* wird gebildet aus *would* + Infinitiv.
2. Das *Conditional Perfect* wird gebildet aus *would + have + Past Participle.*

Beachte: In der 1. Person tritt statt *would* gelegentlich auch *should* ein. In der Umgangssprache werden häufig die Kurzformen *'d* und *wouldn't* verwendet.

V

Conditional

in der indirekten Rede

Betty has borrowed all my Agatha Christies.
She said she **would read** them all in the holidays.
(Direkte Rede: "I **will read** them all in the holidays")

Das *Conditional* in der indirekten Rede vom Typ *He said* ... wird oft als *Future in the Past* bezeichnet: Es entspricht einem *will*-Futur in der direkten Rede.
Zum System der Zeitenfolge vgl. § 25.

in Bedingungssätzen: Erfüllung der Bedingung unwahrscheinlich oder unmöglich

I'd be very surprised if he let us use his record-player.
If I were you I **wouldn't lend** that Jones girl anything.

Zu beachten ist, daß das *Conditional* nur im Hauptsatz auftritt, nicht im *if*-Satz. (Vgl. § 27)

Conditional Perfect

in der indirekten Rede

You haven't given me my book back yet –
you told me you **would have finished** it by now.
(Direkte Rede: "I **will have finished** it by next Monday.")

Das *Conditional Perfect* wird in dieser Verwendung auch *Future Perfect in the Past* genannt: Es entspricht einem *Future Perfect* in der direkten Rede.

in Bedingungssätzen: Erfüllung der Bedingung nicht mehr möglich

If I had known how careless he was, I **wouldn't have lent** him my Beatles LP.

Auch das *Conditional Perfect* erscheint nur im Hauptsatz, nicht im *if*-Satz. (Vgl. § 27)

§ 75 Die Zeitformen des Passivs
The Passive Forms of the Verb

F

Passiv: *Simple Forms*

The car	**is checked** regularly.
The brakes	**were repaired** yesterday.
The tank	**has been filled.**
The car	**had been washed** before the trip.
The battery	**will be recharged** this afternoon.
The oil	**would be changed** if ...
The car	**will have been repaired** by 6 p.m.
The car	**would have been washed** sooner if ...

1. In der *Simple Form* können alle Zeitformen des Aktivs auch im Passiv gebildet werden, und zwar folgendermaßen:

Present Tense:	*am / is / are*		+ *Past Participle*
Past Tense:	*was / were*		
Present Perfect:	*have / has*	*been*	
Past Perfect:	*had*	*been*	
Future:	*will*	*be*	
Conditional:	*would*	*be*	
Future Perfect:	*will*	*have been*	
Conditional Perfect:	*would*	*have been*	

Passiv: *Continuous Forms*

The car	**is being repaired** at the moment.
The car	**was being repaired,** so I took the bus.

2. Von der *Continuous Form* sind nur die *Present-* und *Past-Tense*-Formen üblich. Sie bestehen aus

am / is / are / *was / were* } *being* + *Past Participle*

Zum *Past Participle* vgl. § 66 F.

V

Die Passivformen sind im Englischen vielseitiger verwendbar als im Deutschen (vgl. § 3).
Für den Gebrauch der einzelnen Zeitformen gelten die gleichen Grundsätze wie beim Aktiv (vgl. §§ 62–67).
Bei der Verwendung von *Continuous* und *Simple Form* ist zu beachten:

***Continuous Form:* Betonung des Ablaufs**

Our TV **is being repaired** at the moment.
While the Minister **was being interviewed** the sound went off.

Wie beim Aktiv kann die *Continuous Form* nur von Tätigkeitsverben gebildet werden, da nur sie die Vorstellung des Ablaufs und der Dauer zulassen. (Vgl. § 62).

***Simple Form:* Neutrale Betrachtungsweise**

The news **is** generally **followed** by the weather forecast.
The film **was shown** very late in the evening.

Die *Simple Form* wird benutzt, wenn Ablauf und Dauer nicht besonders hervorgehoben werden sollen. Sie beschreibt z. B. Vorgänge, die regelmäßig wiederkehren *(Present Tense)* oder einmalige Vorgänge in der Vergangenheit *(Past Tense).*

H

1. He **got** badly **hurt** in the accident.

   In der Umgangssprache treten gelegentlich auch Passivbildungen mit *get* auf.

2. The gate **is locked** at 7 p.m. every evening. — Das Tor **wird** jeden Abend um 7 Uhr **geschlossen**.
   We can't get in – the gate **is locked**. — Wir können nicht hinein – das Tor **ist geschlossen**.

   Die Passivkonstruktion aus *be*-Form und *Past Participle* kann nicht nur eine Handlung bezeichnen (etwas *wird* getan), sondern auch einen Zustand (etwas *ist* getan; sog. ‚Zustandspassiv').
   Im Deutschen werden im Gegensatz zum Englischen für die beiden Bedeutungen verschiedene Hilfsverben benutzt.

8 Die Hilfsverben

The Auxiliary Verbs

§ 76 Modale Hilfsverben: Formen, Strukturen, Sprechabsichten (Übersicht)

The Modal Auxiliaries: Verb Forms, Structures, Speech Intentions (Table)

F Zu den modalen Hilfsverben gehören *can, may, shall, will, must, needn't, dare, ought to* und *used to.*
Sie unterscheiden sich von Vollverben in folgender Hinsicht:

He **can** swim. (Vollverb: He **swims.**) We **can swim.** (Vollverb: We **like to swim.**) **Can** you **swim?** (Vollverb: **Do** you **swim?**)	1. **Die auffälligsten Merkmale:** — Die 3. Person Singular *Present Tense* wird ohne *-s* gebildet. — Die Infinitivformen anderer Verben werden ohne *to* angeschlossen (außer bei *ought to* und *used to*). — In Frage und Verneinung wird nicht mit *do* umschrieben.
I **can** / She **may** / We **shall** / They **will** } come. I **could** / She **might** / We **should** / They **would** } come.	2. ***Present-* und *Past-Tense*-Formen:** Einige modale Hilfsverben haben nur eine *Present-Tense*-Form. Zu *can, may, shall* und *will* gibt es auch *Past-Tense*-Formen. Diese drücken jedoch oft nicht die Vergangenheit aus, sondern den Konjunktiv (vgl. dt. „könnte", „müßte").
I **may have been** careless. It **might have fallen.** You **could have got** hurt. They **needn't have worried.**	3. **Zusammengesetzte Formen:** Fast alle modalen Hilfsverben (*Present-* und *Past-Tense*-Formen) können mit *have + Past Participle* (Infinitiv Perfekt) eines Vollverbs verbunden werden. Diese Zusammensetzungen haben oft die Bedeutung eines Konjunktivs der Vorzeitigkeit (vgl. dt. „hätte können").
She can meet you. / She **will be able to** meet you. We must start early. / We **had to** start early. They may go. / They **were allowed to** go.	4. **Ersatzformen:** Für die Zeitformen, die von den modalen Hilfsverben nicht gebildet werden können, treten Umschreibungen mit Verben ähnlicher Bedeutung ein.
Everyone should learn a foreign language. [ʃəd] He can speak Chinese. — Oh, can he? [kən] ['kæn] He must be very clever, mustn't he? [məst] ['mʌsnt]	5. **Aussprache und Schreibung:** Die bejahten Hilfsverben werden normalerweise in der Schwachform gesprochen. Die Vollform verwendet man nur, wenn das Hilfsverb besonders betont ist, z. B. in der Kurzantwort. In der Verneinung sind die Kurzformen verbreitet: *mustn't* für *must not, needn't* für *need not,* etc. **Beachte:** *can't* [kɑːnt] für *cannot* *shan't* [ʃɑːnt] für *shall not* *won't* [wəʊnt] für *will not*

Er **kann Englisch.** He **can speak English.** Ich **muß** jetzt **weg.** I **must leave** now.

Im Gegensatz zum Deutschen kann ein modales Hilfsverb nur durch den Infinitiv eines Vollverbs ergänzt werden, nicht durch ein Nomen oder ein Richtungsadverb.

V Die modalen Hilfsverben drücken jeweils eine bestimmte Einstellung zu dem Sachverhalt aus, den das Vollverb des Satzes bezeichnet (z. B. "go out"). Zusammen mit dem Vollverb geben sie auf diese Weise verschiedenartige Sprechabsichten wieder: "You can / mustn't / shouldn't go out", etc.

Sprechabsichten, die durch modale Hilfsverben ausgedrückt werden können		
Erlaubnis / Verbot		
can may / mustn't	§ 77 § 78	You **can** eat as much fruit as you like, but you **can't** have any more cake or sweets. **May** I take part in the swimming gala next week? You **mustn't** drive after taking those tablets.
Ausdruck einer Notwendigkeit / Verneinung einer Notwendigkeit		
must / needn't	§ 79	We **must** be at the youth club by 7 p.m. You **needn't** take the bus — it's near enough to walk. We **needn't have** hurried — the concert didn't start until 8.30.
Rat / Warnung / Tadel / Ausdruck der Verpflichtung		
should / ought to	§ 81	You **shouldn't** cross the road here. They **ought to** do something about this dangerous crossing. The accident was his own fault — he **should have** been more careful.
Wunsch / Bitte		
will / would can / could	§ 80 § 77	**Will / Would** you do me a favour? **Can / Could** you lend me 50p?
Ausdruck der Fähigkeit		
can / could	§ 77	Tom **can** play the guitar very well. We know the words, so we **can** all join in the chorus. I **couldn't** sing because I had a sore throat.
Ausdruck der Annahme / Möglichkeit / Wahrscheinlichkeit		
may / might can / could must	§ 78 § 77 § 79	The French boys **may** not like the food here. Judging by that girl's accent, she **could** be German. They **must have** enjoyed their holiday in England — they're coming again next year.

H

"You **can (may)** go for a swim, but you **mustn't (shouldn't)** lie in the sun."
The doctor said I **could (might)** go for a swim, but I **mustn't (shouldn't)** lie in the sun.

If it stays fine, we **can** go on a picnic tomorrow.

Zur Zeitenfolge bei modalen Hilfsverben in der indirekten Rede und in Bedingungssätzen vgl. § 25 V 2 und § 27 V 1.

§ 77 *Can/could*

V

Verwendungsmöglichkeiten von *can* und *could:* ähnlich wie die von deutsch „können“	
Ausdruck der Fähigkeit I **can** understand French when it is spoken slowly. We **couldn't** understand what the policeman said. I **was able to** translate most of the menu with the help of the dictionary. Ich konnte (es gelang mir) ... Next year **I'll be able** to speak Spanish fluently.	*Can, can't* und die verneinte *Past-Tense*-Form *couldn't* können unbeschränkt zum Ausdruck des Könnens verwendet werden. Die bejahte Form *could* kann jedoch nicht wie das deutsche „konnte“ in der Bedeutung „es gelang“ benutzt werden. Hier tritt — ebenso wie in den übrigen fehlenden Zeitformen — *be able to* ein.
Annahme / Möglichkeit / Wahrscheinlichkeit Where **can** my umbrella be? Wo kann ... It **could** rain again this afternoon. Es könnte ... Surely you **can't have** left your coat at the pub?	*Can/could* sowie *can have/could have* + *Past Participle* können eine Annahme im Sinn von „möglicherweise“ ausdrücken. *Could* steht dabei für eine vorsichtigere Annahme als *can.* *Can't (have)* bedeutet: „es kann nicht sein, daß ...“.
Erlaubnis / Verbot **Can** I go to the cinema tonight? No, you **can't.** You **can** leave your coats in the cloakroom, if you wish.	Für Erlaubnis und Verbot werden vor allem die *Present-Tense*-Formen *can* und *can't* verwendet. Zu *may* und *mustn't* in dieser Bedeutung vgl. § 78.
Höfliche Frage oder Bitte **Can / Could** you give me some change for the phone?	*Could* klingt in Fragesätzen noch höflicher als *can* (vgl.: „Kannst / Könntest du ...“). Zu *will/would* vgl. § 80.

§ 78 *May/might/mustn't*

V

1. *May/may not* und *must not* entsprechen dem deutschen „dürfen“/„nicht dürfen“. Für die fehlenden Zeitformen tritt *be allowed to* ein (im Amtsstil auch *be permitted to*).

Erlaubnis	**Verbot**
***May:* vor allem im Gespräch** **May** I borrow your pencil? — Yes, you **may.** You **may** use a dictionary for this exercise. We **were allowed to** leave the room as soon as we had finished the test. *May* gebraucht man, wenn man um Erlaubnis bittet bzw. wenn man sie gewährt, also vorwiegend in Fragen und Antworten.	***May not:* vor allem in Kurzantworten** **May** I go swimming? — No, you **may not.** ***Must not:* allgemein im Gespräch verwendbar** You **mustn't** try to hitchhike on the motorway. Jim **wasn't allowed to** go cycling with us.

H

Die Ersatzform *be allowed to* drückt eine etwas andere Sprechabsicht aus als *may/must not:* Während *may/must not* betonen, daß der Sprecher selbst etwas erlaubt oder verbietet, wird durch *be allowed to* nur festgestellt, daß etwas erlaubt oder verboten ist.

V 2. *May* und *might* können im Sinn einer Annahme verwendet werden. Sie drücken dabei einen geringeren Grad der Wahrscheinlichkeit aus als *can* (vgl. § 77) und *must* (vgl. § 79).

May/might zum Ausdruck der Annahme/Möglichkeit

Do you know the name of that band? No, but they **may** tell us at the end of the programme. Nein, aber vielleicht ...
The music we heard this morning **may have been** Beethoven's Third. ... könnte Beethovens Dritte gewesen sein.
That sounds like Janis Joplin, but it **might not be** her at all. ... aber vielleicht ist sie es gar nicht.

May/might sowie die zusammengesetzten Formen *may have/might have* entsprechen dem deutschen Adverb „vielleicht". Die verneinten Formen *may/might not (have)* entsprechen dem deutschen „vielleicht nicht".
Might drückt eine vorsichtigere Annahme aus als *may.*

§ 79 *Must/needn't*

V Eine Notwendigkeit und deren Verneinung kann man im Deutschen jeweils durch das gleiche Hilfsverb ausdrücken: „müssen", „nicht müssen". Im Englischen sind zwei verschiedene Hilfsverben nötig: *must* und *needn't.*
Für die fehlenden Zeitformen tritt *have to* ein.

Must zum Ausdruck der Notwendigkeit

You **must** work a lot harder at mathematics.
Dave **had to** stay up till 11 last night learning grammar.

Must/must have zum Ausdruck der Annahme

It's 5 o'clock — the match **must** be nearly over.
Listen to them cheering — our school **must have** won!

Must drückt, wie das deutsche „müssen", aus, daß der Sprecher etwas für so gut wie sicher hält.

Needn't zur Verneinung der Notwendigkeit

You **needn't** bring your history books tomorrow.
Thank God we **won't have to** do any more tests this year.

needn't have

We **needn't have** worked so hard — the test was easy.
Mary is glad she **didn't have to** repeat her exam.

Needn't have + *Past Participle* drückt aus, daß etwas unnötigerweise geschah. *Didn't have to* drückt aus, daß etwas nicht geschah, weil es nicht nötig war.

H 1. Die Ersatzform *have to* drückt eine etwas andere Sprechabsicht aus als *must/needn't:* Während *must/needn't* betonen, daß der Sprecher selbst etwas für notwendig oder nicht notwendig hält, wird durch *have to* nur festgestellt, daß eine Notwendigkeit besteht bzw. nicht vorhanden ist.

2. Statt *have to* kann auch *need to* als Vollverb verwendet werden (vgl. § 82).

⚠ Für „nicht müssen" kann keinesfalls *must not* eintreten.

§ 80 *will/would/used to*

V *Will* und *would* werden von Deutschen gern mit „wollen“ gleichgesetzt und als Ausdruck des Willens verstanden. Diese Verwendung ist im Englischen jedoch seltener als andere Bedeutungsvarianten von *will/would*.

will/would zum Ausdruck des festen Willens (selten)

I **will** buy that record-player, even if I have to borrow the money.	Ich werde diesen Plattenspieler kaufen ...
John **wants** me **to** lend him my new L.P., but I **won't.**	John will, daß ich ..., aber das werde ich nicht tun.
I **wanted to** tape the concert, but my sister **wouldn't** let me use her cassette-recorder.	Ich wollte das Konzert auf Band aufnehmen, aber meine Schwester wollte ... nicht ...

In dieser Bedeutung erscheinen *will* und *would* nur bei besonderer Betonung, zum Ausdruck der festen Entschlossenheit. Die bejahten Formen sind ausgesprochen selten; etwas häufiger kommen die verneinten Formen *won't* und *wouldn't* zum Ausdruck des Nicht-Wollens vor.
Normalerweise aber wird das „Wollen“ durch *want to, be willing to* oder *intend to* wiedergegeben.

will/would zum Ausdruck einer Bitte oder eines Wunsches

Will you keep an eye on my suitcase while I'm getting the tickets?	Würdest du auf meinen Koffer aufpassen ...
Would you help me with the luggage, please?	Würden Sie mir bitte helfen ...
Would you **like to** sit here? — No, **I'd like to** find an empty compartment.	Würdest du gern / Möchtest du ...
Philip **wants to** sit near the window.	Philip will / möchte ...

Will und *would* kommen in Fragesätzen zur Äußerung einer Bitte oder eines Wunsches vor. Dabei wirkt *would* höflicher als *will*. Ein Wunsch kann auch durch *would like to, want to* oder *wish to* geäußert und erfragt werden.

would/used to zum Ausdruck einer früheren Gewohnheit

My great-grandfather **would** always get up at five o'clock.	Mein Urgroßvater stand immer um 5 Uhr auf.
I **used to** play tennis a lot, but now I've got lazy.	Früher habe ich viel Tennis gespielt, ...

Would kann bei den meisten Tätigkeitsverben zum Ausdruck einer früheren Gewohnheit verwendet werden (im Sinn von „tat gewöhnlich“, „pflegte zu tun“). Gebräuchlicher ist in dieser Bedeutung jedoch *used to,* das mit allen Verben verbunden werden kann.
Used to, zu dem es keine *Present-Tense*-Form gibt, entspricht häufig dem deutschen Adverb „früher“.

H

1. Water **will boil** at 100° C. (Water **boils** at 100° C.)

   Will kann wie das *Present Tense Simple* zur Beschreibung einer Eigenschaft oder eines typischen Verhaltens benutzt werden.

2. Im Gespräch drücken *would* und vor allem *wouldn't* oft höfliche Zurückhaltung aus:
   I wouldn't think so klingt verbindlicher als *I don't think so.*

§ 81 *Shall/should/ought to/to be to*

V *Shall, should* und *ought to* decken nicht alle Verwendungsmöglichkeiten des deutschen „sollen“ ab. Sie sind auf wenige Sprechabsichten beschränkt. Für einige Bedeutungen von „sollen“ tritt *to be to* ein.

Shall: **Wunsch / Vorschlag / Versprechen**	***Should / ought to:*** **Rat / Ermahnung / Pflicht**
Shall we go on a picnic if the weather is fine? **Shall** I make the sandwiches? You **shall** have the biggest feast of your lives! He **shan't** spoil our picnic by bringing that dog!	You **shouldn't** drink so much lemonade. Jim **ought to** leave some of the sandwiches for the rest of us! We **should have** remembered to bring some salt and pepper.
Shall wird in Fragesätzen (meist 1. Person) verwendet, um einen Wunsch zu erfragen oder einen Vorschlag zu machen. In Aussagesätzen drückt *shall* – je nach Zusammenhang – ein Versprechen oder eine Drohung aus. („Ich werde dafür sorgen, daß ...“)	*Should/ought to* entsprechen dem deutschen „sollte (eigentlich)“. Die zusammengesetzten Formen *should have/ought to have* + *Past Participle* entsprechen dem deutschen „hätte sollen“.

to be to: **Auftrag / Anweisung / Vereinbarung**
Can you lend me your youth hostel guide? I **am to** make the reservations for the whole group. I have just had the warden on the phone. We**'re** all **to** bring our own sleeping-bags, as they haven't got enough at the hostel. The coach **was to** leave at 6 a.m., but we were held up for two hours because of engine trouble.

H

1. Nobody would have guessed that that little boy **was to** become one of America's greatest athletes.

   Was to/were to kann auch als eine Art *future in the past* verwendet werden. („Es sollte so kommen.“)

2. Peter's sister **is said to** be an excellent tennis-player.

   Dem deutschen „soll angeblich“ entsprechen im Englischen die Wendungen *to be said to, to be supposed to.*

3. Zu *shall* und *should* bei der Bildung von *will*-Futur und *Conditional* vgl. § 69 F und § 74 F.

§ 82 *Need* und *dare* als Hilfs- und Vollverben
Need and *dare* Used as Auxiliary Verbs and as Main Verbs

F

She	**needn't explain.**
How	**dare** he **say** that!
That	**needs** explaining.
He	**dares to speak** to me like that!
We	**didn't need** to ask.

1. *Need* und *dare* können als Hilfsverben verwendet werden. Das bedeutet:
   – Die 3. Person Singular wird ohne *-s* gebildet.
   – Der Infinitiv wird ohne *to* angeschlossen.
   – Frage und Verneinung werden ohne *do*-Formen gebildet.
   – Es gibt nur die Zeitformen *need, need have done, dare, dared* (selten).
2. *Need* und *dare* treten aber auch als Vollverben auf. Das bedeutet:
   – Die 3. Person Singular *(Present Tense)* wird mit *-s* gebildet.
   – Der Infinitiv wird mit *to* angeschlossen.
   – Frage und Verneinung werden mit *do*-Formen gebildet.
   – Es können alle Zeitformen gebildet werden.

V

***Need* als Hilfsverb: Nur in Verneinung und Frage**	***Need* als Vollverb: Auch im bejahten Satz**
We **needn't** water the lawn today: it's going to rain. **Need** we really dig so deep?	You **won't need** to cut the grass again this month. Those plants **need** a lot of water They **need** to be watered/They **need** watering every day.
Als Hilfsverb kommt *need* nur in Verneinung und Frage vor, als Vollverb auch in bejahten Aussagesätzen. Das Vollverb *need* kann nicht nur mit einem Infinitiv verbunden werden, sondern auch mit einem Nomen, einem passiven Infinitiv oder einem *Gerund*.	

Dare* als Hilfsverb: Nur in Verneinung und Ausrufen mit *how	***Dare* als Vollverb: Auch in Fragen**
He **daren't** touch the strawberries. How **dare** you walk on my flowers!	**Did** she **dare** to climb over the fence? The children next door **wouldn't dare** to steal our apples.
Als Hilfsverb kommt *dare* nur in Verneinung und in Ausrufen mit *how* vor. Als Vollverb kommt es hauptsächlich in Verneinung und Frage vor, jedoch nicht in Ausrufen mit *how*.	

§ 83 *Do* als Hilfsverb und Vollverb
Do Used as an Auxiliary Verb and as a Main Verb

F

		Vollformen	Kurzformen
Present Tense:	I / you / we / they he / she / it	**do (not)** **does (not)**	**don't** **doesn't**
Past Tense:	I / you / he / she / it / we / they	**did (not)**	**didn't**

Infinite Verbformen:

Infinitiv	**do**
Present Participle:	**doing**
Past Participle:	**done**

V

***Do* als Hilfsverb in Frage und Verneinung**	***Do* als Vollverb**
Do you like jazz? Yes, I **do,** but I **don't** like this band. Ann plays the guitar, **doesn't** she? Yes, she **does,** and so **do** I. That girl **does** sing beautifully!	We must turn the radio down. My sister **is doing** her homework. Jack always **does** his best to get good marks at school. What **do** you **do** in your free time?
Do wird, wenn kein anderes Hilfsverb im Satz vorhanden ist, zur Bildung von Frage und Verneinung benötigt, ebenso in verschiedenen Arten von Kurzsätzen und zur Hervorhebung einer Aussage. Vgl. § 6—14.	Als Vollverb gehört *do* zur Gruppe der „Tätigkeitsverben", die häufig in der *Continuous Form* auftreten (vgl. § 62). In Frage und Verneinung wird das Vollverb *do* mit dem Hilfsverb *do* umschrieben.

H Zum Gebrauch der Kurz- und Vollformen vgl. § 7.

§ 84 *Have* als Hilfsverb und Vollverb

Have Used as an Auxiliary Verb and as a Main Verb

F

Present Tense					
Vollformen		**Kurzformen**			
I, you, we, they	**have (not)**	I, you, we, they	**'ve (not)**	I, you, we, they	**haven't**
he, she, it	**has (not)**	he, she, it	**'s (not)**	he, she, it	**hasn't**

Past Tense					
Vollformen		**Kurzformen**			
I, you, we, they, he, she, it	**had (not)**	I, you, we, they, he, she, (it)	**'d**	I, you, we, they, he, she, it	**hadn't**

Infinite Verbformen: Infinitiv: **have** *Present Participle:* **having** *Past Participle:* **had**

He's (= **he has**) done it. **He's** (= **he is**) doing it. **He'd** (= **he had**) done it. **He'd** (= **he would**) do it.

V

have als Hilfsverb zur Bildung von Zeitformen

I **haven't taken** the bus since they raised the fares.
Before he bought a bicycle my brother **had** always **gone** to work by car.

Have wird in Verbindung mit dem *Past Participle* zur Bildung der *Perfect Tenses* benützt (vgl. §§ 66, 67, 73, 74, 75).
Wie alle Hilfsverben wird *have* in dieser Verwendung in Frage und Verneinung nicht mit *do* umschrieben.

have to in der Bedeutung „müssen"

You'**ll have to** get up earlier in future.
Do you **have to** spend half an hour in the bathroom?

Have to muß in Frage und Verneinung mit *do* umschrieben werden. (Zu *have to* und *must/need not* vgl. § 79.)

have something done: „etwas machen lassen"

I never wash that blouse — I always **have it cleaned.**
Where **did** you **have your hair done?** It looks great!

In der Bedeutung „machen lassen" muß *have* in Frage und Verneinung mit *do* umschrieben werden. (Näheres s. § 88.)

have/have got in der Bedeutung „besitzen"

Have you **(got)** any brothers or sisters? — No, I **haven't.**
My eldest sister **has (got)** a second-hand car.

Wenn *have* in der Bedeutung „besitzen" auftritt, kann die *do*-Umschreibung in Frage und Verneinung entfallen. In der Umgangssprache wird allerdings *have got* bevorzugt, welches nie umschrieben wird.
Da *have* hier eine Beziehung und keine Tätigkeit ausdrückt, ist nur die *Simple Form* möglich (vgl. § 62).

have a bath/have breakfast

I **didn't have a bath** this morning because the water wasn't hot enough.
The family **were having breakfast** when she came down.

Diese beliebte Kombination aus *have* + Nomen umschreibt meist ein Tätigkeitsverb („baden", „frühstücken" etc.).
Have verhält sich hier selbst wie ein Tätigkeitsverb:
Die *Continuous Form* ist möglich (vgl. § 62).
In Frage und Verneinung tritt *do*-Umschreibung ein.

Weitere Beispiele:
to have a wash (sich waschen), *to have a swim* (schwimmen), *to have a look* (schauen), *to have a talk (with)* (sich unterhalten), *to have a rest* (sich ausruhen), *to have tea/toast,* etc.

H In den Verwendungen *have something done* und *have a wash/have breakfast* sind Kurzformen von *have* nicht üblich. Bei den übrigen Verwendungen von *have* hängt der Gebrauch der Kurz- oder Vollformen von der Stilebene ab. (Vgl. § 7.)

⚠ Die verneinten Kurzformen *haven't, hasn't, hadn't* sind nur bei bestimmten Verwendungen von *have* möglich.

§ 85 *Be* als Hilfsverb und Vollverb
Be Used as an Auxiliary Verb and as a Main Verb

F

Present Tense

Vollformen		Kurzformen	
I **am** (not)		I **'m** (not)	
you / we / they **are** (not)		you / we / they **'re** (not)	you / we / they **aren't**
he / she / it **is** (not)		he / she / it **'s** (not)	he / she / it **isn't**

Past Tense

Vollformen	Kurzformen
I **was** (not)	I **wasn't**
you / we / they **were** (not)	you / we / they **weren't**
he / she / it **was** (not)	he / she / it **wasn't**

Infinite Verbformen: Infinitiv: **be** *Present Participle:* **being** *Past Participle:* **been**

H In Schlagern und anderen Originaltexten trifft man gelegentlich auf die Slang- und Dialektformen *I ain't/ain't I?* [eɪnt] für *I'm not/am I not?*. (Die Form *ain't* wird außerdem auch anstelle von *aren't, isn't, haven't, hasn't* gebraucht.) Beim eigenen Sprechen sind diese Formen jedoch zu vermeiden.

V

Be **als Hilfsverb zur Bildung der *Continuous Form* und des Passivs**	***Be*** **als Vollverb zum Ausdruck einer Beziehung**
Keep quiet, the baby **is sleeping!** The children **have been running** around since 7 o'clock. I **was woken** by a loud noise.	Some people **are** very lazy. It **is** 10 o'clock, and Mike **is** still in bed! We won't wake my parents: they **are** both sound sleepers.
Das Hilfsverb *be* und das *Present Participle* eines Vollverbs bilden zusammen die *Continuous Forms* der verschiedenen Zeitformen. (Vgl. § 63, 65—67, 71) In Verbindung mit dem *Past Participle* dient *be* zur Bildung des Passivs. (Vgl. § 75.)	Wie das deutsche Verb „sein" kann *be* als Vollverb eine Reihe verschiedenartiger Beziehungen ausdrücken (Eigenschaft, Ort, Zeit, etc.). Es bedarf dazu einer Ergänzung, z. B. durch ein Adjektiv, ein Nomen, eine Orts- oder Zeitangabe. Dabei tritt *be* stets in der *Simple Form* auf (außer in der Bedeutung „sich verhalten", vgl. § 62).

H

1. *Be* wird in Frage und Verneinung nicht mit *do* umschrieben, auch als Vollverb nicht (vgl. § 7 und § 9). (Zum verneinten Aufforderungssatz vgl. jedoch § 8.)

2. Der Gebrauch von Kurz- oder Vollformen ist unabhängig davon, ob *be* als Hilfsverb oder Vollverb verwendet wird. Er hängt nur von der Stilebene ab. (Vgl. § 7.)

9 Die infiniten Verbformen: Infinitiv, *Gerund* und Partizip

The Non-Finite Forms of the Verb: Infinitives, Gerunds, Participles

§ 86 Infinitiv, *Gerund,* Partizip: Formen und Verwendung (Übersicht)

Infinitives, Gerunds, Participles: Forms and Use (Table)

F Infinitiv, *Gerund-* und Partizipialformen enthalten im Gegensatz zu den anderen Verbformen (Personalformen) keine Angaben über Person und Zahl. Sie können von allen Verben außer von den modalen Hilfsverben gebildet werden. Infinitiv, *Gerund* und *Present Participle* können in verschiedenen Aktiv- und Passivformen auftreten. Zur Bildung der Passivformen benutzt man das Hilfsverb *be* und das *Past Participle* des Vollverbs.

Aktiv-Formen	Passiv-Formen
to explore a continent **to be exploring** **to have explored**	**to be explored** **to have been explored**
discovering an island **having discovered**	**being discovered** **having been discovered**
	an **explored** region a **frozen** sea

1. Der Infinitiv (Grundform des Verbs) erscheint meistens mit *to.*
   Continuous-Form: *to be + Present Participle*
   Perfect-Formen: *to have (been) + Past Participle.*
2. *Gerund* und *Present Participle* sind der Form nach identisch und werden auch *ing*-Formen genannt. Zur Schreibung vgl. § 63.
   Perfect-Formen: *having (been) + Past Participle.*
3. *Past Participle*
   Regelmäßige Formen: Grundform des Verbs + *-ed* (vgl. § 65 F).
   Unregelmäßige Formen: vgl. Anhang S. 89.

V Infinitiv, *Gerund* und Partizip sind die Formen des Verbs, die andere Wortarten im Satz vertreten können.

Verwendung von Infinitiv, *Gerund* und Partizip an Stelle von Nomen und Adjektiven

Infinitiv und *Gerund* an Stelle eines Nomens	
That sport / **To climb Mount Everest** / **Mountain climbing** } takes a lot of courage. My brother John loves { **the mountains.** / **to climb mountains.** / **climbing mountains.**	Infinitiv und *Gerund* können die gleichen Funktionen wie ein Nomen erfüllen, und zwar vor allem als Subjekt oder als Objekt eines Satzes.
The danger **of** **an accident** made me turn back. The danger **of** **getting hurt** made me turn back. I was afraid **of** **getting hurt.**	Das *Gerund* kann außerdem wie ein Nomen nach Präpositionen auftreten und dabei in verschiedenen Satzteilen erscheinen.
***Present Participle* und *Past Participle* an Stelle eines Adjektivs**	
The captain of the { **old** / **sinking** / **damaged** } ship remained { **calm.** / **standing on deck.** / **unmoved.**	Das *Present Participle* und das *Past Participle* vertreten häufig ein Adjektiv. Sie können wie ein Adjektiv als Attribut beim Nomen oder als Ergänzung zum Verb erscheinen.

H Zum Gebrauch von Infinitiv-, *Gerund-* und Partizipialkonstruktionen an Stelle von Nebensätzen vgl. §§ 18, 19, 21, 22, 24.

§ 87 Der Infinitiv als Ergänzung zum Verb
Infinitives Used as Verb Complements

F

Verb	(Objekt)	Infinitiv +	Ergänzung
We decided		**to go**	by bus.
We expected		**to be given**	a lift to town.
We expected	**her**	**to give**	us a lift to town.
We advised	**them**	**to go**	by bus.

An das Vollverb kann angeschlossen werden:

— der einfache Infinitiv in seinen verschiedenen Formen (vgl. § 86):

— ein Objekt + Infinitiv; das Objekt kann dabei als logisches Subjekt des folgenden Infinitivs aufgefaßt werden. (Vgl. § 19.)

V

Der Infinitiv tritt wie im Deutschen nach einer Vielzahl von Verben auf, die inhaltlich sehr verschieden sind. Folgende Bedeutungsgruppen verdienen jedoch besondere Beachtung:

Verben, die einen Wunsch oder Plan ausdrücken: **Verb + (Objektiv +) Infinitiv** The farmers **want to get** higher prices for meat. We **want *people* to buy** more British products. I **would hate to have** to pay more for food. Most people **would hate *the price of bread* to go up.**	Da sich der Infinitiv besonders zum Ausdruck eines zukunftsgerichteten Wunsches oder Plans eignet, steht er sehr häufig bei *want, wish, expect, intend* sowie *would like/hate/prefer.* Diese Verben können auch mit Objekt + Infinitiv verbunden werden. Im Deutschen entspricht dieser Konstruktion gewöhnlich ein *daß*-Satz (vgl. § 19).
Verben, die eine Aufforderung ausdrücken: **Verb + Objekt + Infinitiv** I **asked *you* to buy** some potatoes while you were in town. She **warned *her son* not to lose** the money on the way to the shops.	Diese Verben benötigen ein Objekt + Infinitiv, weil die Aufforderung immer an eine andere Person gerichtet ist. Zu dieser Gruppe gehören die Verben *advise, ask, order, tell, warn.* (Zu den Verben des Veranlassens und Zulassens vgl. § 88.)
Verben, die eine Meinung ausdrücken: **Verb + Objekt + Infinitiv in gehobenem Stil** We **believe *supermarkets* to be** a serious threat to the small shopkeeper.	Diese Verben können nicht mit einfachem Infinitiv, sondern nur mit Objekt + Infinitiv verbunden werden. In der Umgangssprache wird der *that*-Satz bevorzugt, wobei die Konjunktion *that* meist entfällt. Vgl.: I think (that) supermarkets are great.

H

1. Zu den Verben, die sowohl mit dem Infinitiv als auch mit dem Gerund verbunden werden können (*remember, regret, try, stop,* etc.) vgl. § 91.

2. We are **waiting for him to come.**

   Ein Objekt + Infinitiv ist auch möglich nach einigen Verben, die mit *for* verbunden werden, z. B. *to wait for* (darauf warten, daß), *to ask for* (darum bitten, daß), *to arrange for* (dafür sorgen, daß).

3. He **likes to** go shopping. (Er geht **gerne** einkaufen.)
   I'd prefer to stay at home. (Ich würde **lieber** ...)
   I **happened to** meet her in the street. (Ich habe sie **zufällig** ... getroffen.)
   He **failed to** notice me. (Er hat mich **nicht** bemerkt.)

   Englischen Verben mit Infinitiv entsprechen häufig deutsche Adverbien (gern, lieber, zufällig). Dem Verb *fail* + Infinitiv entspricht ein verneinter deutscher Satz.

4. It ***is*** **to be expected** that the opposition will win the next election.
It ***remains*** **to be seen** whether the new government will do any better.

Es ist **zu erwarten,** daß die Opposition die nächste Wahl gewinnt.
Es bleibt **abzuwarten,** ob die neue Regierung es besser machen wird.

Das Englische unterscheidet oft genauer zwischen Aktiv und Passiv als das Deutsche.
Nach *be* und *remain* muß im Englischen bei passivem Sinn auch der passive Infinitiv stehen.
Im Deutschen steht dagegen trotz passivem Sinn die Aktiv-Form des Infinitivs.

§ 88 Infinitiv und Partizip nach Verben des Zulassens und Veranlassens
Infinitives and Participles after Verbs of Allowing and Causing

F

	Verb	Objekt	Infinitiv/*Past Participle*
They	**allowed**	him	**to leave** the office early.
They	**let**	him	**leave** the office early.
He	**had**	his coat	**cleaned.**

Verben des Zulassens und Veranlassens werden mit folgenden Strukturen verbunden:

– Objekt + Infinitiv (mit oder ohne *to*)

– Objekt + *Past Participle*

V

Das deutsche *lassen* + Infinitiv kann ganz unterschiedliche Handlungen ausdrücken:
Veranlassen, zulassen, etwas machen lassen (z. B. reinigen lassen, reparieren lassen, etc.).
Im Englischen werden diese verschiedenen Bedeutungen durch unterschiedliche Verben und Strukturen ausgedrückt.

1. Im Sinn von „veranlassen" und „zulassen" wird der Infinitiv verwendet.

Veranlassen	Zulassen
make* + Infinitiv ohne *to	***let* + Infinitiv ohne *to***
The car broke down and we couldn't **make the engine start** again. The policeman **made them push** the car to the side.	After checking the man's licence, the police **let him go.** The driver slowed down to **let the children cross** the road.
Make bedeutet: „jdn. dazu bewegen, bringen oder zwingen, etwas zu tun"; „veranlassen, daß etwas geschieht".	*Let* bedeutet: „jdm. etwas erlauben"; „etwas zulassen"; „nicht verhindern, daß etwas geschieht".
cause/force* + Infinitiv mit *to	***allow/permit* + Infinitiv mit *to***
A bad cough **forced the manager to break off** the meeting. The cost of cigarettes **caused her to give up** smoking.	They don't **allow people to smoke** in here. You will certainly understand that we cannot **permit visitors to smoke** in these rooms.
Zwischen *force* und *cause* besteht folgender Bedeutungsunterschied: *To force s.o. to* entspricht dem deutschen „jdn. zwingen zu", *to cause s.o. to* entspricht dem deutschen „jdn. veranlassen zu", „bewirken, daß".	*Permit* gehört eher einer gehobenen Stilebene an („gestatten"), *allow* erscheint auch in der Umgangssprache („erlauben"). Zu *to be allowed to, to be permitted to* vgl. auch § 78.

2. Im Sinn von „etwas machen lassen“ wird das *Past Participle* verwendet.

Etwas machen lassen: ***to have something done (to get something done)***
This blouse can be washed, but it's better to **have it cleaned.** You should **get those shoes mended** — it would be a pity to throw them away.
Während *get something done* umgangssprachlich ist, wird *have something done* auf allen Stilebenen verwendet.

H I'll **leave** you alone now. I **left** my umbrella on the train. I've **left** the window open.

In den Bedeutungen „zurücklassen“, „an einem bestimmten Ort oder in einem bestimmten Zustand lassen“, wird das Verb *leave* verwendet.

⚠

He **had**	his car **washed.**	Er ließ seinen Wagen waschen.
He **had washed**	his car.	Er hatte seinen Wagen (selbst) gewaschen.

Die Struktur *have* + Objekt + *Past Participle* wird häufig mit dem *Present Perfect* und dem *Past Perfect* verwechselt.
Deshalb ist genau auf die Stellung von Objekt und *Past Participle* zu achten.

§ 89 Infinitiv und *Present Participle* nach Verben der Wahrnehmung
Infinitives and Present Participles after Verbs of Perception

F

	Verb	**Objekt**	**Inf./Part.**	+ **Ergänzung**
He	**saw**	the children	**cross**	the street.
He	**saw**	the children	**crossing**	the street.

Nach Verben der Wahrnehmung können eintreten:

— Objekt + Infinitiv ohne *to*
— Objekt + *Present Participle*

V Zwischen Infinitiv und *Present Participle* nach Verben der Wahrnehmung besteht ein Bedeutungsunterschied.

Infinitiv: Wahrnehmung des ganzen Geschehens	***Present Participle:*** **Wahrnehmung des Verlaufs**
I **heard** someone **shout** for help, and then there was silence. They **watched** the two men **carry** a large box from the house and **put** it in the boot of the car.	I can **hear** two men **whispering** in some foreign language — I think it must be Italian. While she was standing at the counter she **felt** someone **pulling** at her handbag. As I turned round, I **noticed** a man **rushing** towards the door.
Der Infinitiv drückt aus, daß ein Geschehen von Anfang bis Ende wahrgenommen wurde. Dies ist häufig der Fall, wenn es sich um ein Geschehen von sehr kurzer Dauer handelt oder um eine Folge von Handlungen. Diese Struktur entspricht ungefähr dem Gebrauch der *Simple Form* im einfachen Satz (vgl. § 63, 65).	Das *Present Participle* drückt aus, daß ein Geschehen sich gerade im Verlauf befindet (oder befand). Diese Struktur wird vor allem dann gewählt, wenn nur ein Teil des Ablaufs wahrgenommen wird. Sie entspricht ungefähr dem Gebrauch der *Continuous Form* im einfachen Satz (vgl. § 63, 65).

§ 90 Das *Gerund* als Ergänzung zum Verb
Gerunds Used as Verb Complements

F

	Verb	Präp.	dir. Objekt / Präpositionalobjekt	
He doesn't	mind			**working** outdoors.
He doesn't	mind		his son	**working** outdoors.
He succeeded		in		**getting** the job.
He didn't bother		about	me	**being** out of work.
			log. Subj.	*Gerund* + Ergänzung

Eine *Gerund*-Konstruktion kann entweder direkt oder mit Hilfe einer Präposition an das Verb angeschlossen werden. Im ersten Fall hat die *Gerund*-Konstruktion die Funktion eines direkten Objekts, im zweiten Fall die eines Präpositionalobjekts.
In beiden Fällen kann dem *Gerund* ein Nomen oder Pronomen (in der Objektsform) vorausgehen. Dieses ist dann das logische Subjekt der *Gerund*-Konstruktion (vgl. § 19).

V

Das *Gerund* wird direkt ans Verb angeschlossen, wenn auch ein Nomen direkt angeschlossen wird. (Vgl. *He didn't mind* ***the work.***)
Es wird mit einer Präposition angeschlossen, wenn auch ein Nomen mit einer Präposition angeschlossen wird.
(Vgl. *He succeeded* ***in the exam.***)
Die Wahl der Präposition hängt vom Verb ab. Die Präposition wird deshalb in den Wörterbüchern beim betreffenden Verb angeführt und muß für jeden einzelnen Fall gelernt werden.

Verben, die ein *Gerund* direkt anschließen

I **enjoy listening** to classical music.
I **can't stand dressing** up for the opera.
Nobody will **mind you going** to the concert in jeans.

Weitere Verben dieser Gruppe sind:
to admit (zugeben), *to avoid* (vermeiden), *to finish, I can't help* (ich kann nicht anders, ich muß einfach), *to imagine, to miss, to practise, to risk* (Gefahr laufen/riskieren zu), *to suggest.*
Einige dieser Verben können auch ein *Gerund* mit eigenem logischem Subjekt anschließen, z. B.

I can't imagine / *I can't stand* / *I don't mind* } *him playing the trumpet.*

Verben, die ein *Gerund* mit Präposition anschließen

I wouldn't **dream of paying** £ 10 for a concert ticket.
Some concert organizers obviously **believe in making** as big a profit as they can.
Few pop groups **succeed in becoming** famous.

Weitere häufige Verben mit Präposition sind:
to complain about (sich beklagen, daß), *to decide on, to insist on* (darauf bestehen zu), *to prevent s.o. from* (jdn. daran hindern zu), *to rely on* (sich darauf verlassen, daß), *to think of, to worry about.*
Viele dieser Verben können auch ein *Gerund* mit eigenem logischem Subjekt anschließen, z. B. *to complain about/to insist on/rely on/worry about s.o. doing s.th.*

Verben mit der Präposition *to* und *Gerund*

We're **looking forward to hearing** you sing with the band.
Betty's father **objects to us practising** in their house.
My parents **are used to hearing** our kind of music.

Bei diesen Verben ist *to* eine normale Präposition (wie in ***to*** *the door).* Dies ist daran zu erkennen, daß auch ein Nomen folgen kann (vgl. *We're looking forward* ***to*** *the concert).* Deshalb folgt das *Gerund* und nicht der Infinitiv (wie in *He wanted* ***to*** *go*).

H

1. You should **give up smoking** and **take up swimming** instead.

   Auch viele *phrasal verbs* (*give up, take up, put off, keep on,* etc.) werden mit dem Gerund verbunden.
   Phrasal verbs verhalten sich, wenn sie allein stehen, anders als Verbindungen aus Verb + Präposition. Vgl.: I tried to persuade him, but I didn't **succeed** (in persuading him). (Präposition *in* entfällt)
   I tried to persuade him, but in the end I **gave up** (trying).
   (Partikel *up* bleibt.)

2. She often complains about her husband's (his) working too much.

   Zum *s*-Genitiv bzw. Possessivbegleiter als Subjekt der *Gerund*-Konstruktion vgl. § 19 H.

§ 91 *Gerund* und Infinitiv nach bestimmten Verben
Gerunds and Infinitives after Certain Verbs

F Zu den *Gerund*-Strukturen vgl. § 90, zu den Infinitivstrukturen vgl. § 87.

V Kann ein Verb sowohl mit dem *Gerund* als auch mit dem Infinitiv verbunden werden, so haben die beiden Strukturen häufig verschiedene Bedeutungen.

Das *Gerund*	Der Infinitiv
bei *remember, forget, regret:* Bezug auf Vergangenes	**bei *remember, forget, regret:* Bezug auf Kommendes**
I know I met you after the exam because I **remember showing** you the maths paper. How could you **forget seeing it?** Sue now **regrets having taken** French instead of German.	You must **remember to show** me the maths paper after the test. Jack **forgot to write** his name on his English essay. I **regret to tell** you that you have not passed your exam.
Das *Gerund* steht für etwas, was schon geschehen ist. Wenn das Ergebnis einer Handlung betont werden soll, kann auch die *Perfect*-Form des *Gerund* benutzt werden.	Der Infinitiv steht für etwas, was noch nicht geschehen ist (oder war), sondern erst noch getan werden muß (oder mußte).
bei *try:* Bezug auf vorhandene Möglichkeit	**bei *try:* Bezug auf ungelöste Schwierigkeit**
Are you having trouble with that bottle? **Try using** this opener. Probier's mal mit diesem Öffner.	Don't **try to open** that bottle with your teeth — use an opener! Versuche nicht, diese Flasche mit den Zähnen zu öffnen.
Das *Gerund* nennt eine Methode, wie man eine Schwierigkeit überwinden kann. (Deutsch: „es probieren mit")	Der Infinitiv nennt die Handlung selbst, die schwierig auszuführen ist. (Deutsch: „versuchen zu")
bei *stop, go on:* Bezug auf bisherige Handlung	**bei *stop, go on:* Bezug auf neue, andere Handlung**
After telling us twenty times how wonderful the washing-machine was, the salesman **stopped talking** at last. She **went on talking,** though no one was listening. Sie redete weiter, . . .	The speaker **stopped to drink** a glass of water. (= . . . stopped speaking in order to drink . . .) After explaining the problem she **went on to make** a suggestion. Nachdem sie . . ., machte sie einen Vorschlag.
Das *Gerund* nennt die Handlung, die abgebrochen bzw. fortgesetzt wird.	Durch den Infinitiv wird der Grund für den Abbruch bzw. die Fortsetzung einer Handlung angegeben.
bei *like, prefer, love, hate:* allgemeine Aussage	**bei *like, prefer, love, hate:* konkreter Fall**
I **like swimming,** especially in the sea. Ann **hates lying** on the beach all day doing nothing.	**Would** you **like to go** for a walk this afternoon? With a cold like mine, **I'd hate to get** caught in the rain.
Das *Gerund* tritt ein, wenn eine allgemeine Vorliebe oder Abneigung geäußert wird. Hier wäre aber auch ein Infinitiv möglich.	Um einen konkreten Wunsch oder Vorschlag zu äußern, wird das *Conditional* zusammen mit einem Infinitiv gebraucht. Das *Gerund* ist hier nicht möglich.

H I **started reading (to read)** *War and Peace* yesterday.
She **continued to write (writing)** detective stories all her life.

Gerund und Infinitiv nach den Verben *start, begin continue* und *intend* sind etwa gleichbedeutend.

§ 92 *Gerund* und Infinitiv nach Adjektiven und Nomen
Gerunds and Infinitives after Adjectives and Nouns

F

	Adj./Nomen		*Gerund*/ Infinitiv + Ergänzung
I'm	**afraid**	**of**	**flying.**
There's	**a chance**	**of**	(us) **catching** the early flight.
It's	**necessary**		**to arrive** on time.
It's	**time**		(for John) **to leave** for the airport.

Adjektive und Nomen können ergänzt werden

— durch eine Präposition + *Gerund*. (Dabei kann das *Gerund* ein eigenes logisches Subjekt haben, vgl. § 19 und § 90.)

— durch einen Infinitiv. (Dabei kann dem Infinitiv manchmal ein *for* + Nomen/Pronomen vorangehen.)

V

Ob ein Infinitiv oder ein *Gerund* folgt, hängt vom jeweiligen Adjektiv oder Nomen ab.
Eine Präposition + *Gerund* ist grundsätzlich immer dann möglich, wenn auch eine Präposition + Nomen folgen kann. (Vgl. *I'm tired of school. — I'm tired of going to school.*) Die Präposition wird in den meisten Wörterbüchern beim entsprechenden Wort angegeben und ist für jedes einzelne Adjektiv oder Nomen zu lernen.

Ergänzung durch Präposition und *Gerund*

Adjektiv + Präposition + *Gerund*

Neil Armstrong is **famous for being** the first man to walk on the moon. ... berühmt dafür, daß ...
Scientists were very **interested in analysing** moon rocks.

Weitere häufig mit Präpositionen verbundene Adjektive:
(to be) ashamed of, bad at, fond of, keen on, tired of, afraid of, proud of, interested in.

Nomen + Präposition + *Gerund*

There is no **hope of finding** life on Mars.
Many people don't see **the point of** the Americans **spending** so much money on space flights.

Zahlreiche Nomen können mit Präpositionen verbunden werden, z. B. *chance of, danger of, reason for, difficulty in, hope of, opportunity of.*

Ergänzung durch Infinitiv

Adjektiv + Infinitiv

The Americans were **anxious to land** on the moon before the Russians. Die Amerikaner waren darauf aus, ... zu ...
It wasn't **easy to beat** the Russians in the 'space race'.

Weitere häufig mit dem Infinitiv verbundene Adjektive:
(to be) able, ready, willing;
(it is/it was) dangerous, difficult, nice, possible, stupid.

Nomen + Infinitiv

The astronauts made a great **effort to correct** the course of the spaceship.
The Commander announced **his decision to return** to Earth.

Weitere Nomen, die den Infinitiv anschließen können:
ability, attempt, courage, right, wish, plan.

Die Konstruktion *for* + Nomen/Pronomen + Infinitiv

It is **important for an astronaut to be** in good health.
Es ist wichtig, daß .../ Es ist wichtig für ... zu ...
It would be **a pity for NASA to stop** their space programme.
Es wäre schade, wenn die NASA ...

Diese Konstruktion tritt vor allem nach *it is/it was* + Adjektiv/Nomen auf, z. B. *it's dangerous/natural/possible/important; it's time/a rule/a good thing.*
Sie kann als Nebensatz verstanden werden und entspricht häufig einem deutschen *daß*-Satz.

H

1. Zum Teil ist sowohl eine *Gerund-* als auch eine Infinitivkonstruktion möglich, z. B. bei *to be interested (in doing/to do), a chance (of doing/to do).*
2. **It's no use (no good) waiting** for him. (Es hat keinen Sinn ...)

   Nach *it's no use / it's no good* sowie nach *to be busy* und *to be worth* folgt im Gegensatz zum sonstigen Gebrauch ein *Gerund* **ohne** Präposition.
3. He is **likely** to be there. (Er ist **wahrscheinlich** dort.)

   Einige englische Adjektive mit Infinitiv *(sure to, certain to, likely to)* entsprechen deutschen Adverbien *(bestimmt, sicher, wahrscheinlich).* (Vgl. § 87 H 3.)

Die wichtigsten unregelmäßigen Verben

The Most Important Irregular Verbs

bear [eə]	bore [ɔ:]	born(e) [ɔ:]	*(er)tragen, gebären*
beat [i:]	beat [i:]	beaten [i:]	*schlagen*
become [ʌ]	became [eɪ]	become [ʌ]	*werden*
begin [ɪ]	began [æ]	begun [ʌ]	*anfangen*
bet [e]	bet [e]*	bet [e]*	*wetten*
bind [aɪ]	bound [aʊ]	bound [aʊ]	*binden*
bite [aɪ]	bit [ɪ]	bit(ten) [ɪ]	*beißen*
bleed [i:]	bled [e]	bled [e]	*bluten*
blow [əʊ]	blew [u:]	blown [əʊ]	*blasen*
break [eɪ]	broke [əʊ]	broken [əʊ]	*(zer)brechen*
bring [ɪ]	brought [ɔ:]	brought [ɔ:]	*(her)bringen*
build [ɪ]	built [ɪ]	built [ɪ]	*bauen*
burn [ɜ:]	burnt [ɜ:]*	burnt [ɜ:]*	*(ver)brennen*
burst [ɜ:]	burst [ɜ:]	burst [ɜ:]	*platzen*
buy [aɪ]	bought [ɔ:]	bought [ɔ:]	*kaufen*
catch [æ]	caught [ɔ:]	caught [ɔ:]	*fangen*
choose [u:]	chose [əʊ]	chosen [əʊ]	*(aus)wählen*
come [ʌ]	came [eɪ]	come [ʌ]	*kommen*
cost [ɒ]	cost [ɒ]	cost [ɒ]	*kosten*
cut [ʌ]	cut [ʌ]	cut [ʌ]	*schneiden*
deal [i:]	dealt [e]	dealt [e]	*handeln (von)*
dig [ɪ]	dug [ʌ]	dug [ʌ]	*graben*
do [u:]	did [ɪ]	done [ʌ]	*tun*
draw [ɔ:]	drew [u:]	drawn [ɔ:]	*zeichnen, ziehen*
dream [i:]	dreamt [e]*	dreamt [e]*	*träumen*
drink [ɪ]	drank [æ]	drunk [ʌ]	*trinken*
drive [aɪ]	drove [əʊ]	driven [ɪ]	*fahren*
eat [i:]	ate [e]	eaten [i:]	*essen*
fall [ɔ:]	fell [e]	fallen [ɔ:]	*fallen*
feed [i:]	fed [e]	fed [e]	*füttern*
feel [i:]	felt [e]	felt [e]	*(sich) fühlen*
find [aɪ]	found [aʊ]	found [aʊ]	*finden*
flee [i:]	fled [e]	fled [e]	*fliehen*
fly [aɪ]	flew [u:]	flown [əʊ]	*fliegen*
forbid [ɪ]	forbade [æ]	forbidden [ɪ]	*verbieten*
forget [e]	forgot [ɒ]	forgotten [ɒ]	*vergessen*
forgive [ɪ]	forgave [eɪ]	forgiven [ɪ]	*verzeihen, vergeben*
freeze [i:]	froze [əʊ]	frozen [əʊ]	*(er)frieren*
get [e]	got [ɒ]	got [ɒ]	*bekommen, gelangen*
give [ɪ]	gave [eɪ]	given [ɪ]	*geben*
go [əʊ]	went [e]	gone [ɒ]	*gehen, fahren*
grow [əʊ]	grew [u:]	grown [əʊ]	*wachsen, anbauen*
hang [æ]	hung [ʌ]*	hung [ʌ]*	*(auf)hängen*
hear [ɪə]	heard [ɜ:]	heard [ɜ:]	*hören*
hide [aɪ]	hid [ɪ]	hidden [ɪ]	*(sich) verstecken*
hit [ɪ]	hit [ɪ]	hit [ɪ]	*schlagen, treffen*
hold [əʊ]	held [e]	held [e]	*halten*
hurt [ɜ:]	hurt [ɜ:]	hurt [ɜ:]	*verletzen, wehtun*
keep [i:]	kept [e]	kept [e]	*(be)halten*
know [nəʊ]	knew [nju:]	know [nəʊn]	*wissen, kennen*
lay [eɪ]	laid [eɪ]	laid [eɪ]	*legen, decken*
lead [i:]	led [e]	led [e]	*führen, leiten*
lean [i:]	leant [e]*	leant [e]*	*lehnen*
learn [ɜ:]	learnt [ɜ:]*	learnt [ɜ:]*	*lernen*

leave [i:]	left [e]	left [e]	*(zurück-/ver-)lassen*
lend [e]	lent [e]	lent [e]	*leihen*
let [e]	let [e]	let [e]	*lassen*
lie [aɪ]	lay [eɪ]	lain [eɪ]	*liegen*
light [aɪ]	lit [ɪ]*	lit [ɪ]*	*anzünden*
lose [u:]	lost [ɒ]	lost [ɒ]	*verlieren*
make [eɪ]	made [eɪ]	made [eɪ]	*machen*
mean [i:]	meant [e]	meant [e]	*meinen, bedeuten*
meet [i:]	met [e]	met [e]	*(sich) treffen*
pay [eɪ]	paid [eɪ]	paid [eɪ]	*bezahlen*
put [ʊ]	put [ʊ]	put [ʊ]	*legen, setzen, stellen*
read [i:]	read [e]	read [e]	*lesen*
ride [aɪ]	rode [əʊ]	ridden [ɪ]	*reiten, fahren*
ring [ɪ]	rang [æ]	rung [ʌ]	*läuten*
rise [aɪ]	rose [əʊ]	risen [ɪ]	*aufstehen, aufgehen*
run [ʌ]	ran [æ]	run [ʌ]	*laufen, rennen*
say [eɪ]	said [e]	said [e]	*sagen*
see [i:]	saw [ɔ:]	seen [i:]	*sehen*
seek [i:]	sought [ɔ:]	sought [ɔ:]	*suchen*
sell [e]	sold [əʊ]	sold [əʊ]	*verkaufen*
send [e]	sent [e]	sent [e]	*senden, schicken*
set [e]	set [e]	set [e]	*setzen, stellen*
sew [əʊ]	sewed [əʊ]	sewn [əʊ]*	*nähen*
shake [ei]	shook [ʊ]	shaken [eɪ]	*schütteln*
shine [aɪ]	shone [ɒ]	shone [ɒ]	*scheinen*
shoot [u:]	shot [ɒ]	shot [ɒ]	*schießen*
show [əʊ]	showed [əʊ]	shown [əʊ]	*zeigen*
shut [ʌ]	shut [ʌ]	shut [ʌ]	*schließen, zumachen*
sing [ɪ]	sang [æ]	sung [ʌ]	*singen*
sink [ɪ]	sank [æ]	sunk [ʌ]	*sinken, versenken*
sit [ɪ]	sat [æ]	sat [æ]	*sitzen, sich setzen*
sleep [i:]	slept [e]	slept [e]	*schlafen*
smell [e]	smelt [e]	smelt [e]	*riechen*
speak [i:]	spoke [əʊ]	spoken [əʊ]	*sprechen*
spell [e]	spelt [e]*	spelt [e]*	*buchstabieren*
spend [e]	spent [e]	spent [e]	*verbringen, ausgeben*
stand [æ]	stood [ʊ]	stood [ʊ]	*stehen*
steal [i:]	stole [əʊ]	stolen [əʊ]	*stehlen*
stick [i:]	stuck [ʌ]	stuck [ʌ]	*kleben*
strike [aɪ]	struck [ʌ]	struck [ʌ]	*stoßen, schlagen*
sweep [i:]	swept [e]	swept [e]	*fegen*
swim [ɪ]	swam [æ]	swum [ʌ]	*schwimmen*
swing [ɪ]	swung [ʌ]	swung [ʌ]	*schwingen*
take [eɪ]	took [ʊ]	taken [eɪ]	*nehmen, (hin)bringen*
teach [i:]	taught [ɔ:]	taught [ɔ:]	*lehren, unterrichten*
tear [eə]	tore [ɔ:]	torn [ɔ:]	*reißen*
tell [e]	told [əʊ]	told [əʊ]	*erzählen, sagen*
think [ɪ]	thought [ɔ:	thought [ɔ:]	*denken, glauben*
throw [əʊ]	threw [u:]	thrown [əʊ]	*werfen*
understand [æ]	understood [ʊ]	understood [ʊ]	*verstehen*
wake [eɪ]	woke [əʊ]*	woken [əʊ]*	*wecken, aufwachen*
wear [eə]	wore [ɔ:]	worn [ɔ:]	*tragen (Kleidung)*
win [ɪ]	won [ʌ]	won [ʌ]	*gewinnen*
write [aɪ]	wrote [əʊ]	written [ɪ]	*schreiben*

* auch die regelmäßige Form auf *-ed* kommt vor

Wortbildung

Word Formation

Unter Wortbildung versteht man das Bilden neuer Wörter aus schon vorhandenen. Durch die Kenntnis der Wortbildungsregeln lassen sich Bedeutung und Wortart eines unbekannten Wortes aus einem bekannten Grundwort erschließen.
Zu den wichtigsten Mitteln der Wortbildung gehören im Englischen der Gebrauch von Vor- und Nachsilben sowie die Konversion (Wortartwechsel bei gleichlautenden Wörtern). Vorsilben verändern die Bedeutung des Grundwortes, die Wortart bleibt jedoch fast immer erhalten. Durch die meisten Nachsilben und durch Konversion wird das Grundwort in eine andere Wortart übergeführt.

1. Vorsilben

re-: Diese Vorsilbe kommt vorwiegend bei Verben vor und gibt an, daß eine Tätigkeit wiederholt wird *(to reread = to read again).*

***in-* (Sonderformen: *im-, il-, ir-*):** Die Bedeutung eines Adjektivs oder Nomens wird verneint und manchmal sogar ins Gegenteil verkehrt. Die Sonderformen werden gebraucht vor bestimmten Konsonanten (*im-* vor *m, p* und *b; il-* vor *l; ir-* vor *r*).

un-: Bei Adjektiven und Nomen hat diese Vorsilbe die gleiche Wirkung wie eine Verneinung; die Bedeutung des Grundwortes kann dabei ins Gegenteil verkehrt werden. Bei Verben bedeutet *un-* ‚etwas rückgängig machen'.

de-: Bedeutet: ‚etwas rückgängig machen'.

dis-: Die Bedeutung des Grundwortes wird ins Gegenteil verkehrt.

mis-: Kommt vorwiegend bei Verben vor und bedeutet ‚etwas falsch machen'. *(to mispronounce = to pronounce incorrectly)*

over-, under-: Diese Vorsilben haben nicht nur eine konkrete örtliche Bedeutung, sondern können auch ‚zu viel' *(over-)* bzw. ‚zu wenig' *(under-)* bedeuten.

super-: Wird häufig in der Bedeutung ‚groß' gebraucht, oder zur Verstärkung einer positiven Eigenschaft.

inter-: Zeigt an, daß etwas zwischen mindestens zwei Teilen oder Partnern geschieht oder besteht.

pre-, post-: Diese Vorsilben bedeuten ‚vor' bzw. ‚nach'. *(prehistoric = before written history; postscript = s.th. written afterwards)*

Nomen	Verb	Adjektiv
	to **re**read	
a **re**play	to **re**play	
reorganization	to **re**organize	
incompletion		**in**complete
imperfection		**im**perfect
illegality		**il**legal
irregularity		**ir**regular
unhappiness		**un**happy
untruth		**un**true
		unknown
	to **un**lock	**un**locked
	to **un**pack	
desegregation	to **de**segregate	
disadvantage		**dis**advantaged
disagreement	to **dis**agree	
disconnection	to **dis**connect	
dishonesty		**dis**honest
misunderstanding	to **mis**understand	
mispronunciation	to **mis**pronounce	
	to **over**turn	
overcrowding	to **over**crowd	**over**crowded
overconfidence		**over**confident
underdevelopment		**under**developed
supermarket		
		supermodern
interview	to **inter**view	
		international
prehistory		**pre**historic
postscript		

2. Nachsilben

Adjektiv + *-ness, -ity, -ence:* Die so gebildeten abstrakten Nomen bezeichnen meistens eine Eigenschaft oder einen Zustand. Abstrakta auf *-ence* werden nur von Adjektiven auf *-ent* gebildet.

Verb + *-ment, -tion* (*-ation, -ition*): Diese Nomen bezeichnen entweder eine Handlung (bzw. einen Vorgang) oder deren Ergebnis.

Verb + *-er* (*-or*): Solche Nomen bezeichnen entweder eine Person, die etwas (berufsmäßig) ausführt, oder auch ein Gerät.

***Verb* + -ing, -ed:** Diese Endungen bilden *Gerund* bzw. *Present Participle* und *Past Participle* des Verbs (vgl. § 86). Das *Gerund* wird häufig zu einem richtigen Nomen, das sogar einen Gegenstand bezeichnen kann. Beide *Participles* können sich zu echten Adjektiven entwickeln.

Verb + *-ive, -able*: Die so gebildeten Adjektive drücken aus, daß etwas geschehen kann *(explosive = can explode)* bzw. gemacht werden kann *(readable = can be read).*

Nomen + *-ous, -al, -ic, -y, -ful, -less*: Mit Ausnahme von *-less,* drücken all diese Adjektive aus, daß etwas vorhanden ist — eine Sache, eine Eigenschaft, ein Zustand usw. Dabei beschränkt sich der Gebrauch von *-ful* auf abstrakte Nomen, der Gebrauch von *-y* auf konkrete Nomen.
Die Nachsilbe *-less* zeigt ein Fehlen an (vgl. dt. ‚nutz*los*').

Adjektiv + *-en, -ize, -ify*: Die so gebildeten Verben bedeuten immer: ‚etwas verändern' (z. B. *to simplify = to make simple/simpler*).

3. Konversion

Konversion liegt vor, wenn ein Wort in eine andere Wortart übertritt, ohne die Form zu verändern. Dieser Vorgang ist im Englischen sehr häufig. So wurde z. B. das Verb *to slow* aus dem Adjektiv *slow* gebildet.
Für das Verständnis der durch Konversion gebildeten Wörter ist es unwesentlich, ob z. B. das Nomen vom Verb abgeleitet wurde oder umgekehrt. Deshalb wird in der Übersicht die Richtung der Konversion nicht durch Pfeile angezeigt.

Nomen	Verb	Adjektiv
dark**ness**		dark
nervous**ness**		nervous
activ**ity**		active
similar**ity**		similar
intellig**ence**		intelligent
differ**ence**		different
move**ment**	to move	
announce**ment**	to announce	
sugges**tion**	to suggest	
organiz**ation**	to organize	
writ**er**	to write	
sail**or**	to sail	
freez**er**	to freeze	
build**ing**	to build	
writ**ing**	to write	
	to surprise	surpris**ing**
	to interest	interest**ing**
	to surprise	surpris**ed**
	to interest	interest**ed**
	to explode	explos**ive**
	to attract	attract**ive**
	to enjoy	enjoy**able**
	to read	read**able**
danger		danger**ous**
mountain		mountain**ous**
music		music**al**
photograph		photograph**ic**
dirt		dirt**y**
cloud		cloud**y**
beauty		beauti**ful**
use		use**ful**
use		use**less**
cloud		cloud**less**
	to sharp**en**	sharp
	to short**en**	short
	to modern**ize**	modern
	to popular**ize**	popular
	to simpl**ify**	simple
	to electr**ify**	electric
rain	to rain	
an answer	to answer	
a photograph	to photograph	
	to slow	slow
	to empty	empty
a musical		musical
the dark		dark

Englisch-deutsches Verzeichnis grammatischer Ausdrücke

English-German List of Grammatical Terms

		Beispiele:
abstract noun ['æbstrækt 'naʊn]	abstraktes Nomen, Abstraktum	*life, music, illness*
active voice ['æktɪv 'vɔɪs]	Aktiv	He *washed* the car. (vgl. passive voice)
activity verb [æk'tɪvɪtɪ]	Tätigkeitsverb	*walk, read, meet* (vgl. static verb)
adjective ['ædʒɪktɪv]	Adjektiv	*good, bad, slow, green*
adverb ['ædvɜ:b]	Adverb	*slowly, today, always, upstairs*
adverb of degree [dɪ'gri:]	Adverb des Grades	*very* good, good *enough*
adverb of manner ['mænə]	Adverb der Art und Weise	*well, slowly, angrily*
adverbial clause [əd'vɜ:bjəl 'klɔ:z]	Adverbialsatz, adverbialer Nebensatz	*when he arrived; because it was late*
adverbial phrase [freɪz]	Umstandsangabe	*at home, in June, as a joke*
apostrophe [ə'pɒstrəfɪ]	Apostroph, Auslassungszeichen	*John's* room, *she's* ill
article ['ɑ:tɪkl]	Artikel	*a, an, the*
auxiliary verb [ɔ:g'zɪljərɪ]	Hilfsverb	*be, have, do, can, may, must, shall, will*
cardinal number ['kɑ:dɪnl]	Grundzahl, Kardinalzahl	*one, two, three, ...* (vgl. ordinal number)
comparative [kəm'pærətɪv]	Komparativ	*faster, more expensive* (vgl. superlative)
comparison [kəm'pærɪsn]	Steigerung	*fast — faster — fastest*
compound ['kɒmpaʊnd]	zusammengesetztes Wort	*washing-machine, playground*
conditional [kən'dɪʃənl]	Konditional I	he *would come*
conditional perfect ['pɜ:fɪkt]	Konditional II	he *would have come*
conditional clause [klɔ:z]	Bedingungssatz, Konditionalsatz	*if I were a millionaire*
conjunction [kən'dʒʌŋkʃən]	Konjunktion	*when, if, because, although*
consonant ['kɒnsənənt]	Konsonant	[b], [s], [d], [f], [g] (vgl. vowel)
continuous form [kən'tɪnjʊəs]	Verlaufsform (des Verbs)	she *was running* (vgl. simple form)
contact clause ['kɒntækt]	Relativsatz ohne Relativpronomen	The food *we got* was awful.
conversion [kən'vɜ:ʃn]	Konversion	*to answer* ⟷ *an answer*
countables ['kaʊntəblz]	zählbare Nomen	*flower, book, boy* (vgl. uncountables)
definite article ['defɪnɪt 'ɑ:tɪkl]	bestimmter Artikel	*the*
demonstrative determiner [dɪ'tɜ:mɪnə]	Demonstrativbegleiter	*this/that* book, *these/those* books
demonstrative pronoun [dɪ'mɒnstrətɪv]	Demonstrativpronomen	*This/That* is Sue. I'd like *these/those.*
direct object ['daɪrekt 'ɒbdʒɪkt]	direktes Objekt	She gave me *a present.* (vgl. indirect object)
direct speech ['daɪrekt 'spi:tʃ]	direkte Rede	He said: *"I'm fine."* (vgl. reported speech)
expression of quantity ['kwɒntɪtɪ]	Mengenangabe	*a pound of, two pieces of*
future tense ['fju:tʃə 'tens]	Futur	he *will come*
gender ['dʒendə]	Genus, gramm. Geschlecht	the boy → *he*; the teacher → *he/she*
genitive ['dʒenɪtɪv]	Genitiv	*Helen's* car, the tyres *of the car*
gerund ['dʒerənd]	Gerundium	I'm fond of *skiing. Skiing* is fun.
imperative [ɪm'perətɪv]	Imperativ	*"Stop!" "Come here."*
indefinite article [ɪn'defɪnɪt 'ɑ:tɪkl]	unbestimmter Artikel	*a, an*
indirect object ['ɪndɪrekt 'ɒbdʒɪkt]	indirektes Objekt	She gave *me* a present. (vgl. direct object)
infinitive [ɪn'fɪnɪtɪv]	Infinitiv	*(to) wash, (to) take, (to) see*
infinitive construction [kənstrʌkʃn]	Infinitivkonstruktion	He went out *to do some shopping.*
interrogative pronoun [ɪntə'rɒgətɪv]	Interrogativpronomen	*who, what, which*
irregular verb [ɪ'regjulə]	unregelmäßiges Verb	*take — took — taken* (vgl. regular verb)
main clause ['meɪn 'klɔ:z]	Hauptsatz	*He left* when I did. (vgl. subordinate clause.)
modal auxiliary ['məʊdl ɔ:g'zɪljərɪ]	modales Hilfsverb	*can, may, must, shall, will*

noun [naʊn]	Nomen (Substantiv)	*man, chair, milk, life*
object ['ɒbdʒɪkt]	Objekt	s. direct object, indirect object
object case	Objektfall (der Personalpronomen)	*me, him, her, us, them*
object clause	Objektsatz	I noticed *that she was smiling.*
ordinal number ['ɔ:dɪnl]	Ordnungszahl, Ordinalzahl	*first, second,* ... (vgl. cardinal number)
participle ['pɑ:tɪsɪpl]	Partizip	s. past participle, present participle
participle structure ['strʌktʃə]	Partizipialkonstruktion	*Seeing the danger,* he ran to help them.
passive voice ['pæsɪv 'vɔɪs]	Passiv	The car *was washed.* (vgl. active voice)
past participle ['pɑ:st 'pɑ:tɪsɪpl]	Partizip Perfekt (Partizip II)	*washed, taken, seen* (vgl. present participle)
past perfect ['pɜ:fɪkt]	Plusquamperfekt	he *had gone* home; he *had been reading*
past tense ['pɑ:st 'tens]	Präteritum	he *went* home; he *was going* home
personal pronoun ['pɜ:snl]	Personalpronomen	*I, you, he, she, it, we, they*
plural ['plʊərəl]	Plural, Mehrzahl	*books, men, children* (vgl. singular)
possessive determiner [dɪ'tɜ:mɪnə]	Possessivbegleiter	*my, your, his, her,* ...
possessive pronoun [pə'zesɪv]	Possessivpronomen	*mine, yours, his, hers,* ...
prefix ['pri:fɪks]	Präfix, Vorsilbe	*un*happy, to *re*open (vgl. suffix)
preposition [prepə'zɪʃən]	Präposition	*in, on, during, for*
present participle ['preznt 'pɑ:tɪsɪpl]	Partizip Präsens (Partizip I)	*washing, taking, seeing* (vgl. past part.)
present perfect ['pɜ:fɪkt]	Perfekt	he *has gone* home; he *has been reading*
present tense ['preznt 'tens]	Präsens	he *goes* home; he *is going* home
process verb ['prəʊses]	Vorgangsverb	*become / grow* nervous, *turn* red
pronoun ['prəʊnaʊn]	Pronomen	*he, someone, anything, who*
prop word ['prɒp wɜ:d]	Stützwort	the small *one,* two big *ones*
question tag [tæg]	Bestätigungsfrage (Kurzfrage)	It's cold, *isn't it?*
question word	Fragewort	*who, where, when, why*
reflexive pronoun [rɪ'fleksɪv]	Reflexivpronomen	*myself, yourself, himself,* ...
regular verb ['regjʊlə]	regelmäßiges Verb	*live — lived — lived* (vgl. irregular verb)
relative clause ['relətɪv]	Relativsatz	the people *who live next door*
relative pronoun	Relativpronomen	*who, which, that*
reported speech [rɪ'pɔ:tɪd 'spi:tʃ]	indirekte Rede	He said *he was fine.* (vgl. direct speech)
sequence of tenses ['si:kwəns]	Zeitenfolge	He *said* he *had been* ill.
short answer	Kurzantwort	Do you smoke? — *Yes, I do. / No, I don't.*
short response [rɪ'spɒns] with *so/nor/neither*	Kurzsatz mit *so/nor/neither*	I know him. — *So do I.*
sibilant ['sɪbɪlənt]	Zischlaut	[s], [z], [ʃ], [tʃ], [dʒ]
simple form (of the tenses)	einfache Zeitform (des Verbs)	she *ran* (vgl. continuous form)
singular ['sɪŋgjʊlə]	Singular, Einzahl	*book, man, child* (vgl. plural)
static verb ['stætɪk]	Zustandsverb	*be, seem, remain* (vgl. activity verb)
subject ['sʌbdʒɪkt]	Subjekt	*She* gave me a present (vgl. direct object, indirect object)
subordinate clause [sə'bɔ:dɪnət 'klɔ:z]	Nebensatz	He left *when I did.* (vgl. main clause)
suffix ['sʌfɪks]	Suffix, Nachsilbe	writ*er*, punish*ment*, ill*ness* (vgl. prefix)
superlative [su'pɜ:lətɪv]	Superlativ	*fastest, most expensive* (vgl. comparative)
uncountables [ʌn'kaʊntəblz]	nicht zählbare Nomen	*water, sugar, music* (vgl. countables)
verb [vɜ:b]	Verb	*arrive, choose, have*
verb of perception [pə'sepʃn]	Verb der (sinnlichen) Wahrnehmung	*see, hear, smell, feel*
voiced consonant ['vɔɪst]	stimmhafter Konsonant	[b], [v], [z]
voiceless consonant ['vɔɪslɪs]	stimmloser Konsonant	[p], [f], [s]
vowel ['vaʊəl]	Vokal	[ɑ:], [æ], [ʌ] (vgl. consonant)
word order	Wortstellung	subject — verb — object
yes/no question	Entscheidungsfrage	*Did he come?* — Yes, he did / No, he didn't.

Wort- und Sachregister

Die Zahlen verweisen auf die Paragraphen.

Index

Inhalt
Contents

Erster Teil: Satz und Text

1 Wortstellung, Satzarten, Satzverknüpfung

2 Nebensätze, Infinitiv-, *Gerund*- und Partizipialkonstruktionen

3 Gebrauch von Zeitformen und Zeitangaben im Text

Zweiter Teil: Wortarten und Satzteile

4 Nomen, Pronomen und Begleiter

Seite

5 Adjektiv und Adverb

6 Zahlen, Zeit-, Orts- und Mengenangaben